AFRICAN AMERICANS

AMERICANS

in the

REVOLUTIONARY

WAR

AFRICAN AMERICANS

in the

REVOLUTIONARY WAR

Lt. Col. Michael Lee Lanning,
U.S. Army (ret.)

CITADEL PRESS
Kensington Publishing Corp.
www.kensingtonbooks.com

CITADEL PRESS BOOKS are published by

Kensington Publishing Corp.
119 West 40th Street
New York, NY 10018

All Kensington titles, imprints, and distributed lines are available at special quantity discounts for bulk purchases for sales promotions, premiums, fund-raising, educational, or institutional use.

Special book excerpts or customized printings can also be created to fit specific needs. For details, write or phone the office of the Kensington sales manager: Kensington Publishing Corp., 119 West 40th Street, New York, NY 10018, attn: Sales Department; phone 1-800-221-2647.

ISBN: 978-0-8065-4116-7

First Citadel trade paperback printing: December 2005

10 9 8 7 6 5 4 3 2

Printed in the United States of America

Electronic edition:

ISBN: 978-0-8065-4169-3 (e-book)

To Allyanna Maeve Corcoran

Contents

Author to Reader

Theoretically, history is first and foremost the chronological record of significant events. In practice, however, the gathering of dates and places is the least complex process of capturing the past. The difficulty in writing history is not the when and where but the what and why. Complicating any effort to record events and their significance accurately and fairly is the fact that, along with inherent problems of locating sources and information, each historian brings his or her own agenda to a project. Rarely is history unfettered by the beliefs, feelings, values, and self-interest of the historian. Ultimately, and all too often, history becomes a record not of what actually happened but the historian's interpretation of those events.

Military history, in particular, offers classic examples of how written accounts reflect not so much the reality of wars and armed conflicts as the perspective of the historian assimilating and analyzing the events. To the victor go not only the spoils of war but also the recorded version of the conflict. A predictable sequence of literature appears. Personal narratives are usually the first books published about a campaign or war. These works provide a valuable but narrow view, covering only the extremely small field of vision of the individual. Unit or ship histories are generally the next accounts to find their way into print, and these works focus almost exclusively on the loyalty, bravery, and dedication of the unit's soldiers or ship's crew. The "official" histories appear soon afterward, written by victors, to whom victory alone stands as the justification for the war and its outcome. Histories by the defeated, if written at all, appear long after the fact as apologetic and remorseful renditions of the facts.

After hostilities conclude, and for hundreds of years thereafter, academicians move in to pick the bones of decisions, actions, and accounts; they harvest the battlefield to assemble their versions of the conflict, which then becomes "history." Unfortunately, many of these learned individuals record and interpret military operations without the insight of personal experience in uniform. Their results then reflect their personal agendas as much as their research.

Nowhere are these factors and influences more evident than in what passes for the Black history of the Revolutionary era.[1] More than 5,000 Black men joined the rebel Americans in the war as soldiers, sailors, and marines; many more supported the rebellion as laborers. Their service went largely unrecognized and unrecorded.

Few letters, journals, or other narratives by Black individuals about the Revolution exist because whites had denied most African Americans an education. White historians of the period, and for years after the war, ignored the contributions and impact of thousands of Black participants for several reasons. First of all, prejudices were so deeply ingrained that it did not even occur to most whites of the time that Black Americans had played a significant role either as individuals who fought or labored or as a segment of the population that affected decisions. Prejudices also prevented some who did witness the contributions of African Americans from honestly reporting that Black soldiers could perform equally with whites on the battlefield if given the opportunity. Others did not mention Black soldiers because of the difficulty of explaining why the United States kept half a million men, women, and children enslaved while fighting for independence and liberty.

Any study of the American Revolution, particularly in respect to participation by Black Americans, faces obstacles in every aspect of the research process. Most writings on the war simply exclude or greatly downplay African American participation. Historians who do include accounts of Black involvement in the Revolution tend to exaggerate their contributions and at times repeat unverified or unfounded stories. The predetermined agendas concerning Black Americans, either positive or negative, of nearly all writers on the American Revolution clearly show through their narratives.

Regardless of their veracity, existing publications contain, in one form or another, most of the information known about the Revolution and its participants. Little additional information is likely to be discovered. Even if an obscure diary or collection of letters surfaces, its impact will be small.

---

[1] Only the histories about the Vietnam War come close in their unrelenting, blatant biases to those of the Revolutionary War.

The most extensive information source on the American Revolution is the cataloged, published, and minutely scrutinized collected papers of George Washington. Military records on file in the archives of the original thirteen states provide other important resources. National records are few because many of the federal government files of the Revolutionary period burned in a fire at the Washington, D.C., storage facility in 1800. The British destroyed other period documents when they occupied the capital in 1814.

As a result of sparse record keeping of the time and the destruction of documents since, it is not possible to compile a complete listing of participants, or even those who died, in the American Revolution. The best estimate is that 300,000 rebel American soldiers and sailors served during the war and that 4,000–7,000 died in battle. Another 18,000 died of disease and from other noncombat causes. Unfortunately, these estimates are suspect.

Available documents rarely mention race, making any estimate of African American participants and casualties in the Revolution all the more difficult. The following chapters are the result of the careful study of each piece of the puzzle, the fitting together of scattered fragments of information, and material deemed reliable to fill the glaring holes.

A brief look at the major publications on Black participation in the Revolutionary War demonstrates the difficulties of research. For more than fifty years after the war concluded, published histories ignored the efforts of Black Americans in the conflict. In 1855, William C. Nell, a free Black native of Boston, published the first detailed history of African Americans. Nell included in his *Colored Patriots of the American Revolution* a chapter on each state's Black military and civilian participants. Nell's work, often described as more enthusiastic than scholarly because of his personal agenda—to promote his race—includes many individual profiles and accounts that otherwise would have been lost forever.

Harriet Beecher Stowe provides the best summary of Nell's book in its introduction, where she states,

> The colored race have been generally considered by their enemies, and sometimes by their friends, as deficient in energy and courage. Their virtues have been supposed to be principally negative ones. This little collection of interesting incidents, made by a colored man, will redeem the character of the race from this misconception, and show how much injustice there may often be in a generally admitted idea.

The next two publications about African American participation in the Revolution were a direct result of the Civil War. Both books provided official documents and letters relating the history and accomplishments of Black Americans in the Revolution, but their real purpose was to promote the emancipation of slaves and their enlistment as soldiers and sailors to help preserve the Union. George H. Moore, the librarian of the New-York Historical Society, published *Historical Notes on the Employment of Negroes in the American Army of the Revolution* in 1862. George Livermore, a member of the Massachusetts Historical Society, produced the much more detailed *An Historical Research Respecting the Opinions of the Founders of the Republic on Negroes as Slaves, as Citizens, and as Soldiers* the following year.

After the Civil War, the only significant work in the latter part of the 1800s was *The Black Phalanx: A History of the Negro Soldiers of the United States in the Wars of 1775–1812, 1861–'65*, written in 1890 by Joseph T. Wilson, a Black Civil War veteran of the Fifty-fourth Massachusetts Volunteers. Although not as detailed as Livermore's writings on the Revolution, Wilson's better understanding of soldiers and the army is evident.

From the latter years of the nineteenth century until the mid-twentieth, African American periodicals, such as the *Negro History Bulletin* and the *Journal of Negro History*, became the primary sources for publishing additional information on Black participation in the Revolution. The beginnings of the Civil Rights Movement of the 1950s and the approach of the Civil War centennial produced greater interest in Black history and influenced the award of academic grants to fund extensive research. Articles began to appear in scholarly university and state-historical-commission journals. In 1962 the University of North Carolina Press published for the Institute of Early American History and Culture the most detailed work to date. Benjamin Quarles, supported by multiple grants, including a John S. Guggenheim Foundation fellowship, and a leave of absence from the faculty of Morgan State College, became the esteemed expert on the subject as a result of *The Negro in the American Revolution*.

Despite his propensity to include every bit of information he discovered in his decade of research, his lack of military experience, and his efforts to placate his funding sources—agendas that occasionally show through—Quarles's book is magnificent. The opening sentence of his preface has become the most quoted single sentence on Black involvement in the rebellion: "In the Revolutionary War the American Negro was a participant and a symbol."

Sidney Kaplan, who was an emeritus professor of English and Afro-American studies at the University of Massachusetts, and Emma Nogrady

Kaplan, former reference librarian at Smith College, added the wonderfully illustrated *The Black Presence in the Era of the American Revolution*. The Kaplans include a section on Black military participation, but their major contribution is in telling the story of African American businessmen, clergymen, artists, and other contributors to arts and commerce of the period.

Today, African Americans serve in every specialty and at every rank in the U.S. Armed Forces. The story of their long struggle for opportunity and equality, much of which began during the Revolution, has not always been told well, if at all. The author's hope is that the following chapters will give credit where it is due and fill in pages about African American contributions to the Revolutionary War previously left blank.

AFRICAN AMERICANS

in the

REVOLUTIONARY WAR

1

African American Heroes
of the Revolution

IT WAS EARLY ON THE EVENING OF APRIL 18, 1775, when Paul Revere and William Dawes spotted the two lanterns hung in the steeple of Boston's North Church. In response to this prearranged signal, the two men spurred their horses and rode into the night to warn American rebels. "The British are coming! The British are coming!" shouted the riders as they raced from village to farm. At the alarm, local militiamen rose from their beds in mansions, small houses, and slave quarters to secure their weapons and assemble with their units.

The British were indeed advancing north from Boston toward the villages of Lexington and Concord with six companies of light infantry totaling nearly 400 men. Their orders from Gen. Thomas Gage were simple:

> Having received intelligence that a quantity of ammunition, provisions, artillery, tents, and small arms have been collected at Concord, for the avowed purpose of raising and supporting a rebellion against His Majesty, you will march the Corps of Grenadiers and Light Infantry, under your command, with the utmost expedition and secrecy to Concord, where you will seize and destroy . . . all military stores whatever.

Revere's and Dawes's warnings provided the local Minutemen time to prepare for the British advance. By morning, Lexington militia company commander Capt. John Parker stood with about seventy-five men in a staggered line across the two-acre common located in the center of the village. The captain's orders to his company typified the feelings of many of the colonists: "Stand your ground. Don't fire unless fired upon. But if they mean to have a war, let it begin here."[1]

Parker and his militiamen, tired of British taxation and oppression, were determined to defend their village and their perceptions of freedom and liberty. The irony, of course, was that neither Parker nor any of the other white participants appear to have appreciated the fact that their ranks contained several men to whom freedom would not apply. The very patriots who professed the desire for liberty for all did not mean literally "all." In the small company, several armed African Americans[2] stood alongside their owners, prepared to secure a freedom hitherto denied their race.

The ragtag white and Black militia company made little impression on the more experienced, much larger British force. Even the first gunfire of the Revolution, the famous "shot heard round the world," initiated by an unidentified source, failed to convince the British that the Americans were serious. The British commander, Maj. John Pitcairn, merely ordered a volley of fire over the heads of the Lexington militia. He then demanded the surrender of weapons. When Parker apparently instructed his men to comply, some laid down their muskets, while others began to walk away. But then more shots rang out, again their source unidentified, and Pitcairn ordered another volley, this time into the dispersing ranks of the Lexington militiamen.

In a matter of a few minutes, nine American soldiers lay dead, and another eight were injured. The casualty list itself is telling of the war effort by *all* participating Americans, for among the wounded was Prince Estabrook, "a negro man," according to the roster of participants and casualties on Lexington Green that appeared in the *Salem* (Massachusetts) *Gazette* of April 21, 1775. Another mention of him, in the *Journals of the Provincial Congress of Massachusetts*, also noted the African American's participation in the battle, describing him as "Prince, a negro."

Later broadsides also listed the veterans of Lexington Green. An undated one, probably published a few days after the battle and currently on file at the Massachusetts Historical Society, includes the name "Prin-

---

[1]As with many other famous quotes and stories from the American Revolution, the accuracy of Parker's words is difficult to verify. As glorious and patriotic as they may sound, they did not appear in print until 1858 and were credited to the recollection of Parker's grandson.

[2]As noted earlier, enlistment documents and unit rosters, if they exist at all, seldom recorded the race of participants in the American Revolution, making it difficult to determine the exact numbers and origins of those who fought.

cie Easterbrooks, a negro Man,"[3] among the casualties at Lexington. No "Mr." designation appears in front of his name, as it does before the names of the other participants.

As the British marched from Lexington toward Concord, they encountered more colonial militia units. Again, these ranks contained Black members as well as white, for African Americans, both free and slave, assembled with their fellow Minutemen to fend off the British. Among those Black Americans taking part in the ensuing battle were Peter Salem and Samuel Craft of Newton, Cato Bordman of Cambridge, Cuff Whittenmore and Cato Wood of Arlington, and Pomp Blackman, hometown unknown.

While Prince Estabrook had been among the first to shed blood for American independence at Lexington, another Black person, unidentified, suffered one of the last wounds of the war's initial day. When blocked by the rebels at Concord Bridge, the British retreated. As they retraced their steps, militiamen pursued, adopting the Native American tactic of firing at the withdrawing force from behind trees, fences, and impromptu fortifications. Just outside Boston, at Charlestown Neck, according to the journal of a British lieutenant in the Royal Welsh Fusiliers, "a Negro was wounded near the houses close to the Neck, out of which the Rebels fired to the last."

Although African Americans were among the earliest casualties of the Revolutionary War, Estabrook and his fellow Black militiamen were not the first to shed their blood for American independence from Great Britain. Five years earlier, Crispus Attucks, an escaped slave turned sailor, played a major role in the first confrontation between the rebellious colonists and the British military.

In 1770, Americans were chafing under increasing taxes and harsh military occupation by the British Crown. The citizens of Boston particularly disliked the oppression and arrogance of the local British army garrison, and the long, cold winter did little to cool their tempers.

Early in the evening of March 5, Crispus Attucks joined several of his fellow sailors as they warmed themselves around a public-house fire while they awaited their ship to sail from Boston Harbor. Much of their talk focused on the unfair treatment they received at the hands of the British and their animosity toward the redcoat soldiers. Attucks participated lit-

---

[3]Revolutionary War documents often include different spellings of the same name. "Estabrook" is the most accepted spelling of the name of the Black veteran of Lexington.

tle in the white men's conversation, but he shared their feelings of injustice, perhaps even more so, for the Black sailor had escaped slavery to go to sea more than twenty years earlier.

Suddenly, the group sharing the fire became aware of excited voices in the street followed by the ringing of the town's alarm bell. Attucks raced to the door to discover the snow-covered street filled with men moving toward the British headquarters on King Street. Some of the men seemed to be agitating the crowd, while others attempted to stop the mob's progress. A few began to flee.

Attucks stopped a young man leaving the scene and asked what was causing the commotion. The youth explained that a British soldier had refused to pay after receiving a haircut and then beat the barber when he demanded his money. Other colonists came to the support of the barber as more soldiers appeared and threatened to shoot if the mob did not disperse. The colonists made a few more verbal retorts at the men in uniform and reluctantly began to drift away. Laughing at the verbal threats, the soldiers marched back to their customhouse barracks.

Several accounts of eyewitnesses describe what happened next. Although the stories vary somewhat, all agree that a "short, stout, curly haired" Black man pushed forward and urged the hesitant crowd to stand up against the soldiers. With a leader now in charge, the colonists followed Attucks to the customhouse, where they threw snowballs and rocks at the building and its guards. The frightened sentinels called for reinforcements.

Attucks picked up a heavy piece of firewood and shook the club at the soldiers as he dared them to fire. The swelling mob behind him surged even closer to the customhouse. Despite the missiles hurled by the crowd and the threats of the club-wielding Attucks, the disciplined British soldiers adhered to their instruction to fire only upon the orders of their officers.

British captain Thomas Preston arrived and ensured that his men held their fire as he unsuccessfully attempted to convince the mob to disperse. His efforts only made the Bostonians angrier. Attucks, along with a dozen other men, advanced still closer, and the escaped slave began striking a soldier's bayonet with his wooden stick. He then swung his club at Preston's head. As the officer countered with his arm to ward off the blow, he bumped into one of his soldiers, causing the man to drop his weapon.

Instantly, Attucks seized the musket. The soldier also grabbed for the gun, and the two struggled for control. In wresting the musket from the Black man, the soldier stumbled and fell into the icy slush. The colonists laughed and, now confident that the soldier would not shoot, began to chant, "Why don't you fire? Why don't you fire?" Attucks, leaning on his stick, mockingly stared at the wet, muddy redcoat. Humiliated, the British soldier regained his feet and fired directly into Attucks's chest. Instantly, the other soldiers shot into the crowd.

Attucks and five others lay dead or dying in the street. Despite his color, the colonists hailed the dead Attucks as a hero and the first casualty of what would become the American Revolution. Few acknowledged, however, that Attucks, an escaped slave, would not have been able to share the freedoms for which he sacrificed his life. Attucks would not be the last Black man to die for a country and a cause that did not recognize him as an equal or ensure that he turn from the liberty for which he fought.

The "Boston Massacre," as it became known, fanned the flames of revolution that, in turn, led to open warfare at Lexington and Concord. Two months after those skirmishes, the war's first major battle took place. Once again the action occurred in Boston, and as in every fight that followed, Black Americans were in the forefront.

After the Battle of Concord Bridge, the British withdrew to Boston. During the following weeks the colonial militias united to surround the port city. In June 1775, as they tightened their cordon around Boston, the rebel commanders decided to send a force to occupy Bunker Hill, on the narrow peninsula at the end of Charlestown Neck, at the city's edge. Upon arrival, the American commander discovered that adjacent Breed's Hill offered more defendable ground and established his force there. History would record the upcoming battle as Bunker Hill, but in actuality it was on Breed's Hill that the patriots' and their opponents' blood would soak the ground.

In the militia ranks on Breed's Hill were at least a dozen African Americans, including several veterans of the earlier skirmishes. On June 17 the British attacked in waves from the beach. The dug-in Americans waited, as ordered by Col. William Prescott, until they could "see the whites of their eyes" and initially slowed the attacking redcoats. Black and white Americans stood together to resist the assault, but ultimately a shortage of ammunition and the superior numbers of the British finally forced the rebels to retreat.

One of the last to withdraw was Cuff Whittemore of Capt. Benjamin Locke's Arlington, Massachusetts, militia company. According to Samuel Swett, the earliest historian of the battle, in his *Notes to His Sketch of Bunker-Hill Battle*, published in 1825, Whittemore "fought bravely in the redoubt. He had a ball through his hat," and he "fought to the last, and when compelled to retreat, though wounded . . . he seized the sword" of a dead British officer.[4]

Another Black soldier achieved even more fame for his valor at the Battle of Bunker Hill. Peter Salem, claiming as his last name the town near his Farmington, Massachusetts, birthplace, was born in about 1750 to a slave held by Jeremiah Belknap. Peter grew into a tall young man of great physical strength and vigor. Sold shortly before the Revolution began to Maj. Lawson Buckminster, Peter Salem joined his owner's militia regiment and saw his first military action at Concord Bridge on April 19, 1775.

Still enslaved, Salem enlisted a few weeks later in the First Massachusetts Regiment, commanded by Col. Thomas Nixon, and on June 17 stood in the trenches on Bunker Hill with his fellow white and Black soldiers. Varying accounts exist of Salem's performance in the battle, but all agree as to his courage under fire.

At the center of all the stories is the fate of British Royal Marine major John Pitcairn. Major Pitcairn, a veteran of the Battles of Lexington Green and Concord Bridge, anticipated the battle with relish. Shortly before the fight, the major stopped in a Boston tavern for a glass of brandy. As he spun his finger in the glass, he boasted, "I will thus stir the Yankee blood before night."

After the initial volleys of rebel fire from Bunker Hill into the advancing British, Pitcairn and his fellow officers rallied their troops for repeated assaults. As the British line closed on the rebel trenches, Pitcairn shouted, "The day is ours." Amid the hail of gunfire and smoke, Salem took careful aim at the British officer and calmly shot him through the chest. The mortally wounded Pitcairn fell into the arms of his son, a marine lieutenant in his father's regiment.

Several of the battle's witnesses noted Salem's actions in their diaries or later writings. Jeremiah Belknap, Salem's original owner, wrote in his diary in 1787 that a Bunker Hill veteran told him, "A negro man . . . took aim at Major Pitcairn as he was rallying the dispersed British troops and shot him thro' the head."

An eyewitness report, referenced in a letter by Aaron White of Thompson, Connecticut, provides what appears to be the most accurate account. According to White, the eyewitness told him in 1807:

---

[4]That white officers allowed a Black private to keep—and later sell—a captured officer's sword is substantial evidence of the respect his superiors had for Whittemore and his performance in the battle.

The British Major Pitcairn had passed the storm of our fire and had mounted the redoubt, when waving his sword, he commanded in a loud voice, the rebels to surrender. His sudden appearance and his commanding air at first startled the men immediately below him. They neither answered or fired, probably not being exactly certain what was to be done. At this critical moment, a negro soldier stepped forward and aiming his musket at the major's bosom, blew him through.

Salem's officers later introduced him to Gen. George Washington as "the man who shot Pitcairn." More acclaim for the performances of Salem and other Black men at Bunker Hill resulted from a painting by John Trumbull, who witnessed the battle from Roxbury across the harbor. Eleven years after the battle, Trumbull unveiled *The Battle of Bunker Hill*, which prominently shows a Black servant handing a Connecticut officer a musket in the midst of the fight. At the center-top of the painting is another Black soldier.

Trumbull's work, hailed as a classic of realistic military-history paintings, today hangs in the U.S. Capitol rotunda in Washington, D.C. Engravings of the painting appeared on private notes issued by Boston and other banks.

The painting increased the awareness that Black Americans played a significant role in America's struggle for independence, but some writers have misidentified the prominent servant at the right of the painting as Salem. Actually, the much smaller image of a Black soldier at the top of the painting is more likely the heroic slayer of Major Pitcairn.

While official accounts of the actions by individual soldiers, white or Black, during the Revolution are extremely rare, still another African American performed so well at Bunker Hill that his actions, too, made written history. Salem Poor, a twenty-eight-year-old freeman from Andover, Massachusetts, enlisted in Capt. Benjamin Ames's militia company shortly before the battle. Six months after the fight, fourteen officers petitioned the General Court of the Continental Congress to bestow upon Poor "the reward due to so great and distinguished a character."

The document, signed by all fourteen officers, proclaimed:

The subscribers beg leave to report to your Honorable House (which we do in justice the character of so brave a man) that under our own observation, we declare that a negro man called Salem Poor of Col. Frye's regiment-Capt. Ames's Company-in the Battle at Charlestown [Neck], behaved like an experienced officer, as well as an excellent soldier, to set forth particulars of conduct would be tedious. We would only beg leave to say in the person of this said negro centers a brave and gallant soldier.[5]

The bloody encounter at Charlestown Neck's Bunker Hill convinced both the British and the rebellious colonists that the war for American independence would not be short. Neither the British nor the Americans, however, possessed united fronts in support of the war, nor were they decisive about how to conduct their campaigns.

Great Britain, although a world power, faced possible threats on the European continent from France, Spain, and Holland. Simultaneously, some of its political and military leaders empathized with America's desire for independence and stalled support for efforts to put down the rebel lion. One-third of the American population supported the rebellion; another third, known as Tories or Loyalists, remained loyal to the Crown; still another third were indifferent.

Throughout the long war, which did not conclude until 1783, the capabilities and zeal of both the British and the Americans varied from time to time and battle to battle. The British, distracted by worldwide military commitments to an empire on which "the sun never set," did not have the energy, money, or military assets to devote to defeating the rebels. Although they committed about 42,000 regular troops and reinforced them with 30,000 German mercenaries, the British never marshaled their entire resources against the American rebels.

On the other hand, the Continental army never fielded a force larger than 30,000 men, and often the number dropped to only 20,000. On occasion the Americans had as few as 5,000 men in their army. As a result, except for the war's initial battles, the smaller, weaker American armed forces made little effort to conduct sustained combat or lengthy campaigns. The colonists had to avoid defeat, hoping they could attain victory through survival.

Manpower was a critical issue for the rebel colonists. The white population numbered only 2 million, fewer than 700,000 of whom supported the rebellion. About 500,000 African Americans, mostly slaves, also resided in the thirteen colonies at the beginning of the war. These Black Americans, both slaves and free, had served in local militias since colo-

---

[5]For ease of reading, some of the misspellings and now improper capitalization and punctuation in this document and others cited in this work have been edited to comply with current usage. These emendations in no way change or detract from the content.

nization began, especially in the North, defending their villages against attacks by Native Americans. Despite their military service prior to the rebellion and their brave actions in the war's opening battles, the sheer number of Black people frightened many white Americans, who remained reluctant to accept Black men in uniform in any capacity.

At the same time as the Battle of Bunker Hill raged on at Charlestown Neck, the Continental Congress assumed jurisdiction of the state militias and formed the Continental army, with Gen. George Washington as commander in chief. Washington, a slaveholder himself, recognized that regional differences among the colonists complicated his problems in organizing, leading, and maintaining a unified force. An initial issue that threatened the stability of the new Continental army was the concern the southern states had about arming Black Americans. Many southerners feared a slave rebellion more than the British military.

One of Washington's first actions as commander of the Continental army was to placate the southerners as well as others who shared their fears about African American enlistments. On July 9, 1775, Washington had his adjutant general issue an order to recruiters not to enlist "any deserter from the Ministerial [British] army, nor any stroller, negro, or vagabond."

Over the next several months, Washington issued additional orders excluding Black Americans from serving in the military. Eventually, however, severe manpower shortages and the fear that Black Americans would join the British army forced him to sanction the enlistment of African Americans. In the interim, though, mounting casualties, desertions, and completion of enlistments encouraged many subordinate commanders to ignore the orders and enlist men regardless of their color. As a result, Black soldiers stood in the ranks of practically every infantry company and worked on the decks of each warship, serving as scouts, guides, couriers, spies, wagoners, cooks, orderlies, and seamen from the war's first shots to final victory.

Black participants did more than simply fill slots in military units. They displayed enormous courage and individual bravery. Beginning at Lexington, Concord, and Bunker Hill, heroics were common among the more than 5,000 African American soldiers and sailors who contributed to America's independence. William "Billy" Flora, a freeman from Portsmouth who served in Col. William Woodford's Second Virginia Regiment, typified their efforts. At the Battle of Great Bridge, near Norfolk, Virginia, on December 9, 1775, Flora so impressed his officers that after the battle, Capt. Thomas Nash wrote,

Flora, a colored man, was the last sentinel that came into the brest-work. He did not leave his post until he had fired several times. Billy had to cross a plank to get to the brestwork, and had fairly passed over it when he was seen to turn back, and deliberately take up the plank after him, amidst a shower of musket balls.

Despite having only a third of the white population in support of the rebellion, the Continental Congress confirmed its Declaration of Independence on July 2, 1776, and two days later proclaimed the document to the world. Written by Thomas Jefferson of Virginia, the document began, "We hold these truths to be self evident, that all men are created equal, that they are endowed by their Creator with certain unalienable rights, that among these are life, liberty, and the pursuit of happiness . . ."

One "truth" immediately self-evident was that the declaration's promise of liberty did not extend to the more than 500,000 African Americans held in bondage. Jefferson, a slaveholder himself, nevertheless harbored objections against the practice and included in early drafts of the document a clause that would have ended slavery. However, South Carolina and Georgia raised objections so strenuously that they created a threat to the union of the North and South. Jefferson struck the clause from the final document and sealed the fate of Black Americans for another century.

Despite being denied liberty by their country's formal Declaration of Independence, African Americans still volunteered to endure the hardships and dangers of combat to guarantee the freedom of the United States. Some did so in response to promises of release from slavery in exchange for their service. Others either willingly or unwillingly accompanied their owners into the military as servants. Still others volunteered to leave the monotony of their current life for the prospect of adventure afforded by military campaigns. All believed that their race as a whole could only benefit from their demonstrated loyal service.

The British response to the Declaration of Independence was an increase in military pressure to quash the rebellion. Washington's army suffered defeats on Long Island and at New York in August and September 1776, and by December the rebels were in full retreat southward through New Jersey and into Pennsylvania. The fervor of revolt cooled with the losses and the approaching winter. In a report to the Crown, a British commander described the American army in the winter of 1776 as "almost naked, dying of cold, without blankets, and very ill supplied with provisions." Enlistments faltered, and the future of the United States appeared bleak.

Washington knew he had to improve the morale of his army and the

American public. The only way to do this dramatically was to ignore the eighteenth-century warfare tradition of spending the winter months in encampments. Instead of focusing on the cold, Washington procured every serviceable rowboat and barge available and assembled a force of 2,400 men along the southern bank of the Delaware River.

Early on the evening of December 25, 1776, Washington addressed his men as they prepared for a Christmas attack against the Hessian garrison across the river in Trenton, New Jersey. The general quoted lines from *Common Sense* by Thomas Paine:

> The summer soldier and sunshine patriot will in this crisis shrink from the service of their country; and he that stands now deserves the love and thanks of man and woman. Up and help us; lay your shoulder to the wheel; the heart that feels not now is dead.

Those who stood that day and lay their shoulders against the wheel with Washington on the snowy field included scores of African Americans, both free and slave. For twenty-three-year-old freeman Oliver Cromwell of Burlington County, New Jersey, a member of Col. Israel Streve's Second New Jersey Regiment, the crossing of the Delaware and the Battle of Trenton would be only a small portion of the combat he would see during his nearly seven years of Revolutionary War service.

Another Black soldier served in close proximity to Washington for the entire campaign—so close, in fact, that he appears in many of the paintings of the prebattle preparations and as a rower in the general's boat during the actual crossing of the Delaware. This African American was Prince Whipple, a man with an unusual story.

Information about Whipple is scarce. The most detailed source is a brief description by William C. Nell that appeared in his groundbreaking book *The Colored Patriots of the American Revolution . . .* , first published in 1855. Nell acknowledges that the Black soldier in the paintings of Washington is Whipple and further explains:

> Prince Whipple was born in Amabou, Africa, of comparatively wealthy parents. When about ten years of age, he was sent by them, in company with a cousin, to America, to be educated. An elder brother had returned four years before, and his parents were anxious that their other child should receive the same benefits. The captain who brought the two boys over proved a treacherous villain, and carried them to Baltimore, where he exposed them for sale, and they were both purchased by Portsmouth men, Prince falling to Gen. Whipple.

Prince accompanied his owner, William Whipple, a signer of the Declaration of Independence, into the army at the beginning of the Revolution and served as the general's bodyguard and personal servant. At Trenton, General Whipple acted as a member of Washington's staff, and Prince fought alongside both officers for the entire campaign.[6]

Whipple was not without Black companionship while serving with the American commander's staff. Washington had purchased a young slave in 1768 named William Lee. Lee accompanied the general to Massachusetts when he assumed command of the Continental army and served for the duration of the Revolution as Washington's personal orderly. Shortly after the war ended, Lee, still enslaved, asked Washington if he could bring his wife, Margaret Thomas, a free woman from Philadelphia, to live with him at Mount Vernon. Washington agreed, stating, "I cannot refuse his request . . . as he has lived with me so long and followed my fortunes through the war with fidelity."

Washington's crossing of the Delaware and victory at Trenton produced the morale-building result the general had hoped for, though it had little strategic significance. The British, occupying the major cities and ports, still possessed a far superior armed force. With the arrival of the spring of 1777, the redcoats, not surprisingly, resumed their campaign to crush the American rebellion.

Americans, Black and white, continued their resistance and by the summer were fighting under a red, white, and blue flag composed of stars and stripes; it was adopted by the Continental Congress on June 14. At Brandywine Creek, near Philadelphia, Black soldiers once again proved their bravery. One of the stories of their service in the battle is probably more legend than fact but nevertheless shows the impression the Black warriors made on their fellow soldiers.

According to accounts related throughout the States at the time and immortalized in a poem written a century later by Paul Lawrence Dunbar, a slave named Black Samson played a major role in the battle. Enraged by the battle death of a white soldier whom he considered a friend, Samson picked up a hay scythe and swept through the British ranks. Dunbar poetically described the action:

---

[6]Several other accounts mention Prince Whipple's origins. At least one discounts the story of Whipple's being sent to America for an education and states that he was captured in Africa by slave traders and exported to the colonies in bondage. All of the stories agree that he did eventually become the property of William Whipple and that Prince accompanied him throughout the war.

Flee from the scythe of the reaper,
Flee while the moment is thine,
None may safely withstand him,
Black Samson of Brandywine.[7]

While Black Samson's actions at Brandywine on September 2, 1777, are without substantiation, the bravery and sacrifice of other African American infantrymen in the fight are factual. According to the pension records of the state of Pennsylvania, John Francis, identified as a "negro" in the Third Pennsylvania Regiment, "had both legs much shattered by grape shot at the Battle of Brandywine."

Most Black soldiers in the Continental army at Brandywine and other battles served in the infantry, but a few rode with the cavalry, while others manned the guns of the rebel artillery batteries. An obituary published in the January 15, 1834, edition of the *Norristown* (Pennsylvania) *Free Press* provides details on the service of Edward Hector, who enlisted in Capt. Hercules Cortney's Battery of the Third Pennsylvania Artillery on March 10, 1777.

Hector's obituary states:

During the war of the revolution, his conduct on one memorable occasion, exhibited an example of patriotism and bravery which deserves to be recorded. At the Battle of Brandywine he had charge of an ammunition wagon attached to Colonel [Thomas] Proctor's regiment, and when the American army was obliged to retreat, an order was given by the proper officers to those having charge of the wagons, to abandon them to the enemy, and save themselves by flight. The heroic reply of the deceased uttered in the true spirit of the Revolution: "The enemy shall not have my team; I will save my horses and myself!" He instantly started on his way, and as he proceeded, amid the confusion of the surrounding scene, he calmly gathered up a few stands of arms which had been left on the field by the retreating soldiers, and safely retired with his wagon, team, and all, in the face of the victorious foe.

However, individual valor by Black or white patriots at Brandywine and the following battles in the fall of 1777 failed to stop the advancing British. In September the Continental Congress hastily abandoned

[7]Some accounts identify the white friend as a schoolteacher who had taught Samson and whose daughter had provided him food. None of the rosters of the units that fought at Brandywine, however, list anyone named Samson, and no details other than the oral legends support the story.

Philadelphia and moved to Lancaster and then on to York. On October 4 the redcoats occupied Philadelphia, and shortly thereafter Washington and his army settled into winter quarters at Valley Forge.

Washington later wrote about the long, harsh winter, stating that his army of about 12,000 was "composed of men often times half starved, always in rags, without pay, and experiencing every species of distress, which human nature is capable of undergoing."

Samuel Poor, hero of the Battle of Bunker Hill, was one of the survivors of Valley Forge. Another Black soldier, Phillip Field, a private in the Second New York Regiment, joined the more than 2,500 men who died of the cold and disease during the long winter.

Despite their hardships, Washington's army emerged from Valley Forge rededicated to seeking their country's independence. Reinforced by units that wintered at other locations, Washington led an army of 15,000 against the British at Monmouth Courthouse, New Jersey, on June 28, 1778. Unit reports note that more than 700, or about 5 percent, of the rebel soldiers in the fight were Black. More important, two months later, after many of the white veterans of the battle had finished their enlistments and been discharged, the number of Black soldiers in Washington's army remained the same.

The American army managed to survive, and therefore ensure the continuation of the United States, during the summer campaigns of 1778. The approach of winter, however, once again found the struggling army occupying austere quarters at Valley Forge. Recruits for the rebel army remained a primary concern of Washington and his staff, and while the Continental Congress continued to call upon the individual states for additional battalions, the pool of available and willing manpower continued to diminish.

More and more freemen and slaves, particularly in the Northern states, enlisted in integrated units, but many remained relegated to laborer and support roles. Necessity, however, soon provided additional opportunities for African American soldiers. Rhode Island, with a small population and two-thirds of its land occupied by the British, experienced extreme difficulty in providing sufficient numbers of able men for its two active-duty battalions. At Valley Forge in November 1777, Gen. James Varnum proposed that the two diminished battalions be combined into one and that officers return to Rhode Island to recruit an all-Black battalion.

General Washington and Rhode Island governor Nicholas Cooke conferred and agreed there was no other way for the state to meet its draft quota. The concurring Rhode Island assembly passed a measure authorizing the battalion and granting payment to owners of slaves who volunteered for service. With no reference to the need that necessitated the legislation, the assembly nobly declared, "History affords us frequent precedents of the wisest, freest, and bravest nations having liberated their slaves and enlisted them as soldiers to fight in defense of their country."

Col. Christopher Greene and other white officers organized Black volunteers into five companies assigned to the First Rhode Island Regiment. Shortly after their formation and before completing training, the battalion rushed to counter a British-Hessian offensive in August 1778, in what became known as the Battle of Rhode Island to control the state's major seaport. African Americans now had the opportunity to show their skills and bravery as a unit rather than only as individuals. In the four-hour fight that followed, the Black Rhode Islanders held a critical portion of the Continental line and suffered twenty-two casualties.

As the war continued into 1779, the British altered their strategy of concentrating their efforts on the northern states and refocused their efforts to the South. Washington maintained his army in the North while dispatching his ablest general, Nathanael Greene, to command the American army in the southern states. Even though they now fought on two fronts, the rebels retained their strategy of defense. They avoided sustained combat to maintain their country's survival as well as their own.

On December 29, 1778, Savannah, Georgia, fell to the British, who then used the port to mount offensives into the interior. The concerned Continental Congress adopted a resolution on March 29, 1779, recommending that

> the States of South Carolina and Georgia, if they think the same expedient, to take measures immediately for raising three thousand able-bodied Negroes. . . . That every Negro shall well and faithfully serve as a soldier to the end of the present war, and shall then return his arms, be emancipated, and receive fifty dollars.

White manpower in the southern states was even more sparse than in the North, but slaveholders did not think it "expedient" to arm their slaves. In South Carolina the ratio of Black residents to white ones was six to four; in Georgia, nearly four and a half to five and a half. For slaveholders in these states, putting muskets into the hands of such numbers was tantamount to inviting insurrection. Additionally, these whites, believing themselves superior, were contemptuous of the idea of equality and freedom for their slaves. Furthermore, they did not wish to risk the loss or injury of their valuable property.

Neither South Carolina nor Georgia enlisted Black soldiers, but several African Americans made their way into the ranks as substitutes for their owners. Some slaves, like Austin Dabney of Burke County, Georgia, were freed by their owners in order to fill their enlistment obligation. Dabney served as an artilleryman in Col. Elijah Clark's corps until suffering a musket ball through the thigh at the Battle of Kettle Hill, Georgia, on February 4, 1779. The Georgia legislature later honored Dabney for his "bravery and fortitude" and declared that no soldier was "braver or did better in service during the Revolutionary struggle."

Other slaves who served in their owners' places did not necessarily gain their freedom. In 1781 white North Carolinian William Kitchen deserted his Continental army regiment. When caught, Kitchen agreed to purchase Edward Griffin and deliver him as a substitute. Kitchen also agreed to provide Griffin his freedom upon his completion of honorable service.

Griffin joined his North Carolina regiment in June 1781 and participated in several of the war's final battles. Upon his discharge in July 1782, Kitchen seized Griffin and, instead of granting him the promised freedom, sold him to a neighbor. Griffin remained a slave until he successfully petitioned the General Assembly of North Carolina on April 4, 1784. Along with the petition, Griffin submitted his discharge papers, which declared him "a good and faithful soldier," and an affidavit from a witness who observed Kitchen's verbal promise of freedom for his substitute. The assembly responded by declaring Griffin a "freeman."

In addition to their important roles in the Continental army, African Americans also fought for the independence of the United States with allied forces. France allied itself with the Americans against Great Britain in 1778 and supported the rebellion with ground and sea forces. Spain also declared war against Great Britain in 1779, adding to the list of British opponents on the Continent and in the New World.

In 1779 a French brigade of more than 3,500 men joined the American efforts in Georgia to retake the port of Savannah from its British occupiers. Within this French army were nearly 600 Black freemen and slaves recruited in the West Indies and commanded by Viscount François de Fontages.

The joint American-French offensive against Savannah failed, but the Black soldiers performed well nevertheless. The official accounts of the battle dispatched to Paris commended the Black soldiers, stating, "The legion saved the army at Savannah by bravely covering the retreat."

Several of the soldiers in France's Black legion in Georgia returned home to lead their own revolution and gain independence for their island nation of Haiti. Henri Christophe, a twelve-year-old Black infantryman wounded at Savannah, became the leader of the Haitian government.

In Spanish Louisiana, Gov. Bernardo de Gálvez also employed Black soldiers to defend his territory from the British. Accounts vary on the number of Black soldiers in Gálvez's force—10–50 percent, with 15–20 percent the most likely to be accurate. Whatever their numbers, Black soldiers performed well. Gálvez's army pushed the British out of Louisiana at Baton Rouge in 1779 and then continued their offensive, capturing Mobile in 1780 and Pensacola in 1781.

Gálvez attributed much of his success to his Black soldiers, declaring that his companies of "Negro and Free Mulattoes" had "conducted themselves with as much valor and generosity as the white."

The collective Black service and the bravery of individual African Americans in the Revolution extended beyond land combat to service at sea. Black sailors played a heroic role in U.S. naval battles and other seaborne operations during the war. Service at sea in the eighteenth century on fishing and commercial vessels or warships proved extremely difficult and dangerous. Experienced in the difficulties of finding and keeping crews, captains paid little attention to a man's color if he volunteered to sign aboard. In addition to freemen who sought sea duty, some runaway slaves, like Crispus Attucks, went to sea as a means of escape. Still other African Americans found themselves delivered to ship captains by their owners, who received their pay.

Black sailors fought in every major sea battle of the Revolution, including as a part of John Paul Jones's crew aboard the *Bon Homme Richard* in its epic battle against the *Serapis* on September 23, 1779. Most of their service and sacrifice went unrecognized except for the notation on a crew manifest of a sailor's being "Black," "negro," or "mulatto."

Most available information on Black service at sea in the American Revolution comes from personal accounts written by ship captains and the various petitions filed by veterans in the postwar years. James Barron, commander of the Virginia State ship *Liberty*, recorded in his postwar memoir his recollections of the "courageous patriots who had served on board" his ship during the conflict. Barron concluded:

> Amongst these, I take pleasure in stating there were several colored men, who, I think, in justice to their merits should not be forgotten. Harry (a slave belonging to Capt. John Cooper) was distinguished for his zeal and daring; Cupid (a slave of Mr. William Ballard) stood forth on all occasions as the champion of liberty and discharged all his duties with a fidelity that made him a favorite of all the officers.

The Continental and state navies also welcomed Black men as pilots for their vessels when navigating near the shore and on the inland waterways and when maneuvering ships into ports. As one rebel naval official explained, Black Americans were "accustomed to the navigation of the river" from their prewar experience. One of these Black pilots, Caesar, property of the Tarrant family of Hampton, Virginia, stood at the wheel of the schooner *Patriot* in several major actions, including when the ship captured the British brig *Fanny*.

Black freemen performed with equal distinction. James Forten, the third generation of a free family from Philadelphia, volunteered for naval service at the age of only fifteen. As a powder boy, Forten joined twenty other Black Americans, who made up 10 percent of the crew of Stephen Decatur's twenty-two-gun privateer *Royal Louis*. In July 1781, Forten participated in his ship's successful attack against the British brig *Active*.

Unfortunately, their next engagement against three British warships was not as successful. When their captain surrendered, Forten and the other Black sailors faced sale in the West Indies by their British captors. The young Forten became a favorite of the British captain, however, and the officer offered to send him to England to be educated. Forten refused, saying, "I am here as a prisoner for the liberties of my country."

While the U.S. Marine Corps would not officially accept African Americans until World War II, more than 150 years after the American War of Independence, a few Black men did serve as marines on land and on board ships during the Revolution. Thirteen veterans are identified on the Marine Corps' rolls as Black, with three in the Continental marines and the others spread across the detachments assigned to the state navies of Connecticut, Massachusetts, and Pennsylvania. At least one Black marine died in action aboard the brig *Reprisal* in 1777.

Black soldiers, sailors, and marines fought tenaciously for the liberty of the United States. Black freemen saw the fight for independence from Great Britain compatible with their desire for equality. For slaves, the independence of the United States was a step toward their own freedom, and they willingly fought to share a portion of that liberty. Not all enslaved African Americans, however, rallied to the cause of the Revolution; some turned to whichever side promised the most expeditious route to their personal freedom.

Great Britain, long a major transporter of human cargo, had no desire to free the slaves in America or its other colonies. However, several British leaders and their Loyalist American allies saw distinct advantages in trading freedom to slaves in exchange for their military service in that it added to their fighting numbers while depriving the rebels of potential soldiers, sailors, and behind-the-lines support.

While the Americans were still debating whether to allow Black enlistments, the British took action early in the war to entice slaves to gain
their freedom by taking up arms against their former owners. On November 7, 1775, John Murray, the earl of Dunmore and the governor of
colonial Virginia, issued a proclamation:

I do hereby . . . declare all indentured servants, negroes, or others
(appertaining to the rebels) free, that are able and willing to bear
arms, they joining His Majesty's troops, as soon as may be, for the
more speedily reducing this Colony to proper dignity.

More than 300 escaped slaves joined the British during the first month
following the proclamation. Dunmore named his force the Ethiopian
Regiment and issued uniforms inscribed with the slogan "Liberty to
Slaves." During the next few months, more than 30,000 slaves of all ages,
both male and female, crossed the lines seeking the freedom denied
them by their American owners.

Over the next seven years, 100,000 Black Americans sought refuge and
liberty with the British. Most of these escaped slaves worked as rear-area
laborers, cooks, and servants, but as many as 1,000 served directly as soldiers with Lord Dunmore and in other regiments. German Hessians,
mercenaries hired by the British to help quell the rebellion, also placed
Black men in support roles and accepted some into their ranks as replacements for soldiers lost to wounds or disease.

Although the degree of acceptance by white field officers of African
Americans in their combat ranks and in supporting positions varied during the long conflict, no battle of significance took place on land or sea
during the Revolutionary War in which Black soldiers did not participate—at times on both sides. Official reports and available historical documents show that Black military men played a role in the final victory.

Despite their sacrifices, only a few slaves gained their freedom through
military service. Following the war, the quality of life barely improved for
Black freemen and not at all for those who remained in bondage. The
causes and campaigns of the Revolutionary War were many and complicated. The results are much easier to summarize: White Americans fought
for the right to govern themselves; Black Americans fought for freedom for
themselves as individuals and as members of their race. White Americans
achieved success and established what would become the world's most
powerful and wealthy country. Black Americans, despite brave service and
extreme sacrifice, mostly remained mired in the status quo. Nearly another
century would pass before slavery was abolished in the United States.

2

Pre-Revolution Colonial America

SLAVERY DID NOT, OF COURSE, ORIGINATE with European settlement of the New World. Throughout history, groups and nations enslaved individuals who differed from them in race, religion, or political origins.

Although slavery certainly predates the earliest archaeological evidence of human bondage among the Sumerians of Mesopotamia in 2000 B.C., these founders of the Babylonian Empire established the first known slave laws. Slavery remained the norm among so-called civilized societies for the next 3,500 years.

By the time Spain and Portugal began exploring and settling the New World in the latter years of the fifteenth century, slaves played an important role in the commerce and lifestyle of both countries. They assumed they could continue to enslave defeated local populations to build villages, clear forests, and establish plantations in the Western Hemisphere. The Europeans, with their superior weapons and military organization, had little trouble defeating the Native Americans, but turning them into productive slaves proved much more difficult.

While the major Native American tribes commonly enslaved defeated enemies and used them and their families as servants and human sacrifices, the Indians responded poorly to the European style of bondage. They did not adjust mentally or physically to the hard labor of plantation life, but even more significant were two other barriers to their enslavement. First, they possessed no natural immunity to European diseases, which killed them by the hundreds. More important, runaway Native American slaves, familiar with the terrain, could, and did, escape and easily blend in with non-slave Indians or survive on their own in the surrounding countryside.

The Spanish and Portuguese quickly determined that Native Americans could not meet their huge manpower needs. Fortunately for the European conquerors and unfortunately for the residents of Africa, a new, and seemingly unending, source of excellent slaves presented itself.

Portugal imported their first African slaves in 1444 as an exchange for Moorish prisoners of war. During the next fifty years, the Portuguese increased their slave trade with Africa as they established trading posts along the coast of Guinea. Slaves during these years worked as household servants and field hands alongside local non-slaves but did not play a major economic role.

The potential of African slaves as a cornerstone to occupying and exploiting the New World did not reveal itself until it became evident that the Indians neither would nor could fill the labor needs. Portugal began to expand its trade in African slaves, and by the end of the sixteenth century, Black slaves were an integral part of the Portuguese, Spanish, Dutch, and French colonization of the West Indies and Central and South America.

Neither religious organizations nor governments offered any significant resistance to the capture, enslavement, and shipment of thousands of Africans to the New World. Europeans believed in the absolute rights of property owners, and they considered Black slaves property. European countries did not pass laws concerning the slave trade until the sixteenth century. King Louis XIV established the *Code Noir* (Black Code) in 1685, which contained rather mild rulings against beating and executing slaves, but generally the French, like other Europeans, left the treatment of slaves in the New World up to the local colonial leaders.

Most Africans arrived in the colonies of the West Indies and southern America in chains. However, Black Americans—both slave and free, soldier and sailor—also played a part in the early exploration of the lands that would later enslave so many of their race. The contributions of Africans to the European settlement of the New World began with the first voyage of discovery. At least one man of African heritage, Pedro Alonso Nifio, sailed with Christopher Columbus on his initial voyage to the New World. Another Black sailor, Diego el Negro, accompanied Columbus on his last voyage to America in July 1502.

Africans served in subsequent military expeditions into the New World as servants, laborers, and soldiers. When Vasco Núñez de Balboa crossed Central America to reach the Pacific Ocean, at least thirty Black persons occupied his ranks. Africans also accompanied the small expeditions of Hernán Cortés that defeated the Aztecs in Mexico in 1519 and those of Francisco Pizarro that conquered the Incas in Peru in 1533.

The first Africans to arrive in North America did so as a part of a brief Spanish effort to form a colony near the mouth of the Pee Dee River in present-day South Carolina in 1526. Details are sketchy, but records indicate that 100 Black slaves accompanied 500 Spaniards in an unsuccessful attempt to establish a settlement. The colony lasted only a few months before the survivors returned to Spanish island communities in the Caribbean. Some accounts indicate that the settlement's failure came as the result of an uprising by the slaves, but no factual information exists to substantiate this claim.

The most significant Black man in the early explorations of North America arrived in 1528 via shipwreck on the southeast coast of what is now Texas. Among the survivors were the expedition's leader, Cabeza de Vaca, the Spanish soldier Andrés Dorentes, and his Black slave Esteban (or Estevanico), who quickly became "twice a slave" when local Indians captured the castaways. Eventually, Esteban, Dorentes, Cabeza de Vaca, and several others escaped overland to Mexico City, arriving there after a journey of eight years.

Esteban remained enslaved, but his skills in Indian sign language, learned while a captive, led to his earning another "first" in the New World. In 1536, Esteban, acting as scout and interpreter for an expedition into the American Southwest, became the first non-Indian to visit what would become New Mexico and Arizona. Three years later, Esteban returned to the Southwest as a guide for Spaniards seeking the fabled "seven golden cities of Cibola." Esteban found no gold but did reach the Zuni village of Hawikuh in New Mexico, where the Indians, angered at the intrusion, executed him.

Unlike the Spanish and Portuguese, who brought slaves along on their expeditions and planned to use them as an integral part of their settlement of the New World, the English formed their first colonies in Virginia without slaves in their possession. The English settlers had problems enough after they established Jamestown, the viability of the colony in doubt as a result of harsh winters and fatal illness. By 1619 fewer than 1,000 English settlers occupied a small foothold on the American continent, but several events occurred that year that ensured their longevity and greatly influenced the future of the colonists and their adopted land.

In midsummer the Virginia House of Burgesses, the first American legislative assembly, met to establish a representative government that would eventually lead to the world's most powerful democracy. At about this same time, the Jamestown colonists gathered their first major harvest of tobacco for export in exchange for needed goods from Britain.

The significant third event that occurred the same year usually appears as only a footnote of the time, and yet it was an event that was a turning point in the history of Virginia and the future United States. According to John Rolfe, colonial farmer and husband of the Indian Pocahontas, "about the last of August came in a Dutch man of war that sold us twenty negroes." This single-sentence entry in Rolfe's journal, written several months after the fact, marks the first official record of the arrival of Africans in the colonies.

Even this initial sale of Africans to American colonists was not deliberate or premeditated. The Dutch captain put into port at Jamestown to procure food and water. The exchange of slaves for the needed supplies was merely for the convenience of the seller and the buyer.

As Jamestown became more stable and profitable, surely influenced by the contributions of the first Africans, more English colonists arrived to establish additional settlements. These early settlers, like the Spanish conquerors of Central and South America, also initially considered the Native Americans as a potential labor source. However, the number of whites was few and the number of Indians many. The best the English settlers could do was to maintain a degree of peaceful coexistence with the Native Americans, with no possibility of turning them into slaves.

To meet the need for cheap labor, the colonists imported indentured white servants from Britain. These servants, forced to work in slavery-like conditions, generally endured seven years of servitude to pay for their passage to America or to work off debts incurred in England. A second source of imported labor appeared when slave traders discovered the American market for their cargoes. By 1638, New England colonists as well as Virginians were buying slaves from these flesh merchants. The first written record of Africans sold to New Englanders appears in the journal entry of John Winthrop, governor of the Massachusetts Bay Colony. On December 12, 1638, Winthrop noted the arrival of the ship *Desire* in Boston Harbor, where it delivered salt, cotton, tobacco, and "Negroes."

During the early years of colonization, indentured whites filled most of the cheap-labor needs, with the occasional Africans purchased to fill vacancies as the servants completed their contracts. The importation of Africans into the colonies remained slow for the remainder of the seventeenth century. By 1680 there were only about 1,000 Black individuals in New England and about twice that number in the Virginia settlements.

It was not until the early years of the 1700s that indentured servants and the limited slave trade could not satisfy the demand for labor. This shortage occurred as the population of New England grew and as southern farmers expanded their small tobacco and rice production into a plantation system. With the increased demand for laborers, English merchants readily stepped forward to supply slaves to add to their fortunes.

Ships left England with cloth, beads, and other merchandise to be traded on the west coast of Africa for slaves. They then sailed the notorious "Middle Passage" to the West Indies and North America and exchanged their human cargo for cash and such agricultural products as tobacco and sugar. They then returned to England, completing the triangle of trade that produced full cargoes and large profits.

The fate of many of the newly arrived Africans varied. Small farmers, who could only afford one or two slaves, purchased some of the Africans and worked alongside them. Many more ended up as chattel on large plantations, especially in the South, where they worked in the fields in what was known as a "Gang Plan." Some slaves, particularly those of higher intelligence anddemonstrated loyalty, had specific chores, such as cooks, housekeepers, messengers, and craftsmen in what was called the "Task System." Some also became foundry workers and sailors or shipyard workers.

Both the English slave traders and the American colonists considered Africans their personal property and treated them accordingly. During the early years of settling North America, Black Americans had no legal status, because English law at the time ignored slavery as an issue and allowed their colonies to establish their own regulations concerning the ownership of human beings.

Early regulations for slaves evolved from the statutes that governed indentured servants. In fact, the first Africans sold by the Dutch to the Jamestown colonists lived in an environment that suggested an indentured rather than enslaved status. Although records are sparse, apparently at least some of the original twenty Black people at Jamestown eventually gained their freedom. Two, identified only as Antony and Isabella, married in 1624 and became the parents of William Tucker, the first African American child born in Virginia.

Laws, written and perceived, concerning indentured servants and slaves focused first and foremost on the rights of the owners. Second, they emphasized the protection of the general public from these individuals. No laws existed for the protection or benefit of the involuntary laborers, because most colonists felt superior to the indentured servants, who were from the lowest economic and social classes, and believed that African slaves were subhumans from savage cultures.

It did not take long for the colonies to legalize these perceived differences. In 1640 three servants indentured to Hugh Gwyn ran away from his Virginia farm and fled into Maryland. Gwyn pursued, apprehended, and returned them to stand before a colonial court. On July 9 the court ruled that Victor, a Dutchman, and James Gregory, a Scotsman, were to receive thirty lashes and have one year added to their period of indenture. The other runaway also was to receive thirty lashes, but the court concluded "that the third being a Negro named John Punch shall serve his said master or his assigns for the time of his natural life here or elsewhere."

In the same year, only three years after Governor Winthrop first acknowledged the purchase of slaves in his colony, Massachusetts passed Section 91 of the *Body of Liberties* of 1641, which not only recognized a Black individual as a slave but also declared that the enslavement of the entire race was a valid endeavor. Twenty years later, Virginia passed statutes, known as slave codes, that other colonies soon adopted. The 1661 Virginia statute declared that any child born of an enslaved mother was the property of the mother's owner. Furthermore, it denied slaves the right to leave their owner's property or to assemble without permission. They could not own weapons, nor could they testify against a white person in court. The codes also authorized the execution of slaves found guilty of rape or murder and sanctioned the use of the whip, branding iron, and other punishments for minor crimes.

Slave codes, particularly in the South, continued to evolve and become more detailed with the passage of time. South Carolina passed legislation in 1712 that typified the colonies' legal as well as ethical outlook on slavery and slaves. "An Act for the Better Ordering and Governing of Negroes and Slaves"[1] opened with a preamble that admitted that "the plantations and estates of this Province cannot be well and sufficiently managed and brought into use, without the labor and service of negroes and other slaves."

The act continued with a declaration that codes were necessary because slaves "are of barbarous, wild, savage nature, and as such renders them wholly unqualified to be governed by the laws, customs and practices of the Province." Subsequent sections of the South Carolina act spelled out the same restrictions mandated by the Virginia law of 1661.

In these colonial regulations, laws prohibiting the possession of weapons by slaves were safeguards to prevent the slaves from killing their white enslavers. Their fears were not groundless. The first documented slave revolt in the colonies occurred in Gloucester County, Virginia, when white indentured servants and Black slaves conspired against their owner. Another servant betrayed the plot before the conspirators could act.

A slave revolt of greater magnitude took place in New York City on April 7, 1712, when twenty-seven slaves set fire to an outhouse in an orchard near the center of town. When whites responded to the fire, the rebel slaves killed nine of them. The slaves then fled, with the colonial

---

[1]Additional information on this legislation can be found in Appendix B, "Slave Codes."

militia in pursuit. Six of the rebels committed suicide rather than face capture; the militia caught and executed the others. The primary result of the revolt was the extension of the New York slave code to include death sentences for slaves guilty of arson and conspiracy to commit murder.

A more organized slave revolt took place in South Carolina in 1739. On September 9 a slave named Cato, along with about thirty-five to forty-five other fellow slaves, killed two warehouse guards in the village of Stono, about twenty miles west of Charleston. Taking arms and ammunition from the warehouse, the escaped slaves fled toward Spanish Florida and killed at least twenty-five more whites along the way. A mob of whites finally caught up with the runaways and killed Cato and most of his followers. A few escapees, however, apparently outdistanced their pursuers and reached freedom.

By the 1740s white America so feared slave insurrections that Black Americans were the first suspects in any disaster. During the evening of February 28, 1741, a series of fires broke out in New York City. With the slave revolt of 1712 still in mind, the New Yorkers immediately arrested Black residents and held them responsible despite a lack of evidence of their participation. Over the next month the city tried 134 African Americans for arson. The court discharged thirty-three to their owners with no punishment; it then ordered thirteen burned alive, eighteen hanged, and seventy deported in chains to the West Indies.

The slaves were not completely without champions in their resistance to enslavement. Not all the colonists supported the harsh punishment of rebellious slaves or the belief that slavery itself was justifiable or right. On February 18, 1688, Quakers at Germantown, Pennsylvania, adopted the first formal antislavery resolution in the colonies. The Society of Friends, in a document called the Germantown Protest, stated that slavery was in opposition to the basic rights of man and the Christian faith and that all men, regardless of race or color, should be treated the same. The protest also warned of possible slave insurrections and asked, "Have these negroes not as much right to fight for their freedom as you have to keep them slaves?"

Many New England Puritans, however, believed that Black Africans bore a biblical curse and that slavery served as an atonement for their sins. Nevertheless, some colonial church leaders, other than Quakers, joined the protests against slavery. Samuel Sewell, a Calvinist church leader, merchant, and magistrate in Boston, published a three-page antislavery pamphlet in 1700. Sewell began "The Selling of Joseph" with a statement that provides an excellent summary of his writings: "Forasmuch as liberty is in real value next unto life; none ought to part with it themselves, or deprive others of it, but upon most mature consideration."

The Quakers continued their antislavery campaign after the German-town Protest, but their efforts, like that of Sewell, received little attention outside their own communities. That changed in 1754 when John Wool-man of Mount Holly, New Jersey, published his Quaker beliefs on slavery in a pamphlet that became the most circulated antislavery document in the colonies. Woolman began his tract, entitled "Some Considerations on the Keeping of Negroes: Recommended to the Professors of Chris-tianity of Every Denomination," with the New Testament verse of Matthew 25:40, "Forasmuch as ye did it to the least of these my Brethren, ye did it unto me." In 1762, Woolman revised his pamphlet with addi-tional information, asking his fellow Christian colonists to conform their actions to their religious beliefs.

Although widely distributed, Woolman's pamphlet had minimal im-pact outside the Quaker community. Most colonists continued to believe in the absolute right of ownership of what they considered inferiors. Slave insurrections rather than emancipation remained much more on their minds.

Ironically for the whites, the very situation that they feared—weapons in the hands of slaves—was also sometimes critical to their survival. For the Black Americans, the irony was twofold. First, the possession of weapons did not liberate them from the whites; rather, it put them in the position of defending their owners as well as themselves. Second, Native Americans did not distinguish between the colors of the enemy and held these Black individuals equally responsible for their intrusion.

As additional Englishmen arrived and cleared more territory for vil-lages and farms, the Native Americans reacted to the occupation of what they considered their lands. They attacked isolated farms and small vil-lages, treating all the residents, white and Black, as intruders. Because the numbers, and therefore the odds, favored the Native Americans, whites had to arm their slaves for defense.

During the early years of colonial exploration and settlement, the de-cision as to whether or not to arm slaves to resist Indian attacks hinged on the same factor that would influence the use of Black Americans in the American armed forces for the next three centuries: the need for manpower. When whites could not resist the enemy threat on their own, they looked to African Americans to reinforce their numbers. As soon as the smoke cleared from the battlefield, though, white men reclaimed the weapons, and the Black men returned to their former status.

For the century and a half before the American Revolution, white colonists faced the quandary of how to balance the threat from the Na-tive Americans against the possibility of slaves turning their weapons against their owners. As colonial lawmakers wrestled with the problem, they issued a myriad of regulations that changed with the tides of the most pressing threats.

Most frequently, laws regarding the arming of Black Americans, both slave and free, evolved as a part of the regulations for each colony's militia—laws that simply legitimized certain standards already in practice. Some communities disregarded the laws of their colony and organized their militia in accordance with local custom and in response to the real or perceived threats from Native Americans. In other instances, militia commanders interpreted regulations in whatever manner met their needs.

Virginia passed the first universal-service law enacted in colonial America during a period of temporary peace between the English settlers and the Native Americans. On January 16, 1639, the General Assembly of Virginia specifically barred the arming of African Americans, declaring, "All persons except negroes are to be provided arms and ammunition."

The northern colonies, which held fewer slaves and faced a more prevalent threat from hostile Indians, recognized Black residents as an important manpower asset. Early settlements established lists of eligible men for their militia. Most did not indicate the race of each potential soldier, but notations did make their way into the records. The 1643 militia list for Plymouth, Massachusetts, includes Abraham Pearse, identified as a "Blackmore."

By 1652, Massachusetts required all males between the ages of sixteen and sixty to undergo military training and specifically included "all negroes." The wording of the Massachusetts militia act changed slightly in 1656 and again in 1660 to require military service by "every person above the age of sixteen years."[2] The law did not specifically mention Black men but included them in the "every person" phrase. This 1660 adaptation of Massachusetts militia law, with minor variances, remained in effect for the next century.

When Leonard Calvert and his followers arrived in Maryland in 1634 to establish a colony based on religious freedom, they introduced slavery to the region at the same time. The settlers, threatened by both Indians and Virginia whites, who believed the Maryland claims infringed on their property, immediately armed their slaves to assist in the colony's defense.

On October 20, 1654, the General Assembly of Maryland formalized its military organization with an act that required each county to main-

[2]Most of the colonial militia acts refer to persons and do not denote gender. However, their definition was strictly for males, as there was no role for females in the colonial military.

tain a militia composed of "all persons" sixteen to sixty, who were to be ready at all times with "serviceable arms and sufficient ammunition of powder and shot." The act further directed that "every master of families provide arms and ammunition as aforesaid for every such servant"— meaning that every Black male between sixteen and sixty would have to fight for the survival of the colony, notwithstanding the fact that they would be fighting to protect those who exploited them.

Other colonies enacted similar legislation in the mid-seventeenth century to formalize their militias and define who had to serve. Rhode Island, in an act dated May 3, 1665, included "servants" among those required to bear arms. New Jersey's Militia Act of November 3, 1668, required all persons sixteen to sixty years of age to serve, with the exception of a few religious and civic leaders. Being excluded from the exceptions paragraph meant that Black men were eligible for militia service. In 1672, Connecticut passed an act similar to New Jersey's in that it authorized Black participation in the militia by not specifically excluding them in the exceptions clause.

Along with internal strife between the colonies about their borders and the constant threat of Indian attacks, the English settlers also faced hostile French forces that wanted to expand their Canadian territory southward. When England and France clashed in the Queen Anne's War of 1702–1713 over properties in New England and along the St. Lawrence River, the northern colonies renewed or reaffirmed militia acts that authorized the arming and military training of Black men.

The southern colonies, where slaves already outnumbered whites, continued their formal exclusion of Black Americans from military service until manpower needs forced change. While the French increased their threat against the northern colonies in the first decade of the eighteenth century, the Indians also advanced their hostilities in the South. In response, the General Assembly of South Carolina passed some of the most detailed legislation yet enacted concerning military service by slaves. Section XXV of the act stated: "That it shall and may be lawful for any master or owner of any slave, in actual invasion, to arm and equip any slave or slaves with such arms and ammunition as any other person."

Parts of the legislation also provided rewards for military service that other colonies would emulate in later years. The act declared, "Whereas, it is necessary for the safety of this colony in case of actual invasions, to have the assistance of our trusty slaves to assist us against our enemies, and it being reasonable that the said slave should be rewarded for good service." It then defined this reward as being freedom if a slave killed or captured an enemy soldier or became disabled from combat wounds but promised nothing to "trusty slaves" merely for their service. In addition, the act promised that public funds would compensate the owners for slaves freed for their performance or who might be killed or disabled by wounds.

A year later, on November 4, the South Carolina assembly enacted more regulations requiring militia commanders in each province to compose a list of slaves in their area and to inform owners that their property should be available for military service. Again, the colonial government promised to pay for any slave killed or disabled.

North Carolina did not respond as quickly with formal legislation but finally took action when Indian attacks intensified. In 1715, North Carolina passed an act requiring all "freemen and servants" to serve in the militia.

For the next half-century colonial assemblies continued to require and then exempt Black men from military service, depending on the level of threat from the Indians and the French. Colonies also began to explore the use of slave populations in their militias in positions other than as armed infantrymen.

Virginia reconfirmed its policy of exempting Black soldiers from the military in 1705. In 1723 the colony amended its policy of excluding Black men from militia service by authorizing their "employment as drummers or trumpeters." Another section of the same act stated that in time of need Black Americans would be required to perform "pioneer" or labor duties as directed. Virginia again redefined their military policy on African Americans in 1756 by adding that Black men could enlist and serve as "drummers, trumpeters, or pioneers, or in such other servile labor as they shall be directed to perform" but that this service would be "without arms."

Generally, the colonies, especially in the South, officially excluded Black soldiers from military service, but need often won out over regulations, and commanders did employ slaves and freemen in their ranks. Such a need came to the forefront with the outbreak of the French and Indian War in 1754, a confrontation that escalated the previous border disputes between France and England into full-scale warfare.[3]

Both the French and the English mounted expeditions in North America to seize frontier posts in order to solidify their territorial claims. The climax of the conflict came with the successful British attack led by

---

[3]The French and Indian War was an extension of the Seven Years' War in Europe, which primarily pitted England and Prussia against France, Russia, and Saxony.

James Wolfe against the French garrison under Louis Joseph de Montcalm in Quebec on September 13, 1759. By September 8 of the following year, the remainder of Canada had fallen to the British.

The regular British army conducted the major campaigns of the war, but colonial militia units supported them. On a few occasions, including George Washington's unsuccessful expedition against Fort Duquesne in Pittsburgh, Pennsylvania, in 1754, American militia units operated independently against the French and their Indian allies.

Few records exist from this period, but without a doubt the colonies relaxed their Black exclusion laws in order to meet the manpower requirements of the war. One of the few unit rosters of the period to note the race of its enlistees was that of Col. William Eaton's company in Granville County, North Carolina. On October 8, 1754, it listed five negroes and two mulattoes. Rosters of other Granville County companies on the same date included three negroes in Capt. John Glover's company and five more in Capt. Osborn Jeffery's unit.

Commanders also found uses for Black recruits in various support roles. On March 17, 1755, British general Edward Braddock wrote government official Robert Napier: "There are here numbers of mulattoes and free negroes of whom I shall make bat men [personal servants], whom the province are to furnish with pay and frocks." Braddock also used many Black men as wagoners during his campaigns, including one identified as Sandy Jenkins of Fairfax County, Virginia.

While all of the colonies employed Black soldiers to one degree or another in the French and Indian War, the northern colonies used them more extensively. New York, Connecticut, and Massachusetts employed the largest numbers and percentages of Black Americans. Typical of the numbers is that which is reflected in a recruiting report from Hingham, Massachusetts, in 1758, which states that two Black soldiers, Primas Cobb and Flanders, were among the thirty-six enlistees in Capt. Edward Ward's company.

African American soldiers as a group displayed the same courage and tenacity in the French and Indian War that would later mark Black service in the Revolution. Some individual Black soldiers served loyally in both conflicts. Barzillai Lew of Chelmsford, Massachusetts, fought as a teenager against the French and Indians and enlisted again on May 6, 1775, in his state's Twenty-seventh Regiment. In addition to participating in the Battle of Bunker Hill, Lew served for a total of seven years as an infantryman, fifer, and drummer during the Revolution.

Lew's story is verifiable through his unit's muster lists. Accounts of other Black veterans of the French and Indian War are available from other sources. One of the more interesting is the story of Garshom Prince, who, like Lew, fought in both the French and Indian War and the American Revolution. Prince was born in either Connecticut or Rhode Island in about 1733. He joined the militia as a slave of Capt. Robert Durkee, at whose side he fought in both wars.

Prince, like many soldiers, occupied his time in camp carving bits of wood and other materials and became quite a skilled craftsman. His etchings on his powder horn, taken from his body after his death defending the United States at the Battle of Wyoming in 1778 and later preserved at the Wilkes-Barre Geological Society in Pennsylvania, provides a graphic record of the African American's military service. In addition to carved sketches of houses and ships, one side of the horn proudly states, "Prince Negro His Hornm [sic]." On the other side, the Black soldier added a bit of more specific information: "Garshom Prince his horn made at Crown Point, Septm. ye 3rd day 1761."

Lew, the more fortunate, survived both wars and lived until 1821. Other Black soldiers, however, suffered lifelong debilitating wounds while assisting their white owners against the French. A petition to the General Court of Boston on December 14, 1780, stated that George Gire, "a negro man living in Grafton became infirmed by reason of the hard service in the French War" and recommended the continuance of a modest pension.

African Americans assisted in the final victory over the French that gave the British claim to Canada and stabilized their colonial borders. However, as soon as the war ended, whites withdrew arms and uniforms, and Black men returned to the chains of slavery or to the much-discriminated-against class of freemen.

A few Americans, particularly the Quakers, continued their protest against slavery. Other colonists began to express concerns about how the institution of slavery fit with the thoughts of independence now taking hold. The majority of white Americans, however, continued to look upon Black Americans as property and cheap labor to advance their own and their colonies' economic status.

3

On the Verge of Revolution

PRIOR TO THE FRENCH AND INDIAN WAR, the British looked to the American colonies as a resource for raw materials and as a market for their manufactured goods. A series of navigation acts required the colonists to route all of their exports through England before being sold in Europe or elsewhere. Never popular, these laws and regulations favoring England over the colonies became even more restrictive with the defeat of the French in 1763.

British ministers, who believed that the colonies should bear a significant portion of the debt incurred in the war, increased their efforts to regulate the economic and political activities of the colonists. They increased taxes to pay off the war debt as well as to fund the 6,000-man army stationed in North America to protect the Crown's territories.

Colonists objected to the new taxes because they no longer needed the king's army to protect them from the French or the Native Americans, which their militias could handle. Consequently, the colonists increasingly looked upon the British soldiers as enforcers to ensure that they complied with the king's laws rather than as protectors. More important, the loss of revenue through taxes also became a sore point with the profit-seeking Americans.

While the British expected the colonists to contribute toward war expenses and the cost of the British military in America, they allowed the colonists no seats in Parliament. "No taxation without representation" became the rallying cry of those opposed to England's policies and spawned the concept of self-rule and liberty, which took root and spread rapidly.

Meanwhile, on March 22, 1765, the British Parliament passed the Stamp Act, a law that required that bills of lading, diplomas, playing cards, dice, pamphlets, marriage licenses, and other legal documents—

about fifty items altogether—be printed on stamped paper or stamped to show the levy paid.

In response, delegates of nine colonies met in New York City in what they called the Stamp Act Congress. After some debate, the delegates drew up a protest statement and forwarded it to the king and Parliament, which mostly ignored it. This Congress was pivotal, however, because it provided one of the first forums in which colonials discussed their collective, rather than individual, interests.

Other colonists took even more direct measures to counter the Stamp Act taxes. Secret groups, known as Sons of Liberty, held rallies with the slogan "Liberty, Property, and No Stamps." Some members attacked and destroyed tax buildings, hung stamp agents in effigy, and even tarred and feathered a few tax representatives for good measure. By the date the tax was due to go into effect, all of the agents had either resigned or disappeared. On March 18, 1766, Parliament repealed the Stamp Act. The first major revolt by the American colonists against the British had been successful.

Parliament did not, however, totally yield to the colonists. At the same time it repealed the Stamp Act, it passed the Declaratory Act, which proclaimed that Parliament maintained the right "to bind" the colonies "in all cases whatsoever."

It did not take the British Parliament long to attempt to "bind the colonies." On June 29, 1767, Parliament passed the Townshend Acts, which called for import duties on glass, white lead, paper, and tea—the revenue to pay the salaries of royal governors and judges in the colonies. The Americans, confident as a result of their Stamp Act victory, renewed their antitax protests. Enterprising colonists also initiated smuggling activities to circumvent the tax, using Boston as their center.

To ensure the collection of taxes and to counter the protests and smuggling, the British dispatched two regiments of soldiers to Boston in September 1768. The presence of the red-coated soldiers inflamed the colonists' anger, and several small incidents paved the way for the protest initiated by Crispus Attucks on March 5, 1770.[1] The resulting Boston Massacre, led by an African American, became the rallying point for liberty-seeking colonists, and March fifth remained the major patriotic American holiday until replaced by the Fourth of July in 1776.

While the colonists were extremely sensitive to any infringements of their rights and freedoms on the one hand, they remained, on the other,

[1]Details are in chapter 1, "African American Heroes of the Revolution."

oblivious to the concepts of rights and freedom for African Americans, whom they continued to regard as property. That an escaped slave had led the protest that resulted in the Boston Massacre at the cost of his own life brought no change in the attitudes of whites concerning the status of Black Americans.

Americans continued to view Black people as subhumans whose value lay not in their humanity but in their ability to provide cheap labor. As the colonies grew in territory and population, the colonial standard of living improved rapidly. What they could not grow or produce, the colonists could import from England or Europe. Educational opportunities, at least for whites, advanced significantly with the establishment of Harvard in Cambridge, Massachusetts, in 1636 as the first American university. William and Mary in Virginia followed in 1693, and over the next sixty years universities including Yale, Princeton, Columbia, and Rutgers opened their doors to advanced education.

These great halls of learning were not only closed to Black students but also reluctant to examine the issue of slavery and the profits the practice generated. When a Baptist university opened in Providence, Rhode Island, in 1764, it took its name from its founders and chief contributors, the Brown brothers, wealthy New England shippers who had made much of their fortune in the African slave trade.

Quakers continued to voice the loudest protests against slavery, and a few other Americans recognized the inconsistency in their pursuit of political and economic freedom from Great Britain while they themselves continued to keep hundreds of thousands Black Americans enslaved. Some of the leading proponents of American independence voiced anti-slavery sentiments in their writings.

James Otis, who joined Patrick Henry as one of the earliest agitators for independence, denounced slavery and supported the Black American's right to freedom in a pamphlet entitled *Rights of the British Colonists*, published in Boston in 1764. Religious leader Isaac Skillman demanded immediate abolition of slavery in his *Oration Upon the Beauties of Liberty*, published in 1772. Benjamin Franklin, Thomas Paine, and Benjamin Rush added their opposition to slavery in speeches and publications of the period.

Despite ethical and moral protests against slavery by a few, economic considerations were much more influential. Owners of small farms in New England did not require large labor forces; many residents of the larger cities were finding that it was less expensive to hire newly arrived white immigrants than to pay the cost of keeping slaves. For these groups, slavery was not an urgent issue; it did not affect their everyday lives. While some became supporters of abolition, most simply were not impassioned either way. Because they were not among the powerful, their opinions had no particular sway.

In the South, however, where the labor-intensive crops of tobacco, rice, and cotton required many workers, slavery flourished and resulted in larger plantations and increased fortunes. For southerners, slavery was everyday life, and on this issue they were passionate. Supported by the wealth produced by slave labor, these whites were influential.

Neither the demands for liberty by white leaders nor the economic impact of slavery went unnoticed by African Americans. However, communications among them on the matter were not easy. Various slave codes prohibited public meetings of Black people and prevented the opportunity to mount united protest efforts. Laws against teaching slaves to read and write also limited their ability to communicate formally.

Despite their illiteracy and lack of opportunity for assembly, slaves across America did possess an informal but fast "word of mouth" network. Black Americans who drove wagons or herded livestock to market exchanged information with other slaves. On a local level, news moved quickly from household to household and from one plantation to another. Regionally, Black sailors on fishing and merchant ships expedited the exchange of information from port to port.

Black Americans who had the advantage of education displayed eloquence and emotion in their condemnation of slavery. Phillis Wheatley of Boston became the first Black person, the first slave, and the third woman in America to write and have published a book of poetry, *Poems on Various Subjects, Religious and Moral,* in 1773.

The poet, born in Africa, came to America in 1761 aboard a slave ship at about age seven. Purchased by Susannah Wheatley, the wife of a wealthy Boston tailor, to become part of her domestic staff, Phillis displayed a remarkable ability to learn and became a household favorite. With the assistance of a few books and lessons from Mrs. Wheatley, Phillis quickly learned to read and write. At the age of twelve she began a correspondence with a local minister and two years later wrote her first poem.

The Wheatley home was on King Street, close enough for Phillis to hear the musket fire of the nearby Boston Massacre. Freedom for the colonies and for her race became an integral part of her writings, which garnered a host of admirers, including Voltaire, George Washington, and John Paul Jones.

The flames of discontent continued to bum in the post–Boston Massacre years. White Americans focused their open protests against British taxation and boycotted many of the products that required large duties.

Black Americans, unable to voice their concerns about their individual liberty, nevertheless shared the desire for freedom of their white owners, but most slaves could only dream of freedom for themselves. A few slaves did attempt to gain their freedom by suing their owners in the colonial courts. Between November 1766 and December 1772 at least six Massachusetts slaves, supported by abolitionists, filed claims that they were being held in bondage illegally. Such cases were expensive and the procedures slow, but in each instance the courts ultimately found in favor of the plaintiffs and set them free.

John Adams, a future leader of the Revolution, witnessed several of these trials in Massachusetts. In a letter dated March 21, 1795, Adams wrote to Jeremy Belnap, "I never knew a jury by a verdict, to determine a negro to be a slave. They always found him free."

However, Adams did not note that the few lawsuits heard took place in the North and not in the South. Moreover, these cases were about the freedom of an individual and did not affect or refer to slavery in general. While the courts could not justify the ownership of a single person, they remained unwilling to make a decision on the institution itself.

On April 20, 1773, four slaves from Thompson, Massachusetts, filed a petition with their colonial legislature "in behalf of our fellow slaves in this province." Peter Bestes, Sambo Freeman, Felix Holbrook, and Chester Joie asked to share in the "divine spirit of freedom" which "seems to fire every human breast on this continent."

On June 23 the Massachusetts legislature formed a "Committee on the Petition of Felix Holbrook, and others, praying to be liberated from a state of slavery." Three days later, after little discussion, the committee tabled the petition. The following May, the slaves sent another petition to the governor, again requesting their freedom and describing themselves as "stolen from the bosoms of our tender parents and from a populous, pleasant, and plentiful country and brought hither to be made slaves for life in a Christian land." Again, except for brief debate, the legislature took no action.

While white Americans continued to debate the ethical and legal aspects of slavery, a new economic development produced the most significant changes in the status of slaves and slavery. By the 1760s, the number of slaves in the northern states exceeded the demand for them among farmers and merchants, who had learned that hiring labor was cheaper than owning it. Slavery was also now so well established in the colonies that the slaves themselves were self-replenishing, the children of slaves becoming property of the mothers' owners. But the factor that made the single most significant difference was the unpopular British import taxes, including those on slaves. Many colonists refused to purchase additional slaves as part of their boycott against British tariffs and taxes.

With the diminishing demand for slaves, the increased number of births of slave children, and the desire to oppose British taxation and control, the colonial legislatures drafted measures to ban or limit the further importation of slaves. On May 26, 1766, Boston officials resolved to end the importation of slaves into Massachusetts by instructing their representatives to bring the issue before the colony's legislature. When no action resulted, Boston representatives, with the support from a town meeting held on March 16, 1767, again introduced the recommendation to the legislature. It was not until 1771 that the Massachusetts legislature finally passed such a bill, but then the governor refused to sign it into law.

Other colonies took similar actions. Connecticut and Rhode Island passed acts in 1774 prohibiting the importation of slaves. The Rhode Island legislation included a preface which declared, "Those who are desirous of enjoying all the advantages of liberty themselves, should be willing to extend personal liberty to others," and added that any Black person brought into the colony in violation of the act would be declared free. The representatives of Rhode Island, however, recognized the influence of slaveholders who had become wealthy in human trade and added provisions that greatly diminished the law's effects. A clause in the act stated that any slaves who could not be disposed of by Rhode Island traders in the West Indies could be imported into the colony as long as they were sold elsewhere within one year.

In 1773, Pennsylvania limited the importation of slaves by enacting a duty of twenty English pounds per person. Even the southern states joined the anti-importation-of-slaves movement. North Carolina and Virginia banned slave importation in 1774, and Georgia enacted similar legislation in 1775. The Continental Congress in October 1774 encouraged the colonies to stop importing slaves and on April 6, 1775, formally voted to prohibit the importation of slaves into all of the thirteen colonies.

The growing American independence movement, coupled with the desire to support boycotts of British imports—and therefore various navigation taxes—was the true motive behind the enacting of the slave-importation bans. It is important to note that none of the laws ended or even limited slavery. The practice remained unabated, and slave imports, although reduced, continued with little effort to curb the practice.

These anti-slave-importation acts, as well as the increased debate over abolition, were integral to, and not separate from, the overall interest in liberty for the colonists and independence for the colonies. Protests by individuals and groups, such as the Sons of Liberty, against British rule evolved into larger, better organized resistance. In 1772, Samuel Adams established the Committee of Correspondence in Boston and over the next weeks founded similar organizations in eighty towns and villages throughout Massachusetts. These committees, through written correspondence and spoken word, exchanged information to stimulate and organize resistance to the British.

In 1773, Virginia formed its own Committee of Correspondence, and the other colonies followed suit during the next few months. By the end of the year, committees linked all thirteen colonies in the desire for liberty from Great Britain. These committees formed the basic organization and provided the representatives for the First Continental Congress that met in 1774.

Aided by the network of committees, Americans increased their boycott of English imports and displayed their objections to British rule more directly. On December 16, 1774, white protesters in Boston donned thin disguises of Indians and forcibly boarded three British merchant vessels. With a crowd of well-wishers cheering from the wharf, the band proceeded to break open 342 chests of tea and pour them into the harbor.

The bloodless Boston Tea Party further united the colonists while at the same time forcing the British to take stronger measures to ensure their dominance over the colonies. The resultant Boston Port Act closed the harbor until the colonists paid for the discarded tea. The Crown further tightened its rein by restricting public meetings and by announcing that any of its officials who, in the line of duty, killed colonists would return to England for trial, a policy which the colonists interpreted to mean that such officials would face no punishment.

These British actions accomplished little except to fan the glowing embers of rebellion. The Committees of Correspondence increased their numbers; planted spies in the British government; and directed local militias to stockpile weapons, ammunition, and other supplies in preparation for war. From September 5 to October 26, 1774, the First Continental Congress met in Philadelphia. The thirteen colonies, previously linked only by the Committees of Correspondence, now had a government. That government would not have a country to govern without a war, and the first shots, those "heard round the world," were soon to echo across Lexington Green and Concord Bridge, where Black and white Americans would stand together in their fight for American independence.

4

"Enlist No Stroller, Negro, or Vagabond"

DESPITE THE GROWING UNREST IN THE COLONIES, the British took no measures to placate the Americans. They did not eliminate or reduce the duties and taxes, nor did they suggest any possibility of home rule at some future date. The British felt confident that they could continue to control the colonies as they saw fit.

At least some of their confidence had merit, for British officials maintained support from Loyalists, American colonists who continued their allegiance to the Crown. These Loyalists actively aided the British, sometimes for political and philosophical reasons, sometimes for personal gain. Among other things, Loyalists spied on the rebels and infiltrated their Committees of Correspondence and other clandestine groups. Benjamin Church, a prominent doctor, joined other Boston leaders in an intelligence-gathering cell known as the Mechanics, who met regularly in the Green Dragon Tavern. Church, a man who tended to live beyond his means, quickly made advantageous financial arrangements with British army commander Gen. Thomas Gage to report on the activities of the Mechanics.

In mid-April 1775, Church informed Gage about the rebels' stockpiling of arms and equipment, providing a map to their locations in nearby villages. On April 18, Gage sent orders to the Tenth Regiment Foot:

> Having received intelligence that a quantity of ammunition, provision, artillery, tents, and small arms have been collected at Concord, for the avowed propose of raising and supporting a rebellion against His Majesty, you will march the Corps of Grenadiers and Light Infantry, under your command, with the utmost expedition and secrecy to Concord, where you will seize and destroy . . . all military stores whatsoever.

The British marched toward Concord, where they met the Minutemen, forewarned by Paul Revere and William Dawes. Neither the British nor the Americans were ready for the rebellion to begin, but the skirmishes at Lexington and Concord Bridge precluded any opportunity for a peaceful solution.

On the surface it appeared that the Americans had no chance of successfully opposing the British. They had no government, no national treasury, and no regular army or navy. On the other hand, Great Britain was a world power with large monetary reserves, a veteran navy of 131 ships of the line and 139 vessels of other classes, and a professional army of more than 50,000 soldiers. The overall British population of 7,500,000 outnumbered the colonials three to one, and one in five—or 500,000—of the Americans were Black slaves. Furthermore, at least one-third of white Americans supported the king and rejected the idea of independence.

Despite the disadvantages, the Americans did have some factors in their favor. Size alone made it difficult to put down the rebellion, for the widely dispersed colonies measured more than 1,500 miles from north to south and 500 miles from the Atlantic Ocean into the settled interior. More important, the colonies lay 3,000 miles from Great Britain, a vast distance from which to provide soldiers and their supplies.

Other factors also limited Britain's ability to oppose the rebellion. Countries much closer to England than America were vigilant in their search for the opportunity to challenge Britain's power. Moreover, the British themselves were not entirely united against the rebels. Edmund Burke, William Pitt, and others formed the Friends of America and declared that the rebels were only exercising their historical right as Englishmen to oppose the tyranny of the Crown. Some of the most competent British military officers agreed with the rebels' aims and refused service in America.

The American population, white and Black, was widely dispersed throughout the colonies. By colony, the populations ranged from about 35,000 in Georgia to nearly 500,000 in Virginia and 270,000 in Pennsylvania in 1776.[1] The largest city in America was Philadelphia, with 34,000 residents, followed by New York City, 22,000; Boston, 15,000; and Charleston, 12,000.

The half million Black Americans, while spread throughout the colonies, had their largest concentrations in the South. Virginia had nearly 200,000 Black residents, while New Hampshire had only about 500.[2] Ap-

---

[1]The U.S. Bureau of the Census lists population numbers at ten-year intervals. Population figures for 1760, 1770, and 1780 are listed in Appendix C.
[2]For the distribution of African Americans of the period, see Appendix D.

proximately 4–5 percent of Black people, the majority of whom resided in the North, were free.

While the rebel colonists were ill prepared to fight a war, especially against the powerful British, the engagements at Lexington and Concord began a conflict that could end only in independence or total defeat. Attempting to gain a quick victory, the Massachusetts militia units pursued the British from Concord back to Boston and then surrounded the city. Other militia units expanded the fight, and troops led by Ethan Allen and Benedict Arnold secured the Lake Champlain region for the rebels on May 17, 1775.

Because communications traveled via horse-mounted and ship-borne messengers, it took weeks for the news of the rebellion to spread throughout the colonies. It was not until May 10 that representatives convened the Second Continental Congress to provide a central government for the colonies. One of its first decisions was to authorize a Regular Army to unite the rebel forces under one command. On June 14, Congress authorized the Continental army and the following day selected George Washington as its commander in chief; his first mission was to assume command of the militia units surrounding Boston.

Although a veteran of the French and Indian War, Washington possessed no specialized military skills. Rather, his selection was the result of his diplomatic ability to unite the divergent factions of the North and South that were frequently hostile in their disagreements.

Washington arrived in Boston on July 3 and found 17,000 militiamen in a loosely organized army with no centralized chain of command. Some commanders did not recognize the authority of those who outranked them, answering and responding only to their local or colonial government officials. None of the militiamen were professional soldiers in spirit or commitment. Accustomed to reporting for short terms of active duty to oppose Indian uprisings, they lacked enthusiasm for long-term service. The enlistments of the entire "Boston Army" were due to expire by the end of the year.

Because the Americans organized their militias as a defense against the Indians, they were neither trained nor motivated to assume an offensive role. Fortunately for Washington and the Revolution, the British were undecided on a strategy to counter the uprising. Their commander, Thomas Gage, seemed satisfied to do nothing, which certainly suited the rebels.

Shortly after Washington's arrival in Boston, a congressional committee visited him there and met with representatives of the surrounding colonies. They decided that each colony would continue to field its own militia for local defense and would also assign these organizations to Washington for occasional operations. In addition, each colony would provide men for the Continental, or Regular, Army.

Initially, Congress called for an army of 20,370 men, organized into twenty-six battalions[3] of eight companies each. Massachusetts would provide sixteen of these battalions, Connecticut, five; New Hampshire, three; and Rhode Island, two. By the end of November, the army had only 6,000 of these soldiers, a situation that forced Washington to request an extension of the current militiamen enlistments.

As it became obvious within a year that the Revolution would not be a brief conflict, Congress increased the allocations for Continental soldiers and required all the states to provide a number of battalions according to their populations. Virginia was to provide nineteen; Massachusetts, fifteen; Pennsylvania, twelve; North Carolina, nine; Connecticut, eight; Maryland, eight; South Carolina, six; New York, four; New Jersey, four; New Hampshire, three; Rhode Island, two; Delaware, one; and Georgia, one.

At the end of 1776, Congress added requirements for 2,040 artillerymen and 3,000 dragoons (horse-mounted infantry) proportionally from the states.

To encourage enlistments, Congress authorized a twenty-dollar bounty and the promise of land allotments of 100–500 acres, depending on the state and the soldier's rank. Even with these incentives, none of the states ever filled its entire quota, and fewer than one-half of the authorized numbers ever came forward to serve the new republic.

Enlistment periods for volunteers varied. Original plans called for Continental army soldiers to enlist for three years or for the duration of the war. Many Americans and their legislators objected to this plan, claiming that a standing army presented a threat to the very liberties for which they were fighting. As a result, most states enlisted men for only three months to a year. They also rotated their militia companies in and out of active service to fill some of their commitments. None of these methods proved fully effective, and at no time during the war was Washington able to field an army of more than 30,000 soldiers.

An obvious solution to the personnel shortfalls lay in the Black population, which made up 20 percent of the country's residents. African Americans believed that their freedom and the liberty of the United

---

[3]The terms battalion and regiment were used interchangeably during the Revolutionary War. The organizational structure called for about 800 men divided into eight 100-man companies.

States went hand in hand and lobbied for the right to fight. Some militia commanders welcomed freemen and slaves into their ranks. As a result, Black Americans, such as Prince Estabrook, Salem Poor, and Peter Salem, were among the first Americans to shed their own blood, and that of the British, during the early months of the rebellion.

Congress, George Washington, and other top military officials, however, believed that the army would not need Black men, whether free or slave. A few saw the irony of enlisting Black slaves to achieve white independence. Others argued that it was not economical, nor fair to owners, to enlist slaves and grant them their freedom for their service. Still others, especially in southern areas where slaves outnumbered whites, feared potential consequences of arming Black Americans.

The Committee on Safety of Massachusetts was the first organization after the rebellion began to take up the question of Black men in the military service. On May 20, 1775, the committee issued a resolution that supported enlisting freemen while stating that admission of slaves would "be inconsistent with the principles that are meant to be supported." The resolution concluded: "Therefore no slaves be admitted into this army upon any consideration whatsoever."

Field commanders actively fighting the British apparently ignored the committee's resolution. A month later, at Bunker Hill, slaves played an important role in the battle.

A week after assuming command of the Continental army, Washington issued instructions to recruiters to secure replacements and additional troops. A Virginian and slaveholder, Washington tempered his policies based on the general prejudices of whites against Black people throughout the colonies and on July 10, 1775, through Horatio Gates, his adjutant general, instructed his recruiters to "engage men of courage and principle to take up arms." However, he also directed: "You are not to enlist any deserter from the Ministerial (British) army, nor any stroller, negro, or vagabond, or person suspected of being an enemy to the liberty of America."

The recruiters followed orders and enlisted only whites, but freemen and slaves already in the ranks continued to serve. British soldiers had little respect for the white American rebels and ridiculed them for serving with Black soldiers. They often shouted jingles critical of the rebel army, including:

> The rebel clowns, oh! what a sight
> Too awkward was the figure

'Twas yonder stood a pious wight
And here and there a nigger.[4]

The number of complaints about Black men in uniform increased with the mobilization of troops from the South. On September 26, 1775, Edward Rutledge, of South Carolina, introduced legislation to force Washington to discharge all Black people, free or slave. The vote split generally between North and South and failed by a narrow margin. While not an endorsement of Black enlistments, it showed some support for the current practice of maintaining Black enlistees. This vote, however, certainly did not end the debate.

The questions about enlisting and retaining slaves and freemen continued despite all the other problems of organizing, training, and equipping a new army in the midst of combating one of the world's most formidable forces. Once again, desires for unity, as well as prejudices, won out over what some considered "right" and others saw as "need."

On October 8, 1775, Washington conferred with his senior officers concerning the advisability of enlisting Black Americans in the new army and whether their policy should made a distinction between free and slave. The officers agreed unanimously to reject all slaves, and the majority recommended rejecting all Black recruits regardless of their status.

After the conference with his senior officers, Washington met with representatives from Massachusetts, Connecticut, Rhode Island, and Congress. On October 23, 1775, he announced his decision that all Black Americans, free and slave, would "be rejected altogether." In general orders dated November 12, Washington declared, "Neither negroes, boys unable to bear arms, nor old men unfit to endure the fatigues of the campaign, are to be enlisted." On October 31 he directed his quartermaster general to supply clothing to all who would reenlist, "Negroes excepted which the Congress do not incline to enlist again."

Despite the lack of desire on the part of the army's senior leadership to enlist Black men or to reenlist those already in the ranks, many junior officers appreciated the performance of their African American soldiers. Col. John Thomas, commander of one of the twelve battalions created by the Massachusetts legislature on May 19, 1775, and transferred to the Continental army on June 14, wrote to John Adams about his Black soldiers on October 24, 1775: "We have some negroes, but I look upon them as equally serviceable with other men, for fatigue [labor]; and, in action many of them have proven themselves brave."

---

[4]That this jingle made its way into later writings about the war supports the fact that there was significant and widespread service in the war by African Americans.

While white Americans were initiating measures to exclude or eliminate Black Americans from their army, the British and Loyalists were taking a different approach. On November 7, 1775, John Murray, the earl of
Dunmore and the royal governor of colonial Virginia, issued a proclamation that declared he would welcome "all indentured servants, negroes,
or others free" who would join the king's army against the American
rebels.[5]

The number of slaves flocking to Dunmore's army, the increasing
protests by free Black Americans and abolitionists, and his own army's
personnel shortages prompted Washington to modify his position. On December 30, 1775, Washington's headquarters issued the following statement: "As the general is informed that numbers of free negroes are
desirous of enlisting, he gives leave to recruiting officers to entertain
them." Washington, combining the roles of military officer and politician, added, "promises to lay the matter before Congress, who he doubts
not will approve it."

The following day, from his headquarters in Cambridge, Washington
wrote John Hancock, the president of the Continental Congress,

> It has been represented to me that free negroes who have served in
> the army are very much dissatisfied at being discarded. As it is to be
> apprehended that they may seek employment in the Ministerial
> Army, I have presumed to depart from the resolution respecting
> them, and have given license for their being enlisted. If this is dis-
> approved by Congress, I will put a stop to it.

On January 16, 1776, Congress passed a resolution stating "that the
free negroes who have served faithfully in the army at Cambridge may be
reenlisted therein but no other."

State governments followed the "no other" guidance of Congress, either officially or unofficially. Pennsylvania exempted "non-whites" from
military service, while Delaware warned recruiters not to enlist any "in-
debted servants," including slaves. New Hampshire was a bit more blunt,
ruling that the "lunatic, idiots, and negroes" were exempt. Several states
passed laws permitting, or even requiring, slaves to be made available for
the construction of fortifications and on other labor details,[6] but none
authorized Black men to serve in the military.

Despite the clear direction from Congress and their state govern-

---

[5] Details are in chapter 5: "'Liberty to Slaves'—Lord Dunmore's Ethiopian Regiment."
[6] More details can be found in chapter 10: "Behind the Lines."

ments that only free veteran Black soldiers could reenlist, many commanders interpreted the resolution as meaning they could recruit all freemen. Some commanders, desperate for manpower, paid little attention to whether or not a volunteer was free or enslaved. Officers who brought their slaves along as personal servants also ignored the orders.

Still other Black men joined the Continental army and the militias as substitutes for their white owners. Plantation owners and shopkeepers alike often bought slaves and sent them to serve in their place. Some owners promised their substitutes freedom after completion of an honorable enlistment, while others not only accepted the slave's soldier pay but also returned them to bondage after their discharge.

Even with these exceptions and violations of policy, the percentage of Black soldiers in the Continental army fell during the initial year of the Revolution. When Washington raised the first Union flag of thirteen red and white stripes in Cambridge on January 1, 1776, it flew over an army that by regulation and individual prejudice represented only white America.

For nearly a year after the Battles of Lexington and Concord, the American Revolution remained rather quiet. A few skirmishes took place at sites as distant as Falmouth, Maine, and Moore's Creek, North Carolina, but most of the action—or more correctly, inaction—occurred around Boston. The Continental army remained too weak to mount an attack on the city, and the British, still not sure just how to handle the rebellion, remained unwilling to counterattack.

On July 4, 1776, colonial representatives signed the Declaration of Independence in Philadelphia. Even though the preamble declared that "all men are created equal," the signatories did not consider Black Americans as full members of their society and therefore assumed their exclusion. In early drafts of the declaration, Jefferson included a clause condemning King George III for interfering with colonial law prohibiting the importation of slaves during the previous decade, but representatives from Georgia and South Carolina so adamantly opposed the clause that he deleted it from the final draft of the document.[7] There is no evidence that either Jefferson, as the document's author, or the signers, as representatives of their states, had any intention of having the Declaration of Independence end slavery in America.

---

[7] The deleted clause appears in Appendix E.

5

"Liberty to Slaves"—Lord Dunmore's Ethiopian Regiment

DESPITE HOW WE HAVE ROMANTICIZED the war of independence, the American Revolution was not simply a clear-cut contest between an idealistic, united rebel force and an overbearing empire. In fact, the conflict was a complex and multifaceted confrontation of values, goals, and ambitions. For the revolutionaries, at that time, declaring independence in order to establish a democracy was an untried concept. The colonists who advocated independence had no guarantees that the colonies could survive economically on their own or that they could unify their diverse agendas and agree on government policies. Ultimately, each colonist had to make his own choice between supporting the Crown or casting his lot with the revolutionaries.

As noted earlier, one-third of the colonists determined that it was in their best interest to remain loyal to the Crown. Colonial officials, placed in their positions by orders from England, were reluctant to give up power and oppose their British benefactors. Many merchants and landowners, who were becoming wealthy as colonists, saw no financial gain in American independence. A few held British titles passed down through generations; they viewed themselves as colonizers, not new nation builders.

As the rebellion approached military confrontation, some Loyalists returned to England or migrated to Canada; others stayed to form their own militia units in order to reinforce the British army against the rebels. So adamantly did both factions of colonists believe in their causes that some of the war's bloodiest engagements were not between rebel and British soldiers but between American revolutionaries and American Loyalists.

One Loyalist who early on opposed the rebels had the most to lose if the Revolution proved successful. John Murray, the Fourth Earl of Dunmore, who was born in 1732 as a direct descendant of the Stuarts, accepted an appointment as the colonial governor of New York in 1770 after having served in Parliament since 1761 as one of sixteen Scots elected to a seat. The following year, Lord Dunmore received a promotion to the governorship of the larger colony of Virginia, where he and his wife received an enthusiastic welcome.

Initially, Dunmore was an extremely popular governor, prompting the colonial legislature to designate two new counties "Dunmore" and "Fincastle" in honor of his titles. Dunmore reciprocated the honor and named his first daughter born in the colony "Virginia." His popularity quickly faded, however, when the governor announced his continued allegiance to his king and his opposition to the mounting independence movement. In 1773, Dunmore dissolved the Virginia House of Burgesses when they proposed forming a Committee of Correspondence. The following year, he again suspended the reconvened House when it moved to set a day of mourning in response to additional British taxation.

Lord Dunmore briefly united the Virginians in the spring of 1774 against hostile Indians in the northwestern portion of the colony, but once the campaign concluded, the division between potential rebels and Loyalists widened. The governor was determined to do everything within his power to maintain British rule, including arming all the men he could muster. Even before the outbreak of hostilities at Lexington and Concord, Dunmore demonstrated just how far he was willing to go to put down any rebellion. In a letter to Secretary of State George Germain in London on March 1, 1775, Dunmore announced his intentions to "arm all my own negroes and receive all others that will come to me who I shall declare free."

Over the next few weeks, Dunmore wrote similar letters to other British military and political leaders. Although he made no official announcement of his plan to arm Black men if the colonists rebelled, word of his intentions spread quickly. Within weeks of the first battles in Massachusetts, runaway slaves were appearing at Dunmore's Williamsburg home to offer their services to the governor in exchange for freedom. White rebel colonists also heard the rumors about the governor's plan and reacted. Although Dunmore did not actually enlist the Black volunteers immediately, he did try to protect his advantage by attempting to move his stores of gunpowder and ammunition from Williamsburg to a British warship in the harbor. When the Virginia rebels blocked the effort, Dunmore left the capital with his family and a detachment of British soldiers and took refuge aboard the man-of-war *Fowey*, offshore of Yorktown, on June 8, 1775.

The House of Burgesses, now fully under control of those desiring independence, informed Dunmore on June 17 that they would not endanger his personal safety but condemned him for his idea of arming Black Americans, declaring: "A scheme, the most diabolical, had been meditated, and generally recommended, by a person of great influence, to offer freedom to our slaves, and turn them against their masters."

Dunmore refused to recognize the new Virginia government and took measures to reclaim his governorship. He shifted his headquarters to the *William* and, with several ships and about 300 soldiers and sailors, sailed along the Virginia coast and inland waterways. Occasionally, he put parties ashore to raid small towns and isolated plantations in order to replenish supplies and enlist any Black men who volunteered to join his force. During these raids of the summer of 1775, more than 100 Black soldiers joined Dunmore, and news that he was freeing slaves for service in his army quickly spread throughout Virginia and the other colonies.

Although Dunmore wanted to expand the opportunity for slaves to abandon their owners and join his force, he had to bide his time until his own situation improved. With no land base, Dunmore's army operated entirely from aboard ships and lived off whatever they could plunder from limited attacks along the shore. His requests for assistance from General Gage in Boston brought the following reply on September 10: "I can neither assist you with men, arms, or ammunition, for I have them not to spare; should you draw upon me I have not the cash to pay your bills."

With the approach of winter, Dunmore realized that if he and his army were to survive, they would have to establish a land base and enlist additional runaway slaves. On November 7, aboard the *William*, he prepared his official proclamation promising freedom to all slaves who joined him. A week later, Dunmore put ashore at Kemp's Landing, on the Elizabeth River, and routed the local rebel militia, capturing two of their senior officers. On November 14, from his new headquarters in the occupied village, Dunmore sent couriers and spies throughout Virginia with copies of a broadside of his proclamation[1] announcing freedom for slaves willing to fight for the Crown against the rebellion.

Within a few days the broadsides and word of mouth spread the news of the proclamation throughout Virginia to slaves and rebel Americans alike. Both groups took immediate action. Slaves began to escape from their owners and make their way to Dunmore's army and promised freedom. Whites quickly initiated measures to stop the fleeing slaves and to retaliate against the British earl.

On November 17, only three days after Dunmore issued his proclama-

---

[1]The complete proclamation appears in Appendix F.

tion, an article in the *Williamsburg Virginia Gazette* noted that Britain had been a leader in promoting slavery and had prevented the colonies from halting the slave trade prior to the beginning of hostilities. It also reported that Dunmore had the reputation of mistreating his own slaves and speculated that after he had used them in his army, he would likely sell them back into bondage in the West Indies.

Another *Gazette* article a week later warned that Dunmore would free only those slaves physically able to bear arms and that the old and feeble who remained with their owners would have to do the work of those who fled. It also again noted the British tendency to sell Black people to West Indian sugar-plantation owners and concluded, "Be not then, ye negroes, tempted by their proclamation to ruin yourselves."

Since few slaves in Virginia or elsewhere at the time could read, the intended audience of these articles is not entirely clear. It is likely that their real purpose was to further arouse the white Virginia population, especially those still wavering as to whether to join the rebels or support the Loyalists.

Whatever the newspaper's intentions, the articles increased the fervor over the proclamation, and the rebels responded quickly. The Virginians increased their patrols along rivers and roads and arrested all slaves without proper travel papers issued by their owners.

On December 8 the Virginia General Convention appointed a committee to prepare an official response to Dunmore's proclamation. The committee had to consider several complex issues in preparing its response, the most difficult being the long-standing slave code that any slave who took up arms against his owner would be put to death. This anti-insurrection law was troublesome to the committee in that if they threatened to put all runaways to death, no Black Americans would voluntarily surrender. Also, slaves were a valuable commodity, and most owners did not support the execution of their property.

The Virginia General Convention intervened during the debates and advised the committee to include in its proclamation provisions for any runaway who voluntarily surrendered within the next ten days. Those who returned would receive pardons; those who did not would receive severe punishment when captured. The next day, December 14, the committee issued a declaration that began with a harsh warning that any slave deserting his master's service to join the British "shall suffer death, and be excluded all benefit of clergy." It then promised that any runaway who saw the evil of his actions and voluntarily returned to his master or surrendered to the rebel army would receive a pardon.

The Virginia General Convention was mindful of financial considerations and prepared contingency policies. It still authorized death for slaves who actually took up arms against the state, but it also hedged its position by announcing that the state would sell recaptured slaves to West Indian plantations, in which case the purchase price would go to the original owners. The convention also outlined policies for slaves captured while escaping or en route to join Dunmore. These individuals were to be returned to their owners after a brief period of imprisonment. For good measure, the convention also authorized the confiscation of slaves belonging to Loyalists and their transfer to state-owned lead mines.

Americans outside Virginia also took note of Dunmore's proclamation to free the slaves. George Washington, in a letter to Joseph Reed on December 15, 1775, declared that Dunmore was an "arch-traitor to the rights of humanity" and that he "should be instantly crushed, if it takes the force of the whole Colony to do it." Washington further expressed his fear that slaves joining the British for their freedom would result in a "snowball, in rolling, his army will get size" and threaten the revolution.

Lord Dunmore ignored the rebels' proclamation against him and after his victory at Kemp's Landing, marched into Norfolk, the Loyalists' stronghold, where he continued to arm and train any escaped slaves crossing the lines into his camp. By the first week of December, Dunmore's army contained about 300 British soldiers organized into what he called "the Queen's Own Loyal Virginians." He also had an equal number of escaped slaves assigned to Lord Dunmore's Ethiopian Regiment.[2] Along with a musket and ammunition, Dunmore issued each member of the regiment a uniform complete with the embroidered slogan "Liberty to Slaves."

Weapons and uniforms did not, of course, immediately transform a slave into a soldier. Few slaves had any experience with firearms or any military soldiering skills. The months of drill required to instill the knowledge and discipline to withstand the close-quarter combat typical of the period simply were not available.

The Virginia militia leaders realized that they must stop Dunmore before he could properly train the growing numbers of runaways, for not only were they losing valuable property, but also they feared that the situation could endanger the Revolution. In early December 1775, Col. William Woodford, in command of about 200 Virginia and North Carolina militiamen, moved against Norfolk. Among the rebel ranks were

---

[2]Some accounts refer to this organization as the Royal Ethiopians and inflate the numbers to as high as 600 members.

several Black soldiers, including Billy Flora, who would exhibit his valor in the pending fight.

Dunmore marched out of Norfolk with his white and Black regiments and met the advancing rebels about nine miles outside of town at a crossing of the Elizabeth River known as Great Bridge. The 120-foot-long wooden causeway connected two small islands with the marshy banks of the fast-moving river and provided an obstacle to the advance of both forces. Dunmore established a fortification on his side of the bridge, while Woodford ordered half his soldiers to dig in at the bridgehead on his side. The other half established a camp on a hill about 400 meters from the causeway.

For several days the two opposing forces enhanced their defenses on their respective sides of the bridge. Then, according to some accounts, Woodford dispatched one of his officer's servants across the river to pose as a deserter, with instructions to inform Dunmore about the strength of the rebel force. Stories differ on the numbers that the "runaway" reported to Dunmore—varying from far fewer to far greater than were actually present—but all agree that he informed the British that the Americans lacked training, ammunition, and motivation to stand and fight. While there is great doubt that this incident of planting false information occurred at all, some historians often cite it as the reason that Dunmore decided to leave his defenses and attack the Americans.

Dunmore ordered Capt. Charles Fordyce and 120 regular British soldiers to advance across Great Bridge on December 9. Lt. Edward Taylor and his ninety American riflemen repulsed the first attack just before dawn. Fordyce withdrew, secured two cannons for support, and again led his men across the bridge. The Americans remained behind their breastworks and held their fire until the British closed to within a few yards.

Fordyce, convinced the rebels had withdrawn, rushed forward and shouted, "The day is ours." That is when the Americans rose from their defenses and fired a volley into the redcoat ranks. Fordyce fell dead,[3] and a second American volley sent the British regulars retreating back across the bridge. Woodward, observing the battle from his hillside position, or-

---

[3]Accounts of Fordyce's death, like many records of the battle in later writings, lack credibility. Several stories say that the British officer fell from fourteen musket balls in his chest. Considering the accuracy of the smooth-bore muskets of the period, this is improbable. Like the claims of a "runaway slave" providing deceptive information to the British, the story is more likely legend than fact, either created on the battlefield to aid in morale or later embellished by overzealous historians more familiar with fiction that with actual military capabilities and procedures.

dered the remainder of his force, under Col. Edward Stevens, to counter-attack across the bridge. Dunmore committed the Ethiopian Regiment to meet the rebel Americans, but the more experienced militiamen, in a battle that lasted only twenty-five minutes, forced the entire British column to retreat.

Dunmore left the bodies of thirteen of his soldiers on the battlefield, including that of Fordyce. Thirty-five wounded managed to withdraw with the main force, but the rebels captured seventeen injured soldiers as well as both cannons that the British had abandoned. The only American casualty was one militiaman slightly wounded in the hand.

The Battle of Great Bridge was the first significant engagement between the British and American soldiers since Bunker Hill. It was also the first Revolutionary War battle in Virginia. Immediately following the fight, Woodward pursued Dunmore's retreating army toward Norfolk. While Williamsburg had been the center of Virginia government, Norfolk was the center for business and the colony's largest town, with a population of 6,000. Most of Norfolk's leading merchants were Scots representing companies based in Glasgow, and they, supporting their fellow countryman Dunmore, remained loyal to the Crown. Many of these Loyalists joined Dunmore and his regiments when they evacuated the town aboard four British men-of-war and support vessels just before Woodford's army occupied the town.

Dunmore, still wanting to reestablish his control over the colony, remained just outside the Norfolk port. Food and water shortages aboard the crowded ships forced him to send foraging parties ashore in search of supplies, but they were killed, captured, or turned back without success. Dunmore then sent word to the rebel Americans that if they did not provide his fleet with food and water, he would bombard Norfolk with his ships' cannons.

Receiving no provisions, Dunmore followed through with his threat. Early on the morning of January 1, 1776, his ships began shelling Norfolk. Dockside warehouses caught fire, and the flames spread to the city. Some of Woodford's soldiers, who harbored grudges against the Scots merchants who had departed with Dunmore, added to the fury by setting afire the houses of the departed Loyalists. The fires burned for three days, destroying 80 percent of Norfolk's buildings and homes. A few weeks later, the rebels razed the few remaining structures to ensure that the British would have no reason to reoccupy the town.

Dunmore remained offshore of Norfolk for several more weeks before shortages of supplies forced him to sail in order to forage along the Virginia coast. Members of the Ethiopian Regiment proved valuable assets to the seaborne army. With their knowledge of the Virginia countryside from their time as slaves, they led small patrols ashore to gather food and water for those remaining on the ships.

The British defeat at Great Bridge and Norfolk did not deter slaves who still saw Dunmore as a symbol of freedom. Runaways escaped in groups on small boats and even swam from shore to Dunmore's fleet to seek freedom in exchange for their military service. At their maximum strength, Dunmore's Ethiopian Regiment numbered about 800 soldiers. However, instead of fighting for their freedom on land, they remained restricted to ships with the rest of Dunmore's force, which was unable to influence land operations.

Dunmore's fleet, now numbering more than 100 vessels, wintered off-shore from Tucker's Mill near Portsmouth, Virginia. Harassed by fire from the shore and weakening from the lack of provisions, the sea-bound army also faced problems from disease, which accomplished what the white rebels could not; it reduced the number of Black soldiers with Dunmore. Smallpox left the Ethiopian Regiment with less than 150 men. Despite these limitations, the force endured the winter and in May attempted to establish a land base on Gwynn's Island in Chesapeake Bay, near the mouth of the Rappahannock River. Black soldiers exchanged their muskets for picks and shovels to build fortifications but they and Dunmore were reaching the end of their endurance.

On June 26, 1776, Dunmore wrote a letter to Lord George Germain, British secretary for the colonies, stating, "I am extremely sorry to inform you your Lordship that fever . . . has proved a very malignant one, and has carried off an incredible number of our people, especially the blacks."

Without his Black soldiers and with no hope for white reinforcements from Britain, Dunmore realized that saving Virginia for the Crown was hopeless. He concluded his letter to Germain by explaining what might have been if smallpox had not struck so severely, "Had it not been for this horrid disorder, I am satisfied I should have had two thousand blacks with whom I should have had no doubt of penetrating into the hearts of this colony."

On July 8–10, Americans attacked Dunmore's Gwynn's Island base, forcing him to once again evacuate by ship. In a final act of desperation and defiance, Dunmore sailed up the Potomac River, burning several plantations along the way. His objective may have been to reach Washington's Mount Vernon estate, but bad weather and the Virginia and Maryland militia forced his retreat after a brief battle near Occoquan Falls.

Defeated militarily and left with ranks decimated by smallpox, Dunmore withdrew his armada to Lynnhaven Roads, just west of Cape Henry, Virginia. In early August, Dunmore burned, sank, or ran aground about half his fleet and prepared to depart from the Virginia coast. On August 6, Dunmore, along with his regular soldiers and the healthiest of his Ethiopian Regiment, sailed north on seven ships to join the British in New England. The remainder, mostly Loyalists, set sail for Bermuda and the West Indies.

Dunmore's proclamation had promised freedom only to those slaves of the rebels and not to those belonging to Virginians who remained loyal to the Crown. Many of these Loyalists maintained their Black property and took them along with them or sold them to plantations in the West Indies. Dunmore did honor his promise to free the slaves who fled their rebel owners. However, by the time he disbanded his floating army, only about 300 former slaves, including women and children, had survived the smallpox epidemic. About half of them went north with Dunmore.

Lord Dunmore's resistance to the rebellion, particularly his proclamation to free the slaves and arm them against their former owners, made him one of the most despised British officers in the colonies. While rebel Americans in the North and South differed in their opinions about the basic legality and the future of slavery, they united in their resentment against any effort to take their property and to place muskets in the hands of slaves.

Shortly after Dunmore issued his proclamation, northern newspapers expressed their anger and resentment more critically than those published in Virginia. On December 6, 1775, the *Pennsylvania Journal* printed Dunmore's entire proclamation, about which the paper editorialized:

> It at once shows the baseness of his heart, his malice and treachery against the people who were once under his government, and his officious violation of all law, justice, and humanity; not to mention his arrogating to himself a power which neither he can assume, nor any power upon earth can invest him with.

The rebel Americans so despised Dunmore that several accused him of dispatching Black soldiers with smallpox back to the mainland to spread the disease among the Virginians. While Dunmore did use his former slaves extensively as onshore foraging parties, there is no evidence that he ever planned or intended to practice "germ warfare" against the rebels.

Colonists favoring independence were not the only Americans affected by Dunmore's free-the-slaves proclamation. The royal governor's actions influenced many colonists who were unsure as to whether to support the rebels or remain loyal to the Crown. When they saw Black men armed to fight whites and the property destroyed by Dunmore's fleet at Norfolk, many decided to support the independence movement.

Dunmore's proclamation and actions ultimately had little short-term impact on slaves and slavery. Only about 800 were able to join his ship-borne army, and about 100 of them were slaves of Loyalists who were not awarded their freedom. Although white Virginians imposed additional restrictions on the movements and gathering of Black Virginians to prevent them from running away to join Dunmore, slaveholders, as always, maintained the priority of preserving and protecting their property. Some whipped their slaves for attempting to escape, and a few maimed the violators by cutting off ears or other appendages that did not interfere with their abilities to work. Although authorized by the Virginia government, execution of escaped slaves was rare. One of the only confirmed instances of the execution of a slave for running away to join Dunmore is documented in the April 13, 1776, edition of the *Virginia Gazette*. Even this article admits that the purpose of the sentence was more to discourage others from joining Dunmore than to punish the individual.

While Dunmore's proclamation did little to immediately assist the half million Black slaves in America, it did have some far-reaching results. Slaves had shown that they would willingly exchange military service for their freedom and that they were capable fighters. As a result, both British and rebel American commanders had to reevaluate the potential of Black men in the military.

Dunmore, except for inspiring the hatred of the American rebels, suffered not at all from his struggle to preserve the royal government or from his proclamation to free the slaves who helped him. By the fall of 1776 he was back in England. Except for a brief return to America in 1782 in an unsuccessful attempt to once again raise a slave army against the rebels, he spent the next decade serving in the House of Lords. As a reward for his long and faithful service to the Crown, he was appointed royal governor of the Bahamas in 1787 and acted in that capacity until 1796, when he returned home to retirement. Dunmore died in Ramsgate, England, in 1809.

6

Opening the Ranks

WHILE LORD DUNMORE ENLISTED SLAVES as soldiers to help maintain British control over Virginia, the war in the northern colonies remained stalemated. George Washington's weak Continental army could do nothing but continue to besiege Boston. The British, relatively comfortable in the occupied town and able to enter and depart the harbor at will, were still without any great resolve to actively oppose the Revolution.

Neither side attempted to gain an advantage until the spring of 1776. In early March, under the cover of darkness, Washington occupied Dorchester Heights, on the south side of Boston, and mounted his artillery in positions that dominated the city. The British attempted to retake the Heights but the rebel force, assisted by a fierce rainstorm, repelled the attack On March 8 a delegation representing Gen. William Howe, who had replaced Gage, met with Washington to tell him the British would not destroy the city if allowed to leave unmolested.

On March 17 the British, along with 1,000 Loyalists, boarded ships and sailed north to Nova Scotia. Washington knew that the British would soon return and correctly anticipated that they would try to occupy New York because of its strategic location, excellent port, and majority Loyalist population. In response, he established defenses around the city, but New York proved too large and the American army too small to resist an attack from the British, who were now somewhat more committed to crushing the rebellion.

The British defeated the Americans in a series of battles on Long Island and around New York in late summer. On September 17, Washington retreated south into New Jersey. Another series of defeats drove the Americans into Pennsylvania. By the close of 1776 the rebel army numbered less than 4,000 soldiers.

Washington's victories at Trenton on December 26, 1776, and at Princeton on January 3, 1777, were much more important to the rebels as morale boosters than as significant outcomes. Fortunately for the rebel Americans, the will of the British to defeat the rebellion remained less than complete, perpetuating operations that were ill planned and poorly executed.

In 1777 the British, recognizing that simply occupying the major American cities would not quell the rebellion, decided to escalate their offensive. Their plan called for Gen. John Burgoyne to march south from Canada toward the Hudson River Valley while Gen. Barry St. Leger cleared the Mohawk Valley to Albany. Gen. Henry Clinton would proceed north from New York to meet the armies from Canada, cutting the state and the colonies into two sections. At the same time, General Howe would advance from New York and capture the American capital at Philadelphia.

Burgoyne, hampered by long supply lines and the thickly forested, rugged terrain of northern New York, progressed slowly. Revolutionary Gen. Horatio Gates, with ample time to receive reinforcements from Washington's army in Pennsylvania, managed to slow the British in a series of fights during August and September. After losing the Battles of Freeman's Farm on September 19 and Bemis Heights on October 7, Burgoyne surrendered his army of 5,000 on October 17, 1777. St. Leger's column retreated shortly after beginning their march, and Clinton never departed from New York at all.

While Gates and his army performed well in New York, Washington did not do so well in Pennsylvania. When he realized that Philadelphia was the British objective, Washington maneuvered his army to intercept them. The Continental army made its stand at Chad's Ford, on Brandywine Creek, on September 11. Because of poor intelligence on the terrain and the stream, Washington placed his army in a position that the British easily outflanked and defeated.

The Americans withdrew toward Philadelphia. After losing another battle at Paoli on September 21, Washington ceased his attempt to defend the capital, and the British occupied Philadelphia on September 26. Washington tried to regain the offensive on October 4 when he attacked the British garrison at Germantown but withdrew his army to winter quarters at Valley Forge when the assault failed.

Despite the loss of their capital and the defeat of Washington in Pennsylvania, the rebel Americans had won a major victory by stopping the British advance in New York. For the first time, many Americans began to believe in the Revolution and the United States. Recruiting became a little easier. More important, after Saratoga, the French recognized the new country on February 6, 1778, and became an ally in its efforts for independence.

The entry of France into the war forced the British to transfer troops and ships from North America to defend their possessions in the West Indies. Gen. Henry Clinton replaced Howe in command of the British occupying Philadelphia on May 18 and a month later withdrew his army back to the more defensible New York.

On June 28 the Americans and British fought to a stalemate at Monmouth, New Jersey. The battle marked the end of large-scale conflict in the northern states, for neither the British nor the Americans were able to gain any significant advantage.

Even though hampered by the escalating war with the French in Europe and the West Indies, the British still believed it necessary and possible to defeat the American rebels. At the urging of King George III and the encouragement from the large numbers of Loyalists in the Carolinas and Georgia, the British shifted their military efforts to the South. On December 29, 1778, the British easily captured Savannah, Georgia, and used its port to mount an offensive into the southern states. Slowly and methodically the British expanded their operations and on May 11, 1780, captured Charleston and then turned their offensive inland, where British and Loyalist forces under Lord (Gen.) Charles Cornwallis defeated the Americans at Camden, South Carolina, on August 16.

Subsequent battles in the fall of 1780 were small but intense. The most important was the Battle of King's Mountain, South Carolina, on October 7, where 1,700 Americans attacked a Loyalist force of 900. The rebels proved victorious, killing or capturing the entire Loyalist army. In addition to a much-needed morale-boosting victory, the results of the Battle of King's Mountain discouraged the British from further enlisting Loyalists.

On October 14, Gen. Nathanael Greene assumed command of the American army in the South and defeated the British at Cowpens, South Carolina, the following January 17. The British regrouped and achieved a bloody victory at Guilford Courthouse, South Carolina, on March 15, 1781. However, Cornwallis, weakened by battle losses, decreased Loyalist support, and increased British commitments on other fronts, could not exploit his advantage.

Cornwallis, with Greene's rebel army in pursuit, withdrew first to Wilmington, North Carolina, and then to Yorktown, Virginia, in hopes of linking up with the British navy. In August, Washington left a small force to hold the British in New York and moved south to join Greene. Supported by French ground and naval forces, the Americans besieged Cornwallis at

Yorktown on September 18. On October 19, Cornwallis, realizing he could neither win nor escape, sent his deputy, General O'Hara, marching to the old British tune "The World Turned Upside Down," to surrender.

O'Hara offered his sword to the French commander, who deferred to Washington. The American commander in chief, recognizing the enemy's slight of surrendering by the deputy rather than the commander, turned and ordered his own deputy, Gen. Benjamin Lincoln, to accept the sword.

The British garrisons in New York, Savannah, and Charleston, though, did not surrender, and limited fighting continued for more than a year. Yorktown, for all practical purposes, however, ended the war. Against all odds and probabilities, the American rebels had won their independence from the most powerful country and military in the world.

Although history would mostly ignore the fact, from the first shot at Lexington to the last siege at Yorktown, African Americans participated in every fight. Washington, Greene, and other American commanders faced many difficulties in the long war, manpower being the most critical one. The inability to fill the ranks with able, willing participants presented the greatest challenge to the success of the rebellion. While at times sanctioned and at other times prohibited, the presence and participation of Black soldiers often meant the difference between victory and defeat.

Politics, prejudice, convenience, and need were the driving forces in the official and unofficial policies of the rebel army's acceptance of Black enlistees, the latter factor by far the most important. Washington had to balance appeasing the southern states and prevailing white prejudices against remedying manpower shortages. Ironically, while many whites resisted the enlistment of Black Americans, they readily provided slaves as substitutes for their own service.

Each state established its own enlistment regulations, passing, repealing, changing, or ignoring the statues throughout the Revolution. During the first months of the war, the states generally followed Washington's order not to enlist "any stroller, negro, or vagabond." The state governments, like Washington, amended this policy when Lord Dunmore promised freedom for slaves who joined his army. Still, they generally restricted enlistments to freemen.

As the war advanced into its second year and beyond, the issue of Black enlistments created more controversy. Some states debated the issue at length as they changed their policy with each year's legislature. Other states passed regulations to meet whatever enlistment practices their field commanders supported. Still others either passed but did not enforce laws or simply ignored the question altogether, letting the militia determine its own course of action.

Again, the numbers in the ranks strongly influenced decisions about enforcements. States with small Black populations were not as fearful of arming African Americans as those with greater numbers. All the states, regardless of population ratios, shared the difficulty of meeting enlistment quotas set by the Continental Congress after 1777. Desperate recruiters often enlisted willing men regardless of their color. Commanders at the front welcomed anyone who could carry a musket.

The longer the war lasted, the greater the opportunities became for Black men to enlist. Late in the conflict commanders were so short of men that neither color nor criminal record barred enlistment. In a letter to the governor of Maryland on April 17, 1781, Zachariah Forrest asked that a warrant for the execution of a Black prisoner be waived because "he is young and healthy and would make a fine soldier."

Each state approached the issue of African American enlistments differently. New Hampshire, with its small number of Black Americans, simply ignored guidance from the Continental Congress and enlisted freemen and slaves along with whites and awarded them the same bounties and pay. Rhode Island initially recruited few Black men, but manpower shortages became so severe in early 1778 that the state sought and received Washington's approval to recruit an all-Black unit led by white officers.[1]

The Connecticut legislature considered a committee recommendation in May 1777 that any slave desiring to enlist "shall be allowed to do so," with the owner receiving all the enlistment bounty and "one-half of the annual wages of such slave during the time he shall continue in said service." The legislature rejected the measure but did approve a bill exempting any white man from the draft if he provided a substitute. Since the vast majority of these substitutes were Black slaves, the legislature approved regulations the following October that released the substitutes' owners from maintenance costs and encouraged them to free their slaves upon completion of their service.

New York, Maryland, and Delaware passed similar substitution laws; other states sanctioned the practice either officially or unofficially. By the fall of 1777, Black substitutes were so common in the American ranks that

---

[1]Details of Rhode Island's Black regiment are covered in chapter 7, "Segregated Freedom Fighters: All-Black Units."

even the British recognized their presence. A Hessian officer with John Burgoyne at Saratoga noted in his journal, "The negro can take the field, instead of his master; and therefore no regiment is to be seen in which there are not negroes in abundance; and among them there are able-bodied, strong, and brave fellows."

Massachusetts militia units continued to accept African Americans in the same manner as they had enlisted Prince Estabrook, Peter Salem, and other Black heroes of the war's early battles. When faced with providing fifteen regiments for the Continental army in 1777, the Massachusetts legislature passed a resolution that exempted only Quakers from the draft. By not specifically exempting Black men, the act allowed recruiters to interpret it as permitting their enlistment. The legislature finally sanctioned Black enlistments with an official measure that authorized their recruitment in April 1778.

The General Assembly of New Jersey passed an act on June 8, 1781, which directed militia commanders to maintain a roll of all eligible for military service within their district. It excluded "slaves and every person exempted by any particular law of this state," but, in fact, New Jersey enlisted freemen and Black slaves as individuals and substitutes throughout the war.

Whites in the southern states remained fearful of slave insurrections if they armed Black Americans. They also looked at their slaves as valuable property meant to produce profit, not fight for the independence of their country. Sharing any degree of equality with Black people, even the dangers and hardships of battle, was unthinkable to most white southerners.

Maryland was no exception to this kind of thinking. Yet when unable to meet its recruitment quotas as early as 1777, the state's military commanders accepted Black recruits. In October 1780 the state legislature directed that "any able-bodied slave between sixteen and forty years of age, who voluntarily enters into service, and is passed by the lieutenant, in the presence and with the consent and agreement of his master, may be accepted as a recruit." When not enough slaves volunteered or received owners' consent to be soldiers, the Maryland legislature, on May 10, 1781, ordered that free Black men, previously exempt, were now subject to the draft.

Still unable to meet recruitment goals in the summer of 1781, Maryland proposed bounties to slaveholders who permitted their slaves to enlist. Once again, economics proved more important than patriotism to many slaveholders. In a letter to his father on June 4, 1781, plantation owner Charles Carroll explained, "I hope none of our negroes will enlist—the price if paid is not equal to the value of a healthy, strong, young negro man."

In Virginia, James Madison proposed freeing a limited number of slaves in exchange for their military service. The legislature, dominated by slaveholders, preferred to keep Virginia's slaves on the plantation rather than risk them on the battlefield. The Virginia militia, however, accepted free Black men as early as July 1775. To prevent runaway slaves from representing themselves as freemen in order to join the army, the Virginia legislature enacted a measure on May 6, 1777, that required recruiters to verify a certificate of freedom signed by a county justice of the peace. The assembly also ordered that, once accepted, freemen could only serve as drummers, fifers, and pioneers.

North Carolina had permitted free Black men to enlist in local militias before the Revolution and continued the practice after the war began. The state, however, never authorized the enlistment of slaves, though it did allow them to serve as substitutes. Nevertheless, critical manpower needs encouraged some North Carolina commanders to accept Black recruits without concern about their ownership.

South Carolina and Georgia had taken the lead in blocking the inclusion of the slavery paragraph in the Declaration of Independence and in the Continental Congress's stance against the enlistment of slaves. These two states, except for allowing a few substitutes and some slaves accompanying their owners as servants, continued to block Black enlistments even after the British shifted their offensive to the South and captured Savannah on December 29, 1778.

Several members of Washington's staff and representatives to the Continental Congress thought it might become necessary to use the large Black slave population in the South as soldiers if they were to defeat the British. Only weeks after the British shifted their operations southward, Lt. Colonel John Laurens wrote his father, Henry Laurens, a distinguished member of the Continental Congress and its former president, declaring, "A well chosen body of 5,000 Black men, properly officered to act as light troops might give us decisive success in the next campaign."

Henry and John Laurens were unusual men for their time. The senior Laurens owned a large plantation in South Carolina, where he had ceased purchasing new slaves in 1770 and begun freeing the remaining ones in 1775. John shared his father's philosophy—that is, his opposition to slavery—but neither Congress nor General Washington immediately favored the proposal to arm slaves in the South.

The senior Laurens warned his son that any proposal to arm slaves in the South would meet with extreme opposition and that the family's reputation and finances in South Carolina would suffer. Eventually, the younger Laurens prevailed, and on March 16, 1779, his father wrote General Washington, "Had we arms for three thousand such Black men as I could select in Carolina, I should have no doubt of success in driving the British out of Georgia and subduing East Florida, before the end of July."

Washington, ever the politician and mindful of regional unity, responded to the senior Laurens on March 20, expressing his concerns about the unrest among those slaves remaining in servitude if some were freed to fight. He also wrote that the issue of using slaves as soldiers had "never employed much of my thoughts." This last statement again seems more political than honest, since Washington had previously issued orders on enlistments of slaves and freemen and only the year before had authorized Rhode Island to form a Black battalion.

Young Laurens's most vocal support in Washington's headquarters came from New Yorker Alexander Hamilton.[2] The two lobbied their commander and Congress to encourage the enlistment of slaves in the South. It took more than a year, and additional losses to the British, for the Continental Congress to finally take action. On March 29, 1779, Congress recommended, but did not order, South Carolina and Georgia to "take measures immediately for raising three thousand able-bodied negroes."

Moreover, Congress recommended that Black soldiers be formed into separate battalions, with white officers and sergeants. Each volunteer would receive arms, clothes, and food at government expense. Neither master nor slave would receive an enlistment bounty, but the government would compensate owners up to $1,000 for "each active able-bodied negro man of standard size, not exceeding thirty-five years of age." At the end of the war each slave who served "well and faithfully" would receive his freedom and a discharge bonus of fifty dollars.

Hamilton and Laurens, aware of the pending recommendation, took action before it was announced. Laurens headed south to begin organizing the slave battalions. On his way, he delivered a letter from Alexander Hamilton to John Jay, the new president of the Continental Congress.

Hamilton's letter[3] contained an eloquent statement on the need, ca-

---

[2]Though young, Laurens and Hamilton did not hesitate to stand up for their beliefs. In 1778, Laurens was twenty-four years of age; Hamilton, only twenty-one. In 1804, Hamilton died in an infamous duel with Aaron Burr. On December 23, 1780, Laurens challenged and wounded Gen. Charles Lee, Washington's former deputy commander, in a duel.
[3]The complete Hamilton letter is in Appendix G.

pabilities, and humanitarian aspects of enlisting slaves to fight for their country's and their personal freedom. The need for the enlistment of slaves as soldiers in South Carolina and Georgia, according to Hamilton, was simple: "I hardly see how a sufficient force can be collected in that quarter without it; and the enemy's operations there are growing infinitely serious and formidable."

Hamilton also expressed confidence in the fighting abilities of African Americans: "I have not the least doubt, that the negroes will make very excellent soldiers." He even suggested that Black soldiers might be superior to whites, speculating, "I think their want of civilization (for their natural faculties are probably as good as ours) joined to the habit of subordination which they acquire from a life of servitude, will make them sooner become soldiers than our white inhabitants.

"I foresee that this project will have to combat much opposition from prejudice and self-interest," Hamilton warned. The letter continued:

> The contempt we have been taught to entertain for the blacks makes us fancy many things that are founded neither in reason nor experience; and an unwillingness to part with property of so valuable a kind will furnish a thousand arguments to show the impracticability or pernicious tendency of a scheme which requires such a sacrifice.

In closing, Hamilton again warned that if the Americans did not use the slaves as soldiers, then surely the British would. With that practical point made, he concluded that enlisting slaves in exchange for their freedom

> will secure their fidelity, animate their courage, and I believe will have a good influence upon those who remain, by opening a door to their emancipation. This circumstance, I confess, has no small weight in inducing me to wish the success of the project; for the dictates of humanity and true policy equally interest me in favor of this unfortunate class of men.

Both Hamilton and Laurens understood how to solve the Continental army's manpower problems and at the same time bring an end to slavery. What they did not comprehend, however, were the absolutely rigid prejudices and economic self-interest of the southerners. South Carolina governor John Rutledge responded in a letter to his state's representatives to the Continental Congress on April 24, 1779: "As soon as I received the Resolve of Congress respecting the raising of three thousand negroes, I called a full Council and communicated it to them. The proposition was unanimously rejected."

When Laurens arrived in South Carolina, he delivered a letter to the governor requesting reconsideration. On May 26, Rutledge responded, "I laid your letter, respecting Black levies, before the Council, yesterday, but they adhere to their former sentiments on that subject."

Rutledge's responses, although to the point, were much less direct and angry than those of individual South Carolina congressmen. Christopher Gadsden, who four years earlier had been a leader in demanding that the Americans revolt against Britain, declared, "We are much disgusted here at Congress recommending us to arm our slaves." Other South Carolina leaders even suggested that their state withdraw from the Union and approach the British for a separate peace agreement.

It is unlikely that the Continental Congress and Colonel Laurens could have approached any group in America at the time that would have more opposition to arming Black Americans than the legislature of South Carolina. Planters whose social and economic futures depended on the institution of slavery dominated the state's government. Many of them preferred to lose the war and resume colonial status under the British than risk the loss of their valuable property, which they saw as the only means of maintaining profitability on their plantations. It is also noteworthy that South Carolinians, outnumbered six to four by their slaves, had a legitimate fear of insurrection if they armed their Black residents.

Despite the rejection, Laurens remained in South Carolina, attempting to gain support for slave enlistments. He also joined directly in the fight against the British, only to be captured in Charleston in May 1780. After he was paroled and exchanged by the British, Laurens sailed to France in the spring of 1781 as a representative of the Continental Congress to help Benjamin Franklin arrange for additional supplies and monetary support. He returned in time to rejoin the army and participate in the Battle of Yorktown.

All the while, Laurens lobbied for the enlistment of slaves as soldiers and for granting them their freedom for honorable service. Some officers, continually suffering from personnel shortages, supported Laurens's quest. Gen. Benjamin Lincoln. desperately attempting to defend Charleston and knowing the fighting ability of African Americans from his observations of the French Saint Domingue Corps, called upon Governor Rutledge to enlist slaves. On March 13, 1780, Lincoln wrote the governor, "I think the measure of raising a Black corps a necessary one; that I have great reason to believe, if permission is given for it, that many men would soon be obtained."

Lincoln continued: "I have repeatedly urged this matter, not only because Congress have recommended it, and because it therefore becomes my duty to attempt to have it executed, but because my own mind suggests the utility and importance of the measure, as the safety of the town makes it necessary."

Neither Rutledge nor the slaveholder-dominated South Carolina legislature looked upon Lincoln's request favorably. Some dismissed the general as a Massachusetts native more interested in the abolition of slavery than the merits of Black soldiers.

Without Black men to reinforce his army, Lincoln lost Charleston to the British on May 11. Lincoln's replacement, Gen. Horatio Gates, also proved unsuccessful in stopping the British offensive in the South, and in October, Gen. Nathanael Greene replaced him. Shortly after his arrival, Greene appealed to the South Carolina legislature for permission to enlist slaves, whom he said would "make good soldiers." Greene received the same response as had the Continental Congress, Laurens, and Lincoln. South Carolinians continued to refuse to lose personal property and arm slaves.

The arrival of French troops and rebel reinforcements from the North reduced personnel shortages and allowed Greene to assume the offensive and then to eventually join Washington in surrounding the British at Yorktown on October 19, 1781. The victory at Yorktown ensured the survival of the United States but did not end the war with the British, who still occupied Charleston and other parts of both the North and South.

Shortly after Yorktown, Greene once again recognized the need to enlist Black men to ensure that the British did not counterattack and retake all of South Carolina. On December 9, Greene wrote Rutledge explaining that there were not sufficient numbers of whites in the state to maintain the army. He wrote: "The natural strength of this country in point of numbers appears to consist much more in the blacks than in the whites."

Greene specifically requested permission to enlist four regiments of infantrymen and a corps of engineers and craftsmen, including harness makers and wagon repairers. He also requested that each slave volunteer be given his freedom and be treated in the same manner as other soldiers, saying that they would not perform adequately otherwise.

Rutledge delayed taking action on Greene's request by referring it to the state council, which then referred it to the entire legislature on December 23. Greene, assisted by Laurens, wrote another letter to the South Carolina legislature to lobby for the enlistment of slaves. A few of the congressmen favored the proposal, but as Greene wrote Washington on January 24, 1782, "The far greater part of the people are opposed to it."

Shortly after the South Carolina legislature turned down Greene's request, news reached the state that British forces in New York were sailing for Charleston to reinforce a pending offensive. On February 6, John Mathews, who had replaced Rutledge as governor, wrote Greene that the legislature might consider a bill to provide Black Americans as noncombatant support personnel for his army. Greene responded on February 11, requesting "140 wagoners, 150 pioneers, 120 artificers, and 20 or 30 servants." Mathews forwarded the request to the legislature with his endorsement. Once again, the combined legislature refused to free slaves for any kind of military service and handily defeated the bill.

Over the next few weeks Washington and Laurens exchanged letters expressing their frustration over the South Carolina decision. On May 19, Laurens wrote his commander in chief: "The plan which brought me to this country was urged with all the zeal which the subject inspired; but the single voice of reason was drowned by the howlings of a triple-headed monster, in which prejudice, avarice, and pusillanimity were united."

On June 12, Laurens again wrote Washington expressing hopes that Georgia might authorize the arming of slaves and reporting that he had the support of Gov. Richard Howley. Washington responded on July 10 with one of his harshest condemnations of self-interest over the freedom of the country:

I must confess that I am not at all astonished at the failure of your plan. The spirit of freedom, which, at the commencement of this contest, would have gladly sacrificed every thing to the attainment of its objective, has long since subsided, and every selfish passion has taken its place.

The general concluded his letter thusly: "Under these circumstances, it would have been surprising if you had succeeded; nor will you, I fear, have better success in Georgia."

Washington's fears proved correct. The Georgia legislature, with little debate, reached the same decision as neighboring South Carolina. Laurens, defeated in his efforts to free slaves to become soldiers, continued to fight for his country. In one of the war's last skirmishes, Laurens fell mortally wounded in an engagement with a Loyalist unit at Combahee Ferry, South Carolina, on August 27, 1782.

Although neither South Carolina nor Georgia permitted Black enlistments, both states did allow slaves to be used as bounties to induce white volunteers. In April 1781, Gen. Thomas Sumter of South Carolina offered slaves to any white man volunteering for ten months of service.

New recruits were to receive one grown, healthy slave, while those with prior service could receive up to four slaves for reenlisting.

In February 1782 the South Carolina legislature formalized "Sumter's Law." In addition to promising a healthy slave between the ages of ten and forty to any white who enlisted, the legislature ruled that recruiters were to receive a bonus of one slave for every twenty-five whites enlisted during a two-month period. Since neither Sumter nor the South Carolina legislature had any slaves of their own to barter for enlistments, they honored the bounty with slaves captured or confiscated from Loyalists.

Georgia broadened the scale of the use of slaves as enlistment bonuses. The state rewarded white soldiers with slaves for their part in successful battles, paid public officials with slaves, and used slaves as tender in exchange for military provisions and supplies. Again, the source of this "Black currency" was the plantations of the Loyalists.

Despite the resistance of the South Carolina and Georgia legislatures to enlisting slaves as soldiers, African Americans served throughout the southern theater with units from the North and as substitutes and servants in regiments from the South. An exact accounting of their total numbers is as impossible to document as are many other aspects of the American Revolution.

7

Segregated Freedom Fighters: All-Black Units

IN EVERY CONTINENTAL ARMY AND STATE MILITIA REGIMENT active during the Revolutionary War, Black soldiers and white soldiers fought side by side on a mostly equal basis. They shared the hardships and dangers of the battlefield in integrated units in which a soldier's skills and courage were more important than the color of his skin. This mixing of Black and white, so prevalent in the American Revolution, would not take place again in the U.S. armed forces until 175 years later, when the military finally again integrated its ranks during the Korean War.

For nearly two centuries following the Revolutionary War, African Americans fought in segregated units under the command of white officers. In every war the U.S. military resisted enlisting Black Americans and only sought their services when manpower requirements exceeded the abilities or motivation of whites. Despite the objections of whites over Black Americans joining the armed forces, African Americans came forward in every conflict to serve their country and defend the freedoms and equality that whites, in turn, often denied them. Nevertheless, Black men and women experienced the same feelings of patriotism as their white countrymen and sought to share the dangers and adventures of military service. More important, African Americans realized that fighting for their country offered the opportunity for personal advancement and a furtherance of racial equality.

While most Black soldiers fought in integrated units during the Revolution, some served in all-Black organizations that would establish the model for future African American military service. On each occasion, these units resulted from the same situation; when too few whites were available or willing, the military turned to the Black population.

As noted earlier, in late 1777 the state of Rhode Island found it impossible to provide sufficient white replacements to man its two allocated

Continental army regiments. Sparsely populated and suffering restrictions from the British occupation of its major port and two-thirds of its territory, the state had few choices in terms of personnel. Gen. James M. Varnum, commander of the Rhode Island troops, proposed to George Washington on January 2, 1778, that his two diminished regiments be combined into one unit and that the surplus officers return to Rhode Island to recruit an all-Black battalion. In a letter outlining his idea and recommending that Col. Christopher Greene, Lt. Col. Jeremiah Olney, and Maj. Samuel Ward recruit a new force in Rhode Island, Varnum noted, "It is imagined that a battalion of negroes can be easily raised there."

Washington endorsed Varnum's request the same day and forwarded the documents to Rhode Island governor Nicholas Cooke. In his endorsement, Washington wrote that Varnum's request was "an important subject" and might help the state fulfill its commitments to the Continental army, but he made no direct mention of the enlistment or service of Black men.

Governor Cooke referred Varnum's letter to the February session of the Rhode Island General Assembly, where, after heated debate, the legislature passed a law[1] authorizing the formation of a Black battalion. The resolution made little mention of the need for Black soldiers to meet critical manpower shortages; instead, it emphasized the nobility of the legislature's own action, stating, "History affords us frequent precedents of the wisest, the freest, and bravest nations having liberated their slaves, and enlisted them as soldiers to fight in defense of their country."

The act promised freedom to any slave accepted into the Rhode Island battalion and authorized for them bounties and pay equal to that of the state's other Continental army soldiers. It also promised that the state would support any soldier disabled by sickness or battle wounds. The act then detailed procedures and compensation amounts for owners providing slaves to the army. The resolution stated that funding was to come from the U.S. Congress rather than the state budget.

Not all of the Rhode Island legislators agreed with the proposal to enlist slaves. In a formal protest[2] six members outlined their many objections, stating that there were too few slaves in the state who would seek enlistment, that having slaves fight for freedom was inconsistent with the principles of liberty and the constitutional government that they would defend, that other states would resent the action, that the policy would be too expensive, and that slaveholders would not be satisfied with the amount of compensation they received. The protest also noted the possi-

---

[1]The complete resolution can be found in Appendix H.
[2]The complete protest document appears in Appendix I.

bility that enlisting African Americans would bring the state the same ridicule as that directed toward Lord Dunmore's efforts and that such action might provoke the British to repeat the practice.

Despite the protest, Governor Cooke supported the original resolution. In a letter to Washington on February 23, 1778, he stated that recruitment was under way and reported, "Liberty is given to every effective slave to enter the service during the war; and, upon his passing muster, he is absolutely made free, and entitled to all the wages, bounties, and encouragements given by Congress to any soldier enlisting into their service.

"The number of slaves in this State is not great," Cooke concluded, "but it is generally thought that three hundred and upwards will be enlisted."

The recruiting effort was not without problems, however. Whites who opposed making slaves into soldiers and then freeing them often hampered Colonel Greene and his officers' enlistment and training of African Americans. Capt. Elijah Lewis, a recruiting officer in Kingston, wrote the state assembly on February 19, 1778, that local whites were telling their slaves that if they joined the regiment, they would be sacrificed as "breastworks" and that if taken prisoner, they "would be sent to the West Indies and sold as slaves."

Support from the Rhode Island legislature to enlist slaves did not last long. The citizens of Rhode Island showed their displeasure at the ballot box, and a statewide election in April replaced thirty-nine of the state's sixty-three legislators. One of the new legislature's first acts at their May session was to repeal the slave-enlistment law and to declare that the resolution had never been intended as anything other than a temporary measure.

The new act stated: "It is therefore voted and resolved, that no negro, mulatto, or Indian slave, be permitted to enlist into said battalions from and after the tenth day of June next; and that the said act then expire, and be no longer in force."

The number of slaves joining the Rhode Island regiment during the four months of authorization is verifiable through accounts of the state treasurer. From February 14 to June 10, 1778, a total of eighty-eight slaves enlisted in order to gain their freedom. It is likely that a few free Black men also joined the regiment during this period, but it is doubtful that African Americans ever numbered more than 140 in the "Rhode Island Black regiment."

Much of this confusion apparently derives from the assumption by various authors that Colonel Greene's entire combat experience was in the lead of this Black regiment. Actually, he first served as a lieutenant with the Kentish Guards in the Lexington and Concord campaign and later joined General Varnum as a major in the Rhode Island army. In 1777 he advanced in rank to colonel and commanded the defense of Fort Mercer, also called Red Bank, on the Delaware River, near Philadelphia. After a valiant fight, Greene supervised the successful evacuation of the fort. Historians often cite the Rhode Island Black regiment's participation in this campaign. In reality, Greene's force at Red Bank was white, not Black; the Black Rhode Island regiment would not exist for another year.

Greene recruited much of his First Rhode Island Regiment from the towns of North Kingstown and South Kingstown. On July 6, 1778, he held the first muster of his regiment and organized his 175 officers, noncommissioned officers, and men into four companies. He later added another company of fifty more men.

Few of the former slaves had any experience handling muskets or other weapons, and Greene and his officers worked long hours to turn the volunteers into soldiers. After only six weeks of training, the regiment assisted the joint American and French effort to drive the British out of Newport in what became known as the Battle of Rhode Island. Some accounts make no mention of the Black regiment's contributions, while others make it sound as though the First Rhode Island was the only regiment involved in the fight. Neither is correct.

While there is no doubt that the Black Rhode Islanders fought well in the battle and contributed to its success, their role was fairly minor. The Battle of Rhode Island began with an indecisive naval battle between the British and French fleets off Sandy Hook. During the battle at sea, American general John Sullivan advanced on land with an army of about 1,500, including the First Rhode Island.

Sullivan besieged Newport and planned to attack the city's defenses once the French defeated the British fleet and could support his assault with naval gunfire. When the sea battle stalemated and the French sailed away to refit, Sullivan's army, too weak to assault the British fortifications alone, was stranded. On August 28, Sullivan began to withdraw, but the British, now holding the advantage, and with their ships positioned to shell the American lines, counterattacked.

Early on the morning of the twenty-ninth, the Americans hastily fortified Butt's Hill, near Bristol Ferry, about twelve miles from Newport. At 7:00 a.m., the British and Hessians attacked, beginning a battle that lasted into the extremely hot, humid afternoon. Later that evening, General Sullivan wrote Governor Cooke:

> The enemy then advanced to turn our right under fire of their ships, and endeavored to carry a redoubt a little in front of the right wing.

Major General Nathanael Greene,[3] who commanded the right wing, advanced upon them with two or three regiments, and being reinforced, drove them back in great confusion. The enemy repeated the attempt three times and were as often repulsed with great bravery, our officers and soldiers behaving with uncommon fortitude, and not giving up an inch of ground through the whole day.

Sullivan did not mention the Black regiment in his initial correspondence to the governor, and stories among white units began to circulate that the former slaves had not performed well under fire. On August 30, Sullivan put an end to these rumors by praising the Black regiment in an order that concluded, "From the best information the commander-in-chief thinks that regiment is entitled to a proper share of honor of the day."

The Marquis de Lafayette, a French officer in service of the rebels, observed the battle. Although he made no specific mention of the Black soldiers, he did note that the fight was "the best fought action of the war."

The enemy also noticed the fighting abilities of the Black soldiers they faced. Colonel von der Malsbury, who commanded the Hessian unit in the attack against the American right side, noted in his journal,

> The Hessians now rushed up the hill under fire in order to take the redoubt. Here they experienced a more obstinate resistance than they expected. They found large bodies of troops behind the works and at its sides, chiefly wild looking men in their shirt sleeves, and among them many negroes.

Other proof of the involvement and importance of the Black regiment in the Battle of Rhode Island comes from their casualty figures. Total American losses numbered thirty killed, 137 wounded, and forty-four missing. Casualties in the First Rhode Island were three killed, nine wounded, and eleven missing.

Despite the outstanding performance by the African Americans, the Rhode Island General Assembly continued to block the enlistment of additional slaves. In July, October, and November of 1780, General Washington called upon the state to provide a total of 1,350 additional men for the Continental army. On each occasion, the General Assembly of Rhode Island passed acts calling for towns to produce volunteers and including provisions for a draft to meet unfilled quotas. Each act specified that "Indians, mulattos, and blacks" were to be excluded from the enlistment quotas.

[3]General Nathanael Greene and Colonel Christopher Greene were distant kinsmen.

Although Rhode Island restricted future enlistments to whites only, the Black men in the First Regiment continued to serve. The original enlistees, unlike white volunteers, who enlisted for three to twelve months, entered the service for the duration of the conflict. Many of the original Black enlistees in the First Rhode Island Regiment who volunteered in 1778 served for more than five years before their discharge.

The state's legislation allowed no slaves to enlist to replace the Black regiment's casualties, such as those sustained in the Battle of Rhode Island, or others lost to sickness and accidents. Colonel Greene reluctantly accepted the assembly's decision and issued his own instructions to his officers to enlist only whites. In an order dated January 4, 1781, Greene specifically stated, "Negroes will not be received." A few free Black men volunteered, but not enough to maintain the unit's numbers. While the First Rhode Island continued to be known as the "Black regiment," it survived only because whites began joining the unit from the time shortly after the Battle of Rhode Island until the end of the war, making it an integrated unit.

The First Rhode Island Regiment served for the duration of the conflict. It is significant to note that Washington had enough confidence in the Black regiment that he assigned them to duties with his Continental army rather than approve the request of the Rhode Island governor to maintain the unit in his state.

The First Rhode Island remained in the northern states with Washington for several years after the Battle of Rhode Island; like the rest of the Continental army in that region, the regiment saw little combat. Despite the lack of action, the Black regiment maintained a high level of morale and readiness. On January 5, 1781, the French Marquis de Chastellux, while traveling near Lebanon, Connecticut, encountered the First Rhode Island and recorded in his journal: "At the passage to the ferry crossing I met with a detachment of the Rhode Island regiment. The greatest part of them are negroes or mulattos; but they are strong, robust men, and those I have seen had a very good appearance."

In the spring of 1781, Colonel Greene and the First Rhode Island assumed defensive positions in Westchester County, New York. During the evening of May 14, 1781, a Loyalist unit, commanded by Oliver De Lancey, attacked Greene's headquarters at Points Bridge on the Croton River. Several Black soldiers died or suffered wounds rallying to Greene's side in a futile effort to defend their commander.

The Loyalist troops dragged Greene's body away and mutilated it with swords and bayonets. Even though some of the war's most brutal battles pitted Loyalists against rebels, this bit of butchery exceeded the bloody norm. Neither De Lancey nor his troops ever explained their behavior, but their violence is probably attributable to their anger against the Rhode Island colonel for his leadership of Black soldiers.

Col. Jeremiah Olney, who had assisted in the original recruitment of Black men for the First Rhode Island, assumed command of the regiment upon Greene's death. During this same period, because of personnel shortages, the white Second Rhode Island Regiment combined with the First, forming the Rhode Island Regiment. White men outnumbered Black men in the new unit, but many of the African Americans, now in their fourth year of enlistment, were the most experienced soldiers in the regiment.

The following July, the Rhode Islanders joined Washington's camp near White Plains, New York, where Baron Ludwig von Clasen, a German serving with the French in support of the Americans, observed the regiment. On July 8, 1781, von Clasen wrote in his diary, "Three-quarters[4] of the Rhode Island regiment consists of negroes, and that regiment is the most neatly dressed, the best under arms, and the most precise in its maneuvers."

In September, Olney's Rhode Island regiment accompanied Washington's march south to encircle the British at Yorktown, Virginia. There the Rhode Islanders joined the Second and Fourth Connecticut Regiments and formed a brigade under the command of Col. Herman Swift.

From September 30 to October 18, the Continental army, with nearly 9,000 men, supported by 7,800 French ground troops and an offshore fleet, tightened their circle around the British defenses at Yorktown. The Rhode Island regiment participated in several attacks and counterattacks and then proudly stood in formation with the other Continental army units when the British marched out of their defenses to surrender on October 19.

When the British capitulated at Yorktown, which ensured the stability of the United States, most of the militia units returned home, and many of the Regular Army regiments disbanded, over the next few months. The African Americans, already veterans of almost four years of service, were not yet allowed to enjoy the freedom they had fought so hard to achieve.

For nearly two years after Yorktown, Black soldiers in the Rhode Island regiment continued to defend the country that had once enslaved them.

---

[4]Von Clasen's estimate of the number of African Americans in the regiment is an exaggeration; Black men constituted less than one-half of the regiment on this date.

In February 1783 the regiment participated in the fierce winter campaign to capture the British trading post at Oswego on Lake Ontario and then remained in New York. Finally, on June 13, 1783, at Saratoga, more than five years after the original Black enlistees had volunteered to become soldiers in exchange for their freedom, they received their discharges.

Colonel Olney addressed his regiment one last time and praised them for "faithfully persevering in the best of causes, in every stage of service, with unexampled fortitude and patience through all the dangers and toils of a long and severe war." He then declared his "entire approbation of their valor and good conduct displayed on every occasion when called to face the enemy in the field."

Olney closed his remarks by noting that the Black regiment had never received the bounties promised by the Rhode Island General Assembly, nor had they received pay equal to that of white soldiers. He then expressed his hopes that a grateful state and nation would recognize the Black soldiers and that they would "obtain their just due from the public."

The Black regiment received no welcome-home parade or any other "just due from the public" when they returned to Rhode Island. Most of the state's white citizens seemed to think liberty alone was ample reward for the former slaves' service. Some Black veterans tried in vain to receive their back wages through the courts. Others found themselves before judges fighting to prevent their former owners from re-enslaving them.

Once the battles ended, the participation of the Black population was rarely noted in white-written histories of the Revolution. A few Rhode Island politicians did mention the Black regiment when expedient, but many of their comments were more fanciful than factual. Governor Eustis, in a speech against slavery in Missouri on December 12, 1820, included the incorrect claim that the Black regiment had fought at Red Bank. Eustis stated: "The blacks formed an entire regiment, and they discharged their duty with zeal and fidelity. The gallant defense of Red Bank, in which the Black regiment bore a part, is among the proofs of their valor."

Another Rhode Islander, Tristam Burges, provided a more accurate description of the Black regiment during a speech before Congress in January 1828, stating, "At the commencement of the Revolutionary War, Rhode Island had a number of slaves. A regiment of them were enlisted into the Continental service, and no braver men met the enemy in battle." Burges, however, did not have all his facts straight when he concluded that, "not one of them was permitted to be a soldier until he had first been made a freeman." Actually, none of the Rhode Island slave volunteers were declared free until after they had been accepted into the regiments as soldiers.

Although certainly not without its faults, the Rhode Island act of February 14, 1778, that freed nearly 100 slaves to become soldiers in fact provided the only Black unit of significance to serve in the American army during the Revolution. Other states, including Connecticut and Massachusetts, formed several all-Black companies for brief periods, but none ever engaged the enemy to any extent.

The northern states generally accepted free Black men as soldiers early in the war and then later, because of the shortage of white recruits, made provisions for the emancipation of slaves in exchange for their military service. Not everyone was pleased with the mixing of the races in the ranks, as shown in a letter from Brig. Gen. William Heath to Samuel Adams. On August 27, 1777, after marching Black and white troops from Massachusetts to reinforce the American army at Ticonderoga, Heath wrote that, "there were some men advanced in life and some lads, and a number of negroes, the latter were generally able-bodied but for my own part I must confess I am never pleased to see them mixed with white men."

However, the majority of white officers and soldiers, always desperate to fill the ranks, apparently accepted the Black soldiers and willingly fought as part of the integrated units. Although this blatantly negated the primary reason given for African Americans to serve in all-Black units—that whites would refuse to live and serve with Black people on an equal basis—white military and civilian officials ignored the evidence for the next century and a half.

Connecticut considered enlisting an all-Black unit with white officers at the same time that Rhode Island adopted their slave enlistment act. In May 1777 the General Assembly of Connecticut appointed a committee "to take into consideration the state and condition of the negro and mulatto slaves in this State, and what may be done for their emancipation." A few weeks later, the committee recommended that slaves be allowed to enlist in the Continental battalions and granted them freedom for their service.

The recommendation did not cover whether these slaves would serve in all-Black units or be integrated into the main force. It soon became a moot point. Even though the Connecticut lower house approved the committee's recommendations, the upper house rejected it.

The following October, the Connecticut assembly did pass legislation that ended the responsibility of owners to continue the support of their slaves who joined the army. This permitted owners to send slaves as their substitutes with no further responsibility on their parts other than freeing the soldiers for their service.

Legislation permitting Black substitutes for white owners increased the numbers of African Americans in the Connecticut militia and its Continental army regiments. These Black soldiers, along with freemen volunteers, served mostly alongside white soldiers in integrated units. In June 1780 Black Americans were so numerous in the Fourth Connecticut Regiment that the officers segregated fifty-two former slaves and freemen into the Second Company under the command of Capt. David Humphreys. Payroll records for the Second Company, Fourth Connecticut Regiment, provide the most information on the unit, identifying the names of its Black soldiers. From the other limited information available about the unit, it appears that the company served effectively until November 1782, when, likely due to shortages in other units, it was disbanded, its Black soldiers reassigned within the regiment.

Massachusetts also considered the enlistment of all-Black units during this same period but took no direct action until Thomas Kench, an artillery captain, wrote the state legislature on April 3, 1778. Kench began his letter by highlighting his unit's personnel shortages and the need for men to fill the ranks to counter the anticipated British offensive over the next months. He then explained, "I think it is highly necessary that some new augmentation should be added to the army this summer—all the reenforcements that can possibly be obtained."

Kench then outlined his plan to secure recruits, stating, "A reenforcement can quick be raised of two or three hundred men. Will your honors grant them liberty, and give me command of the party? And what I refer to is negroes." The captain further wrote that Black men were serving well alongside whites, but if organized into their own units, "their ambition would entirely be to outdo the white men in every measure that the fortune of war calls a soldier to endure."

Kench concluded his letter by requesting permission to recruit at least one company with white officers and senior sergeants and proposing that Black soldiers eventually be promoted to fill junior-sergeant and corporal positions as they gained experience. The Black volunteers would serve until the end of the war and then be free men.

Neither the members of the Massachusetts legislature nor others in the state embraced the idea of an all-Black unit. Black Americans and their abolitionist supporters argued that segregating African Americans reinforced old prejudices and that intermingling the races in units did more to ensure equal rights and contribute to ending slavery. Whites generally opposed the idea out of fear of possible revolts by the armed all-Black units.

On April 7, Kench again wrote the Massachusetts legislature expressing his regrets about the protests his first letter had generated. He also stated that he did not desire to give "offence" but concluded, "It is justifiable that negroes should have their freedom, and none amongst us be held as slaves, as freedom and liberty is the grand controversy that we are contending for."

The Massachusetts assembly referred Kench's first letter to a joint committee on April 11 "to consider the same, and report." On April 28 the assembly passed a resolution granting freedom to slaves in exchange for military service, but the act made no mention of authorizing all-Black units. For the remainder of the war, Massachusetts continued to enlist Black men, but they served with whites in integrated rather than segregated companies.

There is, however, evidence that one all-Black company, the Bucks of America, was organized in Boston, but it never left the city or saw action against the British. It apparently was more of a police auxiliary intended to guard against Loyalist sabotage than an actual military organization. There are relics of their service on display today at the Massachusetts Historical Society. One can find in the society's collection a silk flag, forty by sixty-two inches, featuring a pine tree and a buck deer in its center, with a field of thirteen stars in the upper-left corner. Below the pine tree is a scroll with the words "The Bucks of America" and the initials "J.H." and "G.W" Accompanying the flag is a silver shield, likely a coat badge, with the same design of pine tree, buck, and stars over the inscription "The Bucks of America" and an added French fleur-de-lis.

Most of the information on the flag and the Bucks comes from Revolutionary War historian William C. Nell. In his 1855 book *The Colored Patriots of the American Revolution,* Nell wrote:

> At the close of the Revolutionary War, John Hancock presented the colored company, called "the Bucks of America," with an appropriate banner, bearing his initials[5] as a tribute to their courage and devotion throughout the struggle. The "Bucks," under command of Colonel Middleton, were invited to a collation in a neighboring town, and, en route, were requested to halt in front of the Hancock Mansion, in Beacon Street, where the Governor and his son united in the above presentation.

Sometime before writing his book, Nell acquired the flag, and possibly the silver badge, from a "Mrs. Key," reputedly the daughter of one of the

[5]The G.W. initials are presumed to be those of George Washington.

original Bucks. In 1858 the flag was exhibited in Boston, and in 1862, Nell presented it to the Massachusetts Historical Society.

No official military record of the existence of the Bucks has yet surfaced. There is mention of "an association of colored men" known as "the Protectors," who guarded the property of Boston merchants during the war, and this might have been another name for the Bucks. A paramilitary status is likely the more accurate term rather than an actual Revolutionary War army unit.

Some historians speculate that the Bucks were formed in 1776, shortly after the British evacuation of Boston, but again, there is no proof. Several also write that the unit disbanded in 1780, while others, citing the fact that Hancock made his presentation at the end of the war, contend that the unit existed until 1783.

As with the Bucks, there is no proof that "Colonel Middleton" ever held a commission in the Continental army or the Massachusetts militia. Nell does not provide his first name but does include a postwar description of him credited to Lydia Maria Child, a Boston neighbor of the former commander of the Bucks: "He was an old horse-breaker, who owned a house that he inhabited at the end of Belknap Street. He was greatly respected by his own people, and his house was thronged with company."

According to Nell, Child added that Middleton was "not a very good specimen of colored man" and that "his morals were questioned." She concluded, however, that his leadership on an unspecified date was largely responsible for preventing a riot between Black and White Americans.

While there is no record of an African American officer in the Revolutionary War by the name of Middleton, or of any other Black officer for that matter, there is ample evidence of the life of George Middleton of Boston, who was likely the commander of the Bucks. Records exist to show Middleton's marriage in 1778 and his membership in the Prince Hall's African Lodge of Freemasons the following year. The 1790 Boston census lists Middleton as the head of a family of three. In 1796, George Middleton assisted in the organization of the Boston African Benevolent Society, and four years later he signed and submitted a petition from Black leaders to a Boston town meeting requesting the establishment of a school for African American children. Except for a later mention in the records of the Boston African Lodge of Freemasons that he became their grand master, the record of Middleton, like that of the Bucks of America, reveals no additional information.

The sketchy records of Black companies from Connecticut and Massachusetts leave the First Rhode Island Regiment as the only recognized, segregated Black unit to participate in the Revolution as a part of the

Continental army. The Rhode Island regiment was not, however, the only Black unit to fight in defense of American liberty. Both France and Spain committed Black units to fight against the British in America.

In early September 1779 a French fleet of thirty-three ships arrived off-shore of Savannah, Georgia, to assist in the Continental army's attempt to recapture the important seaport. On September 12 an army of 3,500 put ashore eight miles south of the city and joined the American siege. Within the French army were 545 Black men, known as the Volunteer Chasseurs, recently recruited in Santo Domingo. Some accounts also refer to the unit as the Fontages Legion, after its commander, Viscount François de Fontages.

On September 12 the joint American-French force attacked the British defenses, only to be beaten back with severe losses. The Volunteer Chasseurs did not directly participate in the assault but played an important role in the American-French withdrawal following the unsuccessful attack. According to the French official accounts of the battle, "the Legion saved the army at Savannah by bravely covering the retreat."

Two weeks later, the French fleet, along with the Fontages Legion, sailed away from Savannah and returned to the West Indies. The legion played no further role in the Revolutionary War, but many of its veterans would use the skills they had developed at Savannah to lead the second successful revolution against European colonizers in the New World. Two decades after Savannah, several of its members—Jacques Beauvais, André Rigaud, Martial Besse, and Jean-Baptiste Mars Belley—led the revolt that secured the independence of Haiti.

Still another Fontages Legion veteran, Henri Christophe, became the first king of the island nation. Many different accounts exist of Christophe's life, but all agree that he served as a twelve- or thirteen-year-old with the Volunteer Chasseurs at Savannah. His actual duties are more difficult to confirm. Some biographies state that he was a bootblack or a mess boy, while others indicate that his duties were that of an orderly to a French officer. Still others claim that Christophe served as a free volunteer infantryman or that he entered the Fontages Legion as a slave to earn his freedom. Whatever the true story, his time in the Fontages Legion in Savannah certainly must have influenced his desire for personal freedom and his ideas concerning national Haitian independence.

Unlike France, which directly supported the American rebellion, Spain joined the war against Great Britain in 1779 without directly allying with the United States. The Spanish fight against the British did, however, indirectly support the rebellion by requiring the English to commit land and sea forces in the West Indies and Europe that might have been able to join the war against the Americans. Spanish troops also assumed a direct role in combating British forces in their territories south and west of the boundaries of the United States.

Once again, as they did in every other campaign during the American Revolution, Black soldiers played a role in the Spanish battles against the British. Shortly after his country declared war on Great Britain, Bernardo de Gálvez, governor of the Spanish territory of Louisiana, began recruiting an army to expel English settlements from the Mississippi River valley and the Gulf Coast. As of August 2, 1779, he accepted freemen into his army, and by the twenty-third he had enlisted eighty-three Black men and organized them into two companies.

The two Black companies, along with 670 white soldiers, then marched on the British garrison at Baton Rouge. Along the way, another 600 men, Black and white, joined the force. Records do not give the exact numbers of Black soldiers from that point, but estimates are that during the next three years Black men never accounted for less than 10 percent of Gálvez's army and may have at times approximated 50 percent.

On September 21, Gálvez defeated the British at Baton Rouge and secured not only the town but also Fort Pamure in Natchez in the surrender agreement. In his official report of the battle, Galvez wrote, "No less deserving of eulogy are the companies of negroes and free mulattoes who were continually occupied in the outposts, in false attacks, and discoveries, exchanging shots with the enemy . . . conducting themselves with as much valor and generosity as the whites."

In 1780, Gálvez occupied Mobile, Alabama, and began preparations to drive the British from Pensacola, Florida. The following February, 260 Black soldiers from Havana, Cuba, organized into two battalions, joined the Louisiana Spanish army. On April 8, 1781, Gálvez, with his Black and white soldiers, captured Fort George, Florida, forcing Pensacola to surrender on May 9.

While Black soldiers in the Continental army rarely, if ever, rose above the rank of private, both the French legion at Savannah and the Spanish force in Louisiana appointed African Americans as noncommissioned officers. Gálvez placed white captains in command of his Black companies, but Black men filled many of the lieutenant positions. These Black officers were the first of their race to earn official commissions in any army in North America.

Most African American soldiers in the Revolutionary War fought with valor and honor in integrated units alongside whites. Unfortunately, integrated units would end with victory. All-Black units with white officers would provide the only opportunities for African American soldiers to serve their country until the 1950s—nearly two centuries after Black Americans helped secure the freedom and liberty of the United States.

8

Service at Sea: U.S. Navy and Marine Corps

WHILE SOME BLACK AMERICANS SERVED in the Continental army, state militias, and units of U.S. allies, other African Americans fought as members of the new nation's navy. Neither the national government nor the states restricted Black Americans from naval service. Captains welcomed them aboard both war and merchant ships prior to the Battle of Lexington and recruited them for the duration of the conflict.

There were three primary reasons for relative equality in the enlistment of Black and white sailors. First and foremost was the fact that sea captains experienced even more difficulty than ground commanders in finding sufficient numbers of recruits. Harsh discipline, poor food, and the inherent dangers of life aboard sailing ships discouraged many potential volunteers.

Second, most of the early plantations were near the seashore, and prior to the war many slaveholders had launched their own fishing and merchant vessels. They used their slaves as crews for these ships as well as lending them to other captains in exchange for their pay. Along the way, many Black men developed considerable skills as sailors, and some gained knowledge of inland passages and waterways that qualified them as among the colonies' most efficient ship pilots.

Last, and perhaps most important, whites did not perceive that Black sailors would rise up in armed insurrection against their masters. Black seamen often carried powder to cannon crews or even worked on the guns themselves, but they were unlikely to turn these types of weapons against the white population.

Once the Revolution began, African American seamen were the focus of earnest recruiting for Continental, state, and private warships. Shortly after the fights at Lexington and Concord, a recruiting poster, widely circulated in Newport, Rhode Island, boldly solicited: "Ye able backed sailors, men white or Black, to volunteer for naval service in ye interest of freedom."

There were numerous ships in need of crews because the American colonies, soon after the war erupted, began forming their own navies to defend their coastlines and rivers. On June 12, 1775, citizens of Machias, Maine, boarded and captured the British armed schooner *Margaretta*. Three days later, two armed vessels, chartered by Rhode Island and sailing under the command of Capt. Abraham Whipple, captured a tender belonging to the British frigate the *Rose* in Narragansett Bay.

America's first national navy began as a part of the army. On September 2, 1775, George Washington chartered the schooner *Hannah* to attack British transports bringing supplies to besieged Boston. He then commissioned six additional ships over the next few weeks in what became known as "Washington's Navy." Within two years the squadron had captured more than thirty-five prizes, which provided Washington's army much-needed provisions, before the fleet was disbanded and its responsibilities assumed by the newly formed Continental navy.

On October 13, 1775, the Continental Congress authorized the formation of the Continental navy and approved a three-man committee to control the new organization. The same act directed the outfitting of two vessels "of ten carriage guns . . . for a cruise of three months." On November 2 the naval committee received approval and $100,000 to obtain and equip ships of war. The result was the first Continental fleet, composed of eight merchant vessels converted to warships varying in size from the *Fly*, with eight guns, to the *Alfred*, with twenty-four.

The leaders of the Continental Congress understood the importance of a navy to defend America's shores and trading lanes, but they were also aware that a powerful sea force was not necessary to conduct a successful revolution against Great Britain. On October 19, 1775, Massachusetts representative John Adams, in a letter to James Warren, explained the general feelings of American leaders about a navy. Adams wrote that he thought the United States should have a fleet capable of "something" but that he did not advocate, nor could the country support, "100 ships of the line."

Undoubtedly, a few Black sailors joined the crews of these early U.S. naval vessels, but specific information and names are extremely difficult to document. Almost nothing exists in the official archives in the way of reliable statistical information. Crew lists for naval and merchant vessels, if they exist at all, rarely note the race of crewmen.

Information that is available comes from the few musters that do include a sailor's color and from other official reports that mentioned race when citing a specific seaman for unusual activities or injuries. One of the earliest official confirmations of Black sailors is a single, one-line entry in the spring of 1776 muster of the Connecticut state brig *Defense Colony Service,* which notes "George, a negro" as a crewman. A similar list for the *Trumbull* in the summer of the same year includes Peter, Brittain, and Danial Peterson as "negroes." The rosters of the warships *Lexington, Fly, Boston, Alfred,* and *Alliance* each designate at least one crewman as African American. Two Black sailors also accompanied Capt. John Paul Jones aboard the *Bon Homme Richard* and participated in the war's most famous naval battle, against the *Serapis* on September 23, 1779.

While most of the proof of Black sailors having serving aboard American vessels in the Revolution comes from ships' rosters, other official documents also mention them. The logbook for the U.S. Navy ship *Ranger,* as it lay at anchor in Charleston Harbor on February 25, 1780, relates: "At ten this night a negro called Cesar Hodgsdon died."

Another source of information on Black sailors in the Revolution are the miscellaneous letters, diaries, and memoirs of the period. Some of this correspondence not only hailed the abilities of Black sailors but also noted their monetary value to their owners. On February 11, 1777, ship owner Stephen Steward wrote to the Maryland Council of Safety:

> I send you two fine boats to carry the soldiers over the Bay; in order to man them I am obliged to put in two sailor negroes. If there is the least danger of losing them I shall be obliged to you to send them back again, as I would not take less than two hundred pounds for each of them; they are as fine fellows as ever crossed the sea.

A second letter from Stewart to the council also mentions Black sailors and notes the difficulties in recruiting white seamen. On March 7, 1782, Stewart wrote that he gladly would provide one of his schooners for state service but apologized that it would have a Black crew because "no white man would go."

Another factor that limits the information available about Black Revolutionary War sailors is that despite the formation of the Continental navy, various state fleets, and privateer operations, the American naval forces played an extremely limited role in the war. Prior to the Revolution, the colonies depended on Great Britain to protect their shores and merchant vessels from other countries and pirates. While the colonies had armed militias with some combat experience in defending their villages from Indians, the Americans had no saltwater navy or any naval military tradition or experience at the outbreak of the war.

In the early years of the rebellion, the British navy controlled the American coastline, but their dominance resulted more from a lack of opposition than their own true prowess. When the Treaty of Paris ended the Seven Years' War in 1763, the British severely reduced their navy through parliamentary budget-slashing measures. In fact, at the beginning of the Revolution, the British were able to commit only twenty-nine ships to control the 1,800-mile American coastline. Despite this small fleet, the British were able to successfully evacuate their army from Boston in 1776 and later land them near New York unmolested by American naval forces.

It was not until the French allied with the United States in 1778 and sent their fleet to counter the British in American waters that any sense of naval balance occurred. Throughout the war, the American naval efforts were small and mostly ineffective along the Atlantic coast, and on the high seas they had no measurable impact on the outcome of the Revolution. That is not to say, however, that the United States did not make an effort or that individual ships did not perform with vigilance and valor. Any real evaluation of the American navy in the Revolution must first, however, consider the organization of its forces. Just as the rebel army had separate commands of Continental and militia units, the U.S. naval forces were not all under one command or even focused on the same missions.

The U.S. Navy, except for its small size, was similar to the Continental army in its authorization, command and control, and purpose. It was, in fact, a national organization composed of officers, commissioned by Congress, who commanded U.S. ships manned by sailors belonging to the national naval force. Each state also maintained the right, in a manner similar to its militias, to commission its own ships and officers to defend its shores and inland waterways. At one time or the other during the war, eleven[1] of the thirteen states launched their own navies.

In addition to the Continental and individual states' navies, the American sea force had still another source of vessels. These ships, neither federal nor state, were privately owned and operated crafts. Less than two months after authorizing the formation of the U.S. Navy, the Continental Congress approved measures for itself and each state to issue "letters of marque" to any armed vessel to carry out operations of war against the British as "privateers."

---

[1]New Jersey and Delaware were the only colonies not to form their own state navies during the Revolution. Massachusetts, Connecticut, Maryland, Virginia, and South Carolina launched the largest fleets, while Georgia, with four galleys, and New Hampshire, with only one ship, had the smallest.

Privateering was not new to warfare or to the Americans. The term *privateer* had been common as early as the mid-seventeenth century as a shortened version of "private man of war." Much of the pre-Revolution American naval experience came not from service in the Royal Navy but, rather, from service on board privateers commissioned by Great Britain during the French and Indian War of 1754–1763.

Privateers usually sailed independently rather than as a part of a fleet. They rarely engaged enemy military vessels but instead preyed on lightly armed merchant ships. The risks were few and the rewards huge. By law the proceeds from the selling of any captured "prize," along with its cargo, went to the privateers' owners and crews.

The Continental Congress attempted to control the American-authorized privateers through a series of articles. On April 3, 1776, Congress issued instructions to federal and state privateers that stated their mission, rules of engagement, settlement of prize income, and other specific regulations. The instructions read: "You may, by force of arms, attack, subdue, and take all ships and other vessels belonging to the inhabitants of Great Britain." They then spelled out in detail the procedures for disposing of captured ships and their cargoes, treatment of captives, and other administrative matters.

During the remainder of the war the Continental Congress issued several updates to the instructions as "additional articles" that provided more details on the sale of prizes and the care and composition of crews. Congress also reminded privateers that their letters of marque did not authorize them to attack vessels of neutral nations. Particularly interesting is the complete absence of any reference to African Americans in the original instructions as well as the subsequent additional articles. At no time did Congress dictate to the privateer captains any restrictions on the signing of Black sailors as crewmen.

Although no official body—not the Continental Congress, its naval committee, or the state governments—ever presented any formal policies on the status of Black seamen, several unofficial guidelines and traditions did emerge. These practices revolved around the same personnel shortages that influenced the army's use of African Americans, but with a few added twists and turns unique to naval service.

The Continental navy commissioned about fifty warships during the Revolution, and the states, primarily Massachusetts, Virginia, and South Carolina, added about that many more. U.S. Navy captains had the greatest difficulty in recruiting seamen because of enlistment periods of one year or more, longer cruises away from home ports, and the increased dangers from seeking out combat with enemy men-of-war. State navies, like their militias, ordinarily enlisted sailors for three- to six-month tours and performed most of their duties within local waters.

Continental and state ship captains competed to enlist the limited number of experienced seamen and paid little attention to race. They generally welcomed freemen aboard any U.S. or state ship. Slaves served on U.S. ships as substitutes or contract seamen, with their owners receiving their wages. Slaves owned by ship officers also accompanied their owners aboard as servants and cabin boys. State ships also accepted slaves, much like the Continental navy.

Black seamen in both the Continental and state navies served as members of integrated crews primarily because the close confines of shipboard did not permit segregation. Freemen and slaves nevertheless occupied the lowest ranks and occupations. In addition to serving as servants and cabin boys, Black soldiers often were responsible for carrying powder from the ship's magazine to the guns in preparation for firing. An occasional Black man also signed aboard in skilled positions, such as ship's cook or carpenter. A few worked their way up to deck and gunner's positions, but Black men rarely, if ever, had positions of authority over white crewmen.

One of the greatest differences between Black service in the Continental navy and the state fleets was their employment as pilots. In the state navies, particularly in Virginia and South Carolina, where there were many offshore islands, inland waterways, and navigable rivers, Black watermen were frequently the most experienced pilots available. Thomas Anderson, the Virginia State commissioner of provisions, explained in a letter dated August 26, 1781, to William Davies that Black pilots were an asset because they were "accustomed to the navigation of the river."

While never given formal command, Black pilots were often at the helm, guiding vessels through treacherous waters, where the ship and its crew's safety depended on their abilities. Their value, recognized at all levels of command in the rebel forces, translated into monetary rewards. In a letter to Maj. Henry Lee on July 26, 1779, concerning pilots in the southern states, George Washington authorized a "warrant for $1,000.00 promised the negro pilots."

Piloting ships was not necessarily a safe vocation. At least two Black Virginia pilots died in the performance of their duties. According to the Proceedings of the Convention of Delegates in the Colony of Virginia, a Black slave named Minny died in the spring of 1776 while piloting a state vessel in the Rappahannock River when it came under fire from a British ship. The convention records note that Minny "bravely and successfully exerted himself against the enemy, until he was unfortunately killed." The Virginia delegates were so impressed with the dead slave's bravery that they voted a reward of $100 to his owner. Another slave pilot, Cuffee, owned by navy lieutenant William Graves, was also killed while piloting a Virginia vessel in 1781.

Size and numbers of ships and crews varied greatly throughout the war. Most privateers were fairly small, ranging between 100 and 500 tons, with a maximum of twenty guns and an average crew of 100. While the total number of Continental and state-commissioned warships did not exceed 100, these governments issued more than 1,500 letters of marque to privateers during the war. Since these letters commissioned ships for as few as one voyage to as many as desired for the duration of the conflict, it is impossible to determine just how many different vessels sailed as privateers. One of the few available quantifiable reports states that in 1781 there were 449 privateers operating under congressional or state letters of marque.

Whatever their exact numbers, the number of privateers dwarfed the number of Continental and state ships and drained off much of the available manpower. The reasons were fairly simple. First, service aboard privateers was much more desirable, for they did not practice the rigid military discipline of the federal and state ships. More important, they avoided combat with enemy war vessels and concentrated on unarmed or lightly armed merchant ships. This not only decreased the personal danger; it provided a greater revenue to be shared by all crew members from the sale of prizes.

Of all the American ships in service during the Revolution, privateers provided the greatest opportunities for Black men—both freemen and slaves—in both the North and South. Officers brought along slaves as servants, and owners provided their property as crewmen in exchange for their wages. Unlike the Continental and state navies, however, the privateers were a haven for escaped slaves. Privateer captains, in need of sailors to fill their crews so they could cast off to capture additional prizes, cared little about the color or the ownership of their crewmen. A runaway could sign aboard a privateer and sail away from the vicinity of his owner and pursuing escaped-slave catchers. Then, weeks or months later, he could go ashore at another port, preferably in the North, as a freeman with money in his pocket from wages and prize-money shares.

Privateering—through numbers, the nature of targets, and the rewards for crews—proved to be more effective in capturing British shipping than were the Continental and state navies. Privateers captured more than 600 British ships, which brought them $18 million in prize money during the war, three times as much as the total of the combined state and federal fleets. It is worth noting, however, that only 16 of the 600 vessels captured by privateers were warships.

While serving in any naval command offered Black soldiers the best opportunities, it also placed them in the most precarious position. Like white sailors they risked their lives in battling the sea and the enemy. However, they bore the additional risk of being at the mercy of the whites' whims if captured. Some Black Americans—both freemen and escaped slaves—found themselves shackled, shipped to the West Indies, and sold back into slavery. Other African American seamen who volunteered for, or were impressed into, British service also faced being returned to their Loyalist owners or sold to the highest bidder. A common fate of Black sailors, caused by the constant shortage of experienced personnel, however, was the offer to change sides and sign aboard the victorious ship or fleet. The promise of freedom for satisfactory service often accompanied the offer.

Opportunities for Black prisoners to change sides usually took place informally at sea, but a few cases did make their way to court and into the official records. On August 13, 1778, the Massachusetts Council granted freedom to David Mitchell, a Black sailor from Bermuda captured on a British vessel, for his voluntary service aboard the American *Alliance*. The council freed another Black British sailor, John Onion, on October 14, 1779, to serve on the Continental frigate *Providence*.

Freemen benefitted from their naval service in the Revolution by receiving wages and reasonably equal rights to those of white sailors. Slaves received different treatment, depending on whether they served on U.S. or state ships or privateers. Even then, policies differed from ship to ship and captain to captain. Some slaves forfeited their pay to their owners during their service and received their freedom upon the completion of their enlistment. Others continued to serve when their owners reenlisted them and kept their wages; they remained slaves at the end of the war.

A few Black sailors who fought for American liberty in the Revolution gained their freedom through legal means. Many of the court decisions, however, did not occur until long after the war's conclusion. It was not until October 30, 1789, eight years after the British surrender at Yorktown, that the Virginia legislature voted to authorize money to buy the freedom of Jack Knight and William Boush for having "faithfully served on board armed vessels."

A Black man identified only as Caesar served for four years in the Virginia state navy and piloted the schooner *Patriot* when it captured the British brig *Fanny*. He was returned to slavery after Yorktown. Despite his heroics, the Virginia legislature did not provide funds to buy his freedom from his owner for his having "entered very early into the service of his country, and continued to pilot the armed vessels of this state during the late war" until November 14, 1789.

The federal government, some of the state navies, and a few privateers provided still another, albeit limited, opportunity for African Americans to serve in the Revolution. On November 10, 1775, the Continental Congress passed a resolution providing for two battalions of "American marines." With Capt. Samuel Nicholas as the Marine Corps' first commandant, the marines were to keep order aboard ships, to engage enemy personnel with their muskets from their vessel's riggings during battle, to assist in manning their ship's main guns, and to man boarding parties and landing forces.

Less than three weeks after their authorization, the Continental marines came under the "Rules and Regulation of the Navy of the United Colonies," prepared by John Adams and approved by Congress on November 28, which provided rules concerning discipline, pay, and rations that applied to all men serving aboard American naval ships. Neither these rules nor any other regulations restricted the race of enlistees.

Marine recruiters had to compete with the navy and the army for the limited number of able and willing recruits. It is not surprising that the marines sought Black enlistees and that they did not always concern themselves about the ownership status of the potential recruit. Marine officers initially sought volunteers in Philadelphia, but poor results soon had them traversing the Delaware River to seek willing men with sea experience. Capt. Miles Pennington, one of the first marine officers commissioned, journeyed as far south as Wilmington in search of qualified individuals for marine duty aboard the *Reprisal*. In April 1776, Pennington enlisted an African American named Keto, also known as John Martin. Neither Keto nor Pennington sought permission from the slave's owner, William Marshall of Wilmington, for the enlistment of the first documented Black marine.

Keto served aboard the *Reprisal* until October 1777, when the ship foundered off the Newfoundland Banks. Only one sailor survived the sinking. Keto and his fellow marines and crew went down with the ship.

During the summer of 1776, marine captain Robert Mullan established his headquarters in the Tun Tavern on Philadelphia's South Water

Street. He experienced the same difficulties in finding suitable personnel that had confronted Pennington and soon extended his recruitment efforts as far west as Lancaster and as far south as Kent County, Maryland. At least two Black men eventually made their way into Mullan's company. Their origins are unknown, but the proof of their service appears in company musters and records on file in the Reference Section, History and Museums Division, Headquarters Marine Corps, in Washington, D.C.

According to the records, "Isaac Walker (Negro)" enlisted on August 27, 1776, and "Orange (Negro)" joined the company on October 1. The company muster rolls for December 1, 1776, through April 1, 1777, again list "Issac Negro" and "Orange Negro" and include their pay and clothing allowance. No other records concerning these two African American marines exist either about how long or where they served. Mullan's company did march out of Philadelphia to support the Continental army in the Battle of Assunpink Creek [Trenton] on January 1, 1777, and the Battle of Princeton the following day. It is likely that Isaac and Orange participated in these fights.

Several of the states formed marine units for their navies. There is proof of at least ten Black men who served as marines in the state navies of Massachusetts, Connecticut, and Pennsylvania. The names of these ten men appear on their state's list of veterans of the Revolutionary War with the designation "negro" or "colored." It is probable that Black men served as marines on the private warships, but there is no documentary evidence to support this assumption.

Although land forces by far played the more significant role in fighting and winning the Revolutionary War, sailors and marines did contribute to the victorious effort by harassing and capturing supply and merchant ships that would otherwise have strengthened the British position. Black sailors, freemen and slave alike, were critical personnel in accomplishing these feats. In exchange for their value to the fleets, Black sailors and marines experienced a greater degree of equality, enlistment opportunity, and financial gain. Because whites did not perceive them as an insurgency threat, Black soldiers in the navies were able to serve diligently and loyally to secure the liberty of their country.

9

Daily Military Life During the Revolution

SHORTLY AFTER THE BATTLE OF SARATOGA in October 1777, Le Chevalier de Pontgibaud, a French officer, visited Gen. George Washington's army and later wrote:

> Soon I came in sight of the camp. My imagination had pictured an army with uniforms, the glitter of arms, standards, etc., in short, military pomp of all sorts. Instead of the imposing spectacle I expected, I saw, grouped together or standing alone, a few militiamen, poorly clad, and for the most part without shoes, many of them badly armed.[1]

In 1775 the Congress of Massachusetts provided Washington with soldiers, offering the following description:

> The greatest part of them have not before seen service; and though naturally brave and of good understanding, yet, for want of experience in military life have but little knowledge of diverse things most essential to the preservation of health and even of life. The youth of America are not possessed of the absolute necessity of cleanliness in their dress, lodging, continual exercise and strict temperance to preserve them from disease.

[1] Accounts of the day-to-day life of soldiers and sailors during the American Revolution are uncommon, and those compiled rarely differentiate between the experiences of Black and white soldiers. Generally, the war's Black and white soldiers and sailors shared the same dangers and terrors of battle and the hardships and boredom of camp life typical of military personnel of all generations. Military service during the Revolution provided one of the few environments in which Black and white men shared a degree of equality not experienced elsewhere.

In 1777, Maj. Gen. Philip Schuyler complained that New England regiments serving under him in New York were "one third negroes, boys, and men too aged for the field." Another French observer of the war, Claude Blanchard, noted at about the same time that the American soldiers were "small, thin, and even some children twelve or thirteen years old."

The small population and the fact that only about one-third of white Americans supported the Revolution meant that the Continental and state forces did indeed have to extend their enlistments to "negroes, boys, and men too aged for the field." Enlistment requirements varied from state to state and at times from unit to unit, but the primary factor influencing eligibility regulations for military service throughout the war remained the shortage of personnel. While states differed in enforcing regulations regarding African Americans, depending on their need for manpower at the time, acceptable age also varied according to these same manpower needs. Generally, a recruit was supposed to be at least seventeen years of age, but boys as young as twelve served in both the army and the navy. The maximum age for conscription was sixty, but if able to carry a musket, volunteers of any age found positions.

Whatever the official restrictions on Black recruits, African Americans found their way into every army unit and onto every navy ship. Black soldiers and sailors experienced the same hardships and dangers as did whites and generally shared in the few comforts and advantages of being in the military. Although Black men in the armed forces continued to endure discrimination, prejudice, and dishonesty, the treatment of white and Black soldiers and sailors during the war came closer to equality than before or after the war.

This aspect of "equality" for African American military personnel must be placed in the context of the times and the conditions under which Black Americans, particularly slaves, experienced the Revolution. As slaves, the Black people were literally the property of their owners and lived not only according to the rules of their masters but also under laws that restricted their travel, ownership of any property, and freedom of assembly. They had no control of their own lives, laboring at mandated tasks on a schedule set by their owners or overseers, who held the power and legal right to whip, maim, or otherwise punish them at will. By law, a child of a slave mother became the property of her owner.

Slaves performed all kinds of work on the plantations and in the villages. Some toiled as skilled coopers, cobblers, bricklayers, carpenters, tailors, cooks, and blacksmiths. Others worked as miners, lumbermen, and longshoremen. A select few became house servants. The vast majority, however, served as field hands on tobacco, rice, indigo, hemp, and cotton plantations and worked from "can see" to "can't see." The normal workweek for slaves, regardless of vocation, was six days, with only Sunday as a day of rest. During harvests or as punishment, slaves worked seven days a week.

For slaves to be productive, owners had to provide food, clothing, shelter, and medical support. Most owners viewed these requirements for slaves in the same way as they approached the care of their livestock: They had to provide nourishment and shelter, but only to the extent of maintaining health, reproduction, and ability to work. While the tables of families of white owners were laden with ham and pork chops, slaves received pig's feet and intestines. Some owners allowed slaves to tend their own gardens to supplement rations, but poor cuts of meat, com, and rice were the more typical staples.

While they considered the acquisition and care of slaves as on a par with livestock, owners held a different view of their contributions. They expected their plantation slaves, men and women alike, to produce most of what they consumed and wore and to build their own shelters. At the time of the American Revolution, the average expenditure per slave per year was less than $15. Only the very old and the very young were exempt from labor. Children worked tending livestock or running errands as soon as they learned to walk. Owners expected a slave to become profitable by the age of nine.

Slave quarters were frequently little more than huts, and clothing received minimal attention. House slaves at times wore castoffs of the white owners. Others wore the cheapest clothing available. Several French visitors to southern plantations during the war noted that slave children, especially during the summer months, wore no clothes at all and that Black adults frequently had little to cover their nakedness. In his journal written during the time he supported the Continental army, Baron Ludwig von Clasen noted the sordid conditions of slave cabins in Virginia and also wrote of slaves grinding maize, which was normally fed only to horses, to make a pancake-like bread.

Since the advent of armies, the promise of "three hots and a cot"—three meals a day and a place to sleep—has lured men to volunteer for military service. Such a promise, especially with the added inducements of wages and potential postwar freedom, surely must have seemed an irresistible opportunity to men facing nothing but forced bondage for the rest of their lives. They were soon to discover that the quality of life in the military certainly was an improvement over that of slavery, but they also learned that the advantages of military service came with extreme dangers and a different set of hardships.

Any soldier, Black or white, faces the possibility of death or debilitating wounds from direct combat with the enemy. Generally, Black and white soldiers and sailors in the Revolutionary War shared these dangers on an extremely equitable basis. It is reasonable to assume that some Black soldiers believed they had to exhibit greater degrees of bravery than their white contemporaries to be a "credit to their race" and to dispel the belief that they could not or would not fight.

Soldiers in most Continental army regiments and virtually all militia units generally came from the same areas. Volunteers and recruits from one or two villages might fill a company. Companies from the same geographic region usually made up a regiment, and regiments from a single state formed a brigade.

Black soldiers in these locally recruited units caused mixed reactions. Initially, white enlisted soldiers, although generally from the lowest classes, felt superior to the African Americans and resented sharing any degree of equality with individuals they considered inferiors. However, the horror of combat and the boredom of camp life create a great camaraderie among soldiers.

As time passed and white and Black soldiers shared the experiences of camp and combat, they developed a soldierly fellowship common to all armies. That is not to say, however, that white and Black soldiers in integrated units developed deep or lasting relationships. Journals of the time and later memoirs mention the races facing the enemy together and having mutual respect for each other's fighting abilities, but they do not mention overcoming racial prejudices.

Black men in the Revolution shared equality in the status of being soldiers but not as individuals. They served almost exclusively in the infantry, with only a few permitted to join the artillery and cavalry. Promotions were practically nonexistent; Black soldiers remained privates for the entire war regardless of their experience and abilities. Sergeants appointed above them were white, as were their officers.

White officers during the Revolution, many not far removed from colonial military service, came from the upper classes that owned land and slaves. Enlisted white soldiers, although from the lower classes, came from a culture that believed that any white person was far superior to a Black person, free or slave. Because of this basic tenet, it was impossible for Black soldiers to experience total equality with white soldiers. In each unit, someone had to receive the most worn-out equipment and weapons; someone had to stand guard duty during the late hours. If bonuses, pay, or rations were in short supply, someone had to be shortchanged. That someone, of course, was often the freeman serving as a volunteer, the slave acting as a substitute for his master, or the former chattel seeking his freedom through military service.

Black and white soldiers in the Revolution shared pay, bounties, rations, arms, shelter, medical care, and discipline with varying degrees of equality. Explaining the details of these areas of soldiers' lives more than two centuries ago in current amounts and contemporary terms is difficult. That the United States did not exist prior to the Revolution and had no existing monetary, military, or even legal system further complicates any comparison.

None of these issues is more difficult to explain than that of money. Prior to the Revolution, coins from England, Spain, France, Holland, and Portugal circulated as legal tender throughout the colonies. Because of coin shortages[2] of all origins, several of the colonies minted their own and also issued various paper notes for redemption in gold or silver. Certain commodities, such as tobacco, also served as tender, with each colony establishing its own exchange rates.

On June 22, 1775, the Continental Congress resolved to finance the war with paper currency backed by the "Spanish milled dollar." Congress initially authorized the printing of $2 million in paper bills of credit in the form of Continental dollars, and by November 29, 1777, it had approved and placed more than $241 million in circulation. During this same period, the states issued another $209 million of paper currency.

Neither the federal government nor the states had anywhere near sufficient hard-money specie to back their paper money. They also lacked a taxation process to raise funds to support their monetary systems. The result, of course, was rapid depreciation of paper money, spawning the phrase "not worth a Continental" to describe anything of inferior value. By 1779, Americans could exchange a Continental dollar for only 10 percent of its value in copper, silver, or gold coins. Despite efforts by the Continental Congress to support the currency through partial redemption and retirement and by passing laws requiring the acceptance of paper money as legal tender, the Continental currency system totally collapsed in May 1781, and only hard money was used thereafter.[3]

At the beginning of the Revolution, privates in the Continental army's

[2]In the eighteenth century, gold, silver, and copper coins were the primary currency; paper money had little value. Coins were in short supply in the American colonies and throughout the British Empire because of the inability of the English government to stabilize the value of silver in relation to gold. As a result, the British minted few silver or copper coins, which were the primary means of exchange between 1760 and 1816.

[3]In 1790, Congress, under a new paper-money system, authorized the exchange of the old Continental currency for U.S. bonds at the rate of 100 to 1.

infantry were authorized $6.67 per month in pay, while the lowest-ranking men in the cavalry, artillery, and military police were to receive $8.33 per month. This higher pay was supposed to lure more skilled and intelligent recruits into these specialties. Infantrymen, despite their greater exposure to enemy fire and the threat of death, ranked as a cheaper commodity.

During the early months of the war, the states authorized payments as high as thirty-six dollars per month to private soldiers in their militias, but many later changed their pay rates to match that authorized for the Continental army. The fairness and adequacy of military pay during the Revolution is a moot point, for rarely did a soldier actually receive his pay.

After the value of Continental currency collapsed in 1779, Congress left the responsibility of paying the army to the states. Unfortunately, their financial status was no better than the national treasury. Money that was available to the states was usually in nearly worthless paper notes. Late in the war the New Hampshire legislature admitted that their state troops "have had no pay for nearly twelve months."

Although each state had its own regulations on the admission of Black men into its militias and Continental army regiments, once enlisted, African Americans were supposed to receive pay equal to that of white soldiers. When money was available to meet unit payrolls, Black soldiers apparently received equal pay to keep for themselves or to turn over to their owners if they were serving as substitutes. More times than not, however, equality in pay meant that no one, regardless of color, received any wages at all.

The financial difficulties in raising, paying, and maintaining the Continental army worsened as the war wore on. American leaders thought initially that volunteers would meet the manpower requirements, but experience soon changed their minds. In a letter to Congress on September 24, 1775, George Washington stated that when the army was first formed at Cambridge, he believed that sufficient numbers of volunteers would come forward to fill the ranks and that since the "contest was not likely to end so speedily as was imagined," the states would now have to pay bounties to meet their quotas.

To bolster enlistments, the Continental Congress issued a proclamation to the states on January 19, 1776, encouraging them to offer a bounty[4] of $6.66 to men who enlisted and provided their own musket.

---

[4]The bounty system of attracting soldiers into the American military outlived the Revolution itself. Not until the Selective Service Act of 1917 did the United States end recruitment bounties.

Congress recommended an enlistment bonus of $4.00 for volunteers who reported without a weapon.

The passage of time and an increase in the level of combat forced Congress to recommend higher bounties to encourage enlistments in the Continental army. On June 26, 1776, Congress increased their bounty recommendation to $10 and a few weeks later suggested that an additional $10 be given to those who agreed to reenlist for an additional three years after completing their initial tour. On October 8, Congress doubled the recommended enlistment bonus and added that volunteers could collect it in either cash or clothing.

State-militia recruiters, who began losing volunteers to the Continental army, were forced to provide their own bounties. By early 1777 several states were offering bounties ranging from $33 to $87 to militia volunteers. Competition between the state militias and the Continental army for recruits, combined with monetary inflation and the small pool of eligible manpower, increased the bounty to $200 in early 1779. In 1780, New Jersey raised the bounty to $1,000 to entice volunteers, but more commonly, the cash-poor states began offering 100 acres or more of land to men who agreed to enlist for the war's duration.

Freemen, especially in the North, and runaway slaves who claimed to be free received bounties equal to those of whites for their enlistment. White owners who provided slaves as their substitutes received the enlistment bounty. However, slaves who enlisted in exchange for their freedom did not receive any state or federal bounty. Whites considered emancipation reward enough.

This unofficial policy of denying enlistment bounties for slaves even took precedence over official resolutions. For example, the February 14, 1778, law approved by the Rhode Island legislature that authorized the enlistment of Black men specifically stated: "Every slave so enlisting shall be entitled to and receive all bounties, wages, and encouragements allowed by the Continental Congress to any soldier enlisting into their service." However, when the Rhode Island Black regiment finally was discharged on June 13, 1783, their commander, Lt. Col. Jeremiah Olney, in his farewell speech, noted that the men had not received the promised bounties. Olney's final words to the long-serving Black regiment were that he hoped someday they would "obtain their just dues from the public." There is no evidence that the state ever fulfilled Olney's wishes.

Unpaid soldiers could fight, but not unfed ones. Colonial America contained vast natural food resources from the forest and the sea, and its lush farmlands produced surpluses of grains, vegetables, and domestic livestock. Most white men entering the military came from farms and villages where food was healthful and plentiful. Although food provided to the enslaved was of inferior quality, slaveholders knew they had to be fed well to maintain their work capacity. As a result, white and Black soldier alike expected the army to provide adequate nourishment.

Private soldiers in the Continental army were authorized "one ration," defined as three meals, per day. The Continental Congress first prescribed the contents and amount of an army ration on September 12, 1775, and the following November 4 modified it as follows:

> Resolved, that a ration consist of the following kind and quantity of provisions: 1 lb. beef, or ¾ lb. pork or 1 lb. salt fish, per day; 1 lb. bread or flour, per day; 3 pints of peas or beans per week, or vegetables equivalent, at one dollar per bushel for peas or beans; 1 pint of milk, per man per day; 1 half pint of rice, one pint of Indian meal [corn], per man per week; 1 quart of spruce beer or cider per man per day, or nine gallons of molasses, per company of 100 men per week; 3 lbs. of candles to 100 men per week, for guards; 24 lbs. soft, or 8 lbs. hard soap, for 100 men per week.

Although not an official part of rations, vinegar was also commonly provided. It made dirty water more drinkable and added flavor to food. Vinegar's antiseptic properties also proved beneficial.

Even in the best of times the army quartermaster department had difficulty providing the authorized rations. Fresh milk proved the most difficult to procure, disappearing from the list early in the war. Much to the approval of the soldiers, the army later added four ounces, known as a "gill," of rum or whiskey per day per soldier to the ration, but little alcohol ever actually made its way into the daily issue.

Other rations also were frequently in short supply. Beef and flour of varying freshness and purity were at times the only food issued, and on occasion, particularly in the winter, even these basic rations were unavailable. Food was in such short supply at Valley Forge in the winter of 1778–1779 that the army threatened to revolt. "No bread, no meat, no soldier," the soldiers chanted. The following winter, at Morristown, New Jersey, soldiers frequently subsisted on rations that amounted to only a half pound of salt beef and a pint of rice every five days. Washington recorded in this journal that during the winter at Morristown his soldiers sometimes went for five or six days without bread, often as long without meat, and, once or twice, for two to three days, with no food at all.

Summer campaigns did not necessarily mean that the Revolutionary

War soldier received any more or better food. Washington noted in his journals that during the summer of 1780 his army often went nearly a week with either only bread and no meat or with meat and no bread. He added that at times the soldiers went for several days without either.

Hungry soldiers often supplemented their official rations with whatever they could gather, hunt, or otherwise appropriate on their own. Livestock, orchards, and gardens of civilians, especially Loyalists, were excellent sources of supplemental foodstuffs. In the spring of 1779, Gen. John Sullivan observed his soldiers in western New York marching into camp with pumpkins and melons on their fixed bayonets, their shirts stuffed with com, nuts, and beans. Streams and rivers also provided food. Several accounts of the miserable winters at Valley Forge mention the spring shad run up the nearby Schuylkill River which briefly ended the army's hunger.

The quartermaster department issued firewood and cooking utensils when possible, but in a manner similar to the rations, the consistency of delivery varied greatly. Generally, the soldiers competed with each other to gather additional firewood from forests near their camps for cooking and warmth. An iron kettle issued by the quartermaster on the basis of one to every six or eight men provided a utensil for the men to combine their rations into a "squad mess" while in camp.

Some of the states, particularly Maryland, issued bowls and spoons to their troops, but usually each soldier provided his own. Eating utensils were simple and ordinarily included a wooden plate or bowl, a cup made of tin or cow's horn, and some sort of knife and a crude fork.

In the field, a soldier often had no more time than to quickly broil a piece of meat stuck on his knife over a fire. Flour mixed with water and cooked in the ashes provided his bread. In camp, squads generally pooled their rations and took turns as cook. If a soldier showed talent, or the will, he might prepare the squad's rations on a regular basis.

Most of the campaigns and battles of the Revolutionary War took place in areas where water was readily available from creeks, rivers, and lakes. The quartermaster issued wooden keglike canteens, which were made of wood staves held together with iron or brass bands, to carry water on the march, but these containers were never in sufficient supply. Soldiers also made their own wooden canteens, preferring oak because it transferred the least amount of taste to its contents. Glass and ceramic containers, sewed into leather or canvas covers, with a carrying strap, also provided soldiers a means of transporting personal water supplies.

The quantity of water was not usually as much a problem as quality. Hundreds, or even thousands, of men, along with draft animals and horses, using the same water sources did not promote sanitation. In December 1777, Elijah Fisher noted in his journal: "The water we had to drink and to mix our flour with was out of a brook that runs along the camps, and so many a dippin' and washin' in it made it very dirty and muddy."

Soldiers, who depended on each other in battle, usually maintained teamwork and cooperation on the march and in camp between skirmishes. Black soldiers shared equally in the distribution of food. When rations were abundant, Black soldiers, especially those who entered the army from slavery, received more and better food than they had prior to their enlistment. When rations were in short supply, Black and white soldiers experienced hunger equally.

Shelter for the Revolutionary War soldier varied with the time of year. During the winter months at camps like Valley Forge, the soldiers built wooden huts which held six to ten men each. Most of these were built of logs the men cut themselves, with some additional wood coming from nearby sawmills and farmers' fence rails. Gaps between logs they filled with clay, moss, and straw. Crude rock-and-mud fireplaces provided heat and a place to cook but also often filled the cabins with smoke. Nevertheless, the huts protected the soldiers from the long, snowy winters.

During campaigns in warmer weather, the army provided tents, which were made of various water-resistant materials manufactured domestically, captured from the British, or procured from the French. These six-by-six foot shelters were designed to house six men, but due to shortages, ten or more often crowded inside. Because of their weight, tents were transported on the battalion supply wagons, which meant that they were often unavailable during marches and impending combat.

Wool blankets were prized possessions, and soldiers generally carried them on their person so that they would be available even if the supply wagons could not reach their positions. Blankets were often the first item discarded in a fight and the first to be recovered from a battlefield once the firing ceased.

Although there are no written records that document the equality in shelter for Black soldiers, it can be assumed that they occupied the same austere huts and tents as did the white soldiers. Again, the teamwork of combat units and the general camaraderie of soldiers exceeded any prejudices. It is also likely that this integration of quarters was the only available option because few companies had sufficient numbers of Black soldiers to segregate them into their own huts or tents.

Paintings, films, and reenactment groups usually show the Revolutionary War soldier dressed in spotless white pants, long blue or green jackets, black boots or leggings, and tricorner hats. None of these depictions are remotely accurate. American soldiers in the Revolution considered themselves extremely fortunate to have any clothing at all, and the idea of uniforms, as depicted today, would have been strictly a far-fetched fantasy.

Military uniforms had only been in use for about a century before the Revolution. From the beginning of time and into the seventeenth century, soldiers provided their own clothing and wore whatever was functional, comfortable, and more important, available. It was only during the mid-1600s that European regimental commanders assumed the responsibility of clothing their soldiers. As a cost-saving measure, they purchased coats and trousers of similar materials in large lots. This "uniformity" led to their name. Commanders quickly realized that in addition to advantageous economic considerations, uniforms also increased unit pride and morale and assisted in unit identification on the battlefield.

In the colonial militias only the wealthiest officers had uniforms; junior officers and enlisted men mostly wore work or hunting clothes. Some of the militias attempted to dress their soldiers in the same color. Massachusetts and Connecticut, for example, adopted brown clothing, while southern colonies opted for dark blue. The manufacture of traditional military uniform cloth, either wool, hemp, or linen, in the colonies was extremely limited, however, and so those colonists who could afford to do so imported the material for uniforms. As a result, the colonial militia and the rebel army wore whatever was available.

George Washington appeared before the Continental Congress to assume command of the army wearing the blue-and-buff uniform that he had had made for his duties with the Virginia militia. When Congress sent Washington to Boston, it recommended that the army adopt brown for uniform jackets. This decision resulted from the ease of obtaining the color and the fact that the militias of Massachusetts and Connecticut, which made up the bulk of the rebel force surrounding the city, already used that shade.

Washington and many of his soldiers favored hunting shirts, which were loose garments similar to smocks worn by farmers and workmen. The long hunting shirts had fringe around collars and at the seams for shedding water. These garments, designed either as pullovers or jacket-type fronts, were large enough to wear over other clothing. Hunting shirts were durable, practical, and the most popular uniform item in the rebel army.

Hunting shirts and other uniform coats were usually fastened with cloth or leather straps or buttons. The most common buttons were made of wood or horn, though a limited number of cast brass or pewter buttons, embossed with "USA" (for Continental army units) and state symbols (for the militias), did exist.

Congress remained silent for several years about uniforms after its recommendation of brown as the color of choice in 1775. As a result, many hunting shirts were either brown or green because of the local availability of these dyes. Finally, on October 2, 1779, Congress, bowing to popularity rather than practicality, reversed itself and adopted blue as the army's official color. In reality, sufficient amounts of replacement clothing rarely reached the American soldiers during the Revolution. At times, the only item between a soldier and nakedness was a blanket draped around his body and tied with a cord at his waist.

Continental soldiers also adopted a great assortment of headgear. A round felt hat, malleable to various configurations—including the tricorner—was common but not always available. Soldiers often wore leather hats or stocking caps made of knitted wool. The unifying factor among headgear, though, was the universally worn single sprig of evergreen or other greenery that symbolized the rebel Americans.

The wide variance in "uniforms" and colors made identifying ranks difficult. Shortly after assuming command of the army, Washington directed the use of distinguishing insignia. Corporals were to sew a strip of green cloth to the right shoulder of their jackets or hunting shirts. Sergeants were to do the same with red cloth. Officers were to wear different color cloth rosettes, known as cockades, on their hats—green for lieutenants, yellow or buff for captains, and pink or red for majors, lieutenant colonels, and colonels. General officers added color sashes to their uniforms to identify their rank—pink for brigadier generals, purple for major generals, and light blue for Washington.

Footwear and leg wear also varied. Only the wealthiest officers could afford boots, and even the simplest of shoes were expensive. For the most part, shoes were of the buckle variety, but some laced types were available. Soldiers used leather, canvas, or other cloth to wrap their calves above their shoes for protection from mud, brambles, and brush. Some soldiers, particularly those from western areas of the colonies, wore leather moccasins modeled after Native American footwear.

Shoe factories did not exist, and one-man cobbler shops were the most common source of footwear. Some quartermasters exchanged the hides of cattle butchered to feed the soldiers with cobblers for shoes. Whatever their source, shoes, like clothing in general, were always in short supply. It was not at all uncommon for the Revolutionary War soldier to campaign barefoot in the summer and endure the winter with nothing but cloth wraps to cover his feet.

After a visit to the American winter camp at Ticonderoga, New Yorker Joseph Wood, on December 4, 1776, wrote in a letter to Thomas Warton Jr., "For all this army at this place, which did consist of twelve or thirteen thousand men, sick and well, no more than nine hundred pairs of shoes have been sent. One third at least of the poor wretches is now barefoot, and in this condition obliged to do duty."

It is difficult to prove how Black soldiers fared in receiving their fair allotment of clothing, but it is not hard to surmise. Most of the documents and letters of the period note the general shortages of uniforms, boots, and other clothing for everyone. Black soldiers would certainly not have fared better than white soldiers in their distribution, and there is a suggestion that at times they fared far worse.

The most concrete example of this discrimination comes from letters between Col. Samuel Parsons and Col. John Lamb. In correspondence during the spring of 1779, Parsons informed Lamb that he was considering resigning his commission because his unit had not received its fair share of clothing.

While Parsons did not specify that the shortages were due to the disproportionate number of Black soldiers in his unit, his brigade—composed of the Third, Fourth, Sixth, and Eighth Connecticut Regiments—did have the largest number of African American soldiers of any Continental army organization. In fact, Parson's brigade had 148 Black soldiers according to the adjutant general's report of August 24, 1778.

Not only did the Continental army, like all other military organizations, have to provide pay, rations, shelter, and clothing; it also had to issue arms to its soldiers. To accomplish its objective of "closing with and destroying the enemy," the army provided a variety of firearms and edged weapons. Because Black soldiers served almost exclusively in infantry units, the musket and bayonet were the primary weapons they employed in contributing to American independence.

While they had been in use by military forces for more than two centuries before the American Revolution, firearms were still extremely difficult to operate. The principal infantry weapon of both sides in the war was the muzzle-loading, smoothbore, flintlock musket. At the beginning of the conflict, most colonial militias carried the English Long Land Service Musket, known as the Brown Bess, or American copies called Committee of Safety muskets, which the Continental Congress authorized in November 1775.

Both the Brown Bess and the Committee of Safety musket weighed about ten pounds each and had forty-six-inch-long, .75-caliber (three-quarters of an inch in diameter) barrels. To load and fire these muskets required twelve separate motions. Newly trained soldiers did well to shoot two rounds a minute, while veterans could squeeze off about five shots in the same amount of time. The muskets' one-ounce lead balls measured only .71 caliber, a factor that shortened the loading time but affected accuracy because the shot bounced from side to side as it traveled out the larger-diameter barrel.

A third primary infantry weapon appeared on the battlefield when the French entered the war and brought their basic Charleville muskets. Other than their slightly reduced .69 caliber, they closely resembled the Brown Bess—right down to their lack of accuracy. Some individual American soldiers and special units armed themselves with yet another type of weapon, one with raised ridges in the barrel known as rifles. The ridges in the smaller-caliber barrels caused the tight-fitting lead shot to spin through its passage and to thus be more accurate to the target. However, two factors limited the use of the rifle in the Revolutionary War. First, the production costs were such that few soldiers could afford one, and, second, it took an excessive amount of time to tamp down the shot.

Perhaps the only items in sufficient supply for the rebels were the various muskets and lead for shot, which came from lead mines in Virginia and other states. Gunpowder, however—like rations and uniforms—was in short supply. Unlike food and clothing shortages, though, the lack of gunpowder was a condition resulting from premeditation. The British had learned from their worldwide colonization efforts that no rebels could conduct a successful revolt against them without sufficient supplies of gunpowder. As a result, they prohibited the manufacture of gunpowder in their colonies and carefully controlled imports. The British march against Lexington and Concord that ignited the Revolution had, in fact, been conducted largely to confiscate stores of gunpowder.

In the early battle at Bunker Hill, the rebel Americans withstood the British attack until they ran low on gunpowder. The British, better trained and disciplined, were then able to sweep the rebels from the hill with a bayonet attack. Gunpowder remained so scarce during the first year of the Revolution that Washington estimated that at no time did any of his soldiers have enough powder to fire more than nine rounds each. Not until the French entered the war on the Americans' side did the gunpowder shortage end.

Access to gunpowder, however, did not solve all the battle problems. Individual marksmanship was dismal as a result of both the smoothbore muskets and lack of training. Few muskets had front sights, and even fewer had rear sights, and so soldiers pointed rather than aimed their weapons. A popular military rhyme of the period about musket shots from both sides summed up the situation: "One went high, and one went low, and where in Hell did the other one go."

Early in the war, American rebel units followed traditional European battlefield protocol and positioned themselves three or four men deep in long lines. Then, in sequence, one line fired a volley and then reloaded while the next lines fired theirs. Such practices emphasized quantity of fire rather than accuracy of shots.

The muskets' and soldiers' inaccuracy dictated infantry tactics; thus, most battles occurred at ranges of less than 100 yards. In traditional maneuvers, enemy soldiers advanced against each other and waited to see which could withhold firing longer in order to position themselves advantageously. Often the opposing sides closed to within fifty yards before initiating fire; the lesser-disciplined unit usually fired first.

British major George Hanger, who fought in the New York campaign with Burgoyne before being captured at Saratoga, later wrote about the accuracy of the Brown Bess and its copies:

> A soldier's musket will strike the figure of a man at 80 yards; it may even at a hundred, but a soldier must be very unfortunate indeed who shall be wounded by a common musket at 150 yards, provided his antagonist aims at him; and as to firing at a man at 200 yards, with a common musket, you may just as well as fire at the moon. No man ever was killed by a musket at 200 yards by the person who aimed at him.

When he first assumed command, Washington fully understood that the lack of uniform training and discipline made his army inferior to the more experienced British force. Of his own troops, Washington wrote in 1776:

> Place them behind a parapet, a breastwork, stone wall, or anything that will afford them shelter, and from their knowledge of a firelock, they will give a good account of their enemy; but I am as well convinced, as if I had seen it, that they will not march boldly up to a work nor stand exposed in a plain.

Adding further to the unpredictability of battle were weather conditions. In rainy periods only one of four flintlocks was likely to fire, for the powder in the flash pan would become damp. Flints also wore out or came loose from their holders and were lost. Accuracy and reliability of the weapons were so poor that Benjamin Franklin, in early 1776, wrote a letter to Gen. Charles Lee seriously recommending that consideration be given to replacing muskets with bows and arrows.

What Franklin was overlooking was that the musket was not just a firearm; it also served as the holder for a fourteen- to twenty-inch bayonet, which made it into an effective pike. After the initial volley, fights frequently evolved into a match of bayonets. Cold steel rather than hot shot became the deciding factor in many battles.

Of course, merely providing a musket, ammunition, and a bayonet to a recruit did not make him into a competent soldier. Discipline and training, attained only through repetitious drill and demanding leadership, converted the civilian into a warrior. By their very nature, the local militias were a composite of friends and neighbors who were unlikely to impose a high degree of training and discipline on one another—even to prepare their ranks to stand against bayonet charges by the veteran British infantry. To help convert the paramilitary militias to Regular Army troops of the Continental army, Washington and his officers referred to whatever literature on the subject was available.

A Treatise of Military Discipline, written by British general Humphrey Bland and first published in 1727, was the most widely used military manual in the early part of the eighteenth century in the American colonies. In the late 1760s many militia captains, particularly in New England, began using the training criteria developed by the county militia of Norfolk, England, in 1759 known as the *Norfolk Discipline*. About the same time, copies of the *Sixty-fourth*, the official 1764 British army manual, made their way into the colonies.

In 1775, Timothy Pickering, of Salem, Massachusetts, adapted and expanded the *Norfolk Discipline* and published *An Easy Plan of Discipline for a Militia*. Pickering's manual listed every responsibility of a soldier in extreme detail. It did not assume that a soldier knew how paper cartridges were made or what they contained; rather, this book spelled out all the information step-by-step. Pickering also provided drawings of exactly how a soldier should position his feet when preparing to fire his musket.

During the first two years of the Revolution, American rebels trained and operated their units according to one or more of these four manuals. Units fighting side by side often followed different procedures, depending on which "book" their commander supported. Washington apparently sought counsel from several of the manuals. In his archives are six copies of the British *Sixty-fourth* and only a single copy of Pickering's manual. The latter, however, is the most worn and displays a greater amount of use and wear.

Consistency and proficiency did not become characteristics of the Continental army until the arrival of Baron Friedrich von Steuben at Valley Forge in 1779. Von Steuben, a Prussian working with the French, brought many lessons he had learned while serving in Europe with Frederick the Great. Von Steuben immediately simplified commands and reduced the number of motions required for fire and maneuver. He also reorganized battle formations from three-rank-deep lines to two ranks, which provided additional flexibility and maneuverability. While Von Steuben had units he was training repeat drills over and over until they became second nature, he wrote his own manual for distribution to other commanders. First published in 1779, Von Steuben's *Regulations for the Order and Discipline of the Troops of the United States* remained the basic manual for the American army for the next quarter century. Under Von Steuben's leadership, the Continental army advanced from a loose organization of militias to a formidable united army. Poorly disciplined militiamen became professional soldiers who could stand toe-to-toe against the British and ultimately defeat the redcoats in a bayonet charge against the Yorktown defenses.

Neither Von Steuben's manual nor any of those used earlier by the Americans included any information for different training or treatment of African Americans. All of the tomes simply and equally referred to "soldiers" with no reference to race.

When not drilling or fighting, the Revolutionary War soldier was far from idle. Clothing and arms required constant maintenance. Procuring food and wood to prepare meals took much of the soldiers' time. Other hours were devoted to making cartridges, repairing huts or tents, and tending horses and livestock. A soldier's day began at sunrise, defined as when a sentry could clearly see a thousand yards, and ended when it became too dark to work. Even the arrival of night did not mean rest for soldiers assigned to sentry duty.

Saturdays were just another workday. Routine camp maintenance and sentry duty continued on Sundays, too, but drill ceased to allow for the reading of orders, unit roll calls, and religious observation. Washington placed a high priority on religion and made his beliefs clear when he issued an order stating, "To the distinguished character of a patriot, it should be our highest glory to add the more distinguished character of a Christian."

The Continental Congress, except for a few southern representatives, agreed with the general's priority, and despite the shortages of food, ammunition, and other materials needed to fight the war, voted on September 11, 1777, to import 20,000 Bibles for issue to the armed forces.

Soldiers being soldiers, enlisted men still found time to play various card games and gamble in other games of chance. When sufficient ammunition was available, they also participated in marksmanship matches. The prevalence of venereal diseases indicates that the soldiers found other means of entertainment as well.

Constant drill not only trained soldiers in battle procedures and prepared them to follow orders quickly and completely; training also increased morale in units. As a result, discipline problems usually occurred not during drill or in battle but in the confines of camp. Minor offenses, such as improper care of equipment, earned the offender the extra duty of digging latrines or sentry detail. More serious offenses, like theft and assault, merited 39–100 whiplashes—a common punishment with which Black civilians were far more familiar than their white counterparts. There is no evidence, however, that Black soldiers received more or harsher punishment than whites.

In the Revolution, as in all wars, desertion was one of the most serious offenses a soldier could commit. Desertion not only removed a man from the ranks but also, if he were not apprehended and punished, set a dangerous precedent that might encourage others to abandon the army. Generally, deserters received whiplashes in front of their regiments and then returned to their squads. Occasionally, deserters received the ultimate sentence, being publicly hanged or shot. As with most aspects of the war, standardization was lacking. Punishment varied from regiment to regiment and commander to commander. Personnel shortages and the level of combat also influenced the fate of deserters.

Executions provided the extreme lesson as to the perils of deserting, but dead soldiers could not return to the ranks. At times, commanders had to set an example while also conserving manpower. Such was the case on July 10, 1779, when three soldiers deserted the First Pennsylvania Regiment. When he caught them, the commander ordered the three to draw lots. The two winners returned to duty. The captors then shot the unlucky soldier, cut off his head, and placed it on a pole in the regiment's camp as a warning to anyone thinking of deserting.

While training and discipline produced an army that could ultimately stand in close-quarter combat against the British and achieve victory and independence, the price of such resolve and courage was high. One-ounce musket balls and sharp bayonets left gaping wounds in their targets. If struck in the chest or head, soldiers on both sides nearly always died; if hit in the leg or arm, they faced amputation as treatment. Drugs—including opium, which was the primary painkiller—surgical instruments, and other medical supplies were always insufficient to meet the demand. Wounded soldiers who survived the initial shock and blood loss faced the danger of dying from infection resulting from unsterilized instruments and the unsanitary conditions in the hospitals and aid stations.

As frightening as was the possibility of battlefield wounds, even more so was the potential for disease, which struck down more Revolutionary War soldiers than actual combat. Late in the war, John Adams wrote, "Disease has destroyed ten men for us where the sword of the enemy has killed one."

Smallpox, typhus, diphtheria, dysentery, malaria, measles, mumps, and even scurvy swept through the military camps. Revolutionary War soldiers, like military personnel in wars before and after, also suffered from venereal diseases. The rate of those afflicted with sexually transmitted diseases became so high early in the war that the Continental army issued a resolution that declared: "That the sum of ten dollars, shall be paid by every officer, and the sum of four dollars, by every soldier, who shall enter, or be sent into any hospital to be cured of venereal disease; which sum shall be deducted from their pay." This resolution did little to reduce the number of soldiers contracting venereal diseases, but it did encourage them not to report their condition and to seek treatment outside of military medical channels.

At any one time, one soldier in five was incapacitated due to illness, and at the height of epidemics, fully one-half of the American army was too sick to fight. Black soldiers, especially former slaves, who had experienced harsher living conditions prior to becoming soldiers, had more resistance to some illnesses than many whites. However, the popular idea that they, because of their African heritage, possessed immunities to tropical diseases, such as malaria, proved untrue; Black soldiers succumbed to these illnesses at about the same rate as white ones. Disease and illness did not discriminate; total equality prevailed.

Similarly, the daily life of the African American sailor during the Revolution included shortages of pay, rations, and quarters, as well as the necessity to endure other hardships of military life. Like the Black soldier who nearly always served in the lowest infantry rank, Black sailors went to sea at the bottom of the rank structure. Also like Black men in the army, those in the navy generally shared the same conditions and dangers as did whites.

Basic pay in the Continental navy for Black and white seaman alike at the beginning of the war was eight dollars per month. State navies and some privateers matched those wages. With the passage of years, all the maritime units added bounties to entice enlistments. Like the army, however, the navy rarely had sufficient funds to meet its payrolls on time. Bonuses represented the greatest difference in incentives between soldier and sailor. While states offered both soldiers and sailors either money or land for joining their militias or navies, the federal government made a distinction. The Continental Congress promised land to army enlistees but not to navy volunteers.

The reason for this discrimination was simple and fairly reasonable. Congress recognized that sailors, unlike soldiers, shared prize money from the auction of captured ships and cargoes that went to the highest bidder.[5] While a portion of the proceeds went to the government, which commissioned the vessel, the remainder went to the crew, which divided it either at a set percentage or into shares based on rank.

At the beginning of the war, the Continental Congress authorized crews to receive only one-third of the prize proceeds gained from the sale of commercial vessels. For the more difficult targets of enemy warships and privateers, Congress granted the crews one-half. In October 1776 the recruiting of seamen became so difficult that John Paul Jones lobbied Congress to increase the prize percentages in order to encourage volunteers. Congress reluctantly raised the crew prize shares from one-third to one-half for transports and from one-half to 100 percent for warships.

Since Black sailors nearly always occupied the lowest ranks on ships, their share was small, but they did receive their authorized portion. The only Black sailors who did not collect booty were those whose owners had placed them in the service of the captain in exchange for prize monies, a practice confirmed by official U.S. Navy records. One notation in the archives records the payment of 120 pounds to Esek Hopkins "for his two negroes share" when the Continental navy *Cabot* captured the British merchant *True Blue* in June 1776. The document further identifies the two African Americans as Surriname Wanton and Loushir.

The Black sailor, along with his white shipmates, worked hard under difficult circumstances for his wages and prize money. Long hours, poor food, and restricted living conditions, combined with the natural hazards of sea life and the dangers inherent in a strong enemy force, made the sailor's job far from idyllic.

Shipboard life revolved around four-hour "watches." Four hours on duty followed by four hours off were routine. "Off hours" did not necessarily mean a sailor was not at work. During the day sailors not on watch

---

[5]Capture and sale of merchant vessels was so common that often the original owners ended up repurchasing confiscated ships and cargoes.

performed maintenance and cleaning duties throughout the ship. Crewmen were fortunate to get four to six hours of sleep a night. These sleeping hours were often shortened by calls of "all hands on deck" in preparation for battle or severe weather.

The "Rules of the Regulation of the Navy of the United Colonies" prescribed the rations for each day of the week, which were adequate, if monotonous. Salt beef or pork, potatoes and peas, and bread or biscuits dominated the menu. While the quality of the fare often depended on the cook's expertise, time at sea had the greatest impact on rations. The longer a ship stayed away from port, the more likely food would become rancid or infested by insects. Like soldiers on land, sailors at sea used vinegar for seasoning their meals. Each ship, in accordance with navy regulations, carried fishing tackle to supplement the crew's diet with fresh fish, but location, weather, and enemy contact often interfered with this supply method.

Ships also sailed with water stored in wooden casks. The most popular liquid by far, though, was a daily ration of a half pint of rum, sometimes diluted with water into a drink known as grog. Prior to battle or after extreme storms, some captains increased this ration.

Sleeping accommodations consisted of a hammock hung on hooks between the ship's guns or in other out-of-the-way places. When not in use, hammocks and blankets were rolled and stowed in netting above the bulwarks.

The American navy, like the army, entered the Revolution with no designated uniforms. On September 5, 1776, the Marine Committee issued its first uniform regulations, which called for officers to wear blue coats with red lapels and cuffs and yellow metal buttons. A red vest, blue breeches, and white stockings completed the uniform. Most of the senior naval officers, including John Paul Jones, preferred blue coats lined in white, with gold lace and buttons, along with white vest, pants, and stocking.

Uniforms for enlisted men remained the responsibility of ship captains. Some issued clothing as a part of the pay; others charged for each item. Most dressed in loose-fitting, wide-bottomed trousers that reached about halfway between knee and ankle. A shirt or vest covered the chest; if fortunate, the sailor had a waistcoat or short jacket for warmth during long watches. White was the most common color of this sailor garb, but long wear and infrequent washing turned it to various shades of tan or gray.

Sailors usually wore cotton handkerchiefs around their necks and stocking hats on their heads. Some had caps made of straw or canvas and covered in tar to repel water during storms. Officers usually wore buckled leather shoes, but most seamen went barefoot regardless of the weather because shoes deteriorated quickly in the salty-air environment. Besides, bare feet provided better traction on wet decks and in the upper riggings. Sailors during the American Revolution, like soldiers, faced greater risk from disease than from the enemy. The close confines of shipboard increased the rapid spread of smallpox, typhus, and other diseases. Although neither medical personnel nor naval captains of the period understood the role of germs in causing sickness and disease, they did know from experience that "a clean ship is a happy ship."

The members of the Marine Committee appreciated the importance of shipboard cleanliness and often issued letters to captains, encouraging them to maintain a high level of sanitation. Typical was the letter sent to Capt. Nicholas Biddle on April 26, 1777, which ordered:

> You should insist that your officers do frequently see the ship thoroughly and perfectly cleansed; aloft and below from stem to stern, burn powder and wash with vinegar between decks—order hammocks, all bedding, bed clothes, and body clothes daily into the quarters or to be aired on deck; make the people keep their persons cleanly and use exercise—give them as frequent changes of wholesome food as you can, fish when you can get it and fresh food in port. Ventilate the holes and between decks constantly. In short cleanliness, exercise, fresh air, and wholesome food will restore or preserve health more than medicine.

Indeed, cleanliness did help prevent diseases such as typhus, which spread via lice, and lowered the rate of dysentery. However, even the highest standards of sanitation could stave off only so many hazards. Extended stays at sea resulted in spoiled food and putrid water that still caused many cases of dysentery. The lack of vitamin C sources, which caused scurvy, led to bleeding gums, loosened teeth, hemorrhaging, and swollen limbs. If scurvy itself did not kill a sailor, it left him weakened and vulnerable to other fatal diseases.

For more than a hundred years before the Revolution, medical personnel had suspected that lemon juice and other vitamin C–rich citrus protected sailors from scurvy. Some captains issued daily dosages of an ounce of lemon juice, often added to the rum or grog ration; others remained ignorant of the preventive measure or simply ignored it. Some captains assumed that available West Indian limes could substitute equally for lemons and issued them instead. Unfortunately, the limes contained only about one-fourth of the vitamin C as lemons, and crew members still came down with the disease.

Black crew members shared sickness, disease, accidents, combat wounds, and other hardships of ship life equally with white sailors. From analysis of the limited information on the causes of death at sea for both sides during the Revolutionary War, fully one-half of the fatalities were the result of disease. The other 50 percent came from accidents on board ship, perils of the sea, such as shipwreck and drowning, and combat against the enemy. The odds of a sailor being killed in battle accounted for only about one in twenty-four. For every sailor who died fighting, twelve died of disease, eight of the perils of the sea, and three of shipboard accidents.

U.S. and state marines likewise shared similar hardships and hazards. Although authorized green uniforms with red facings, few marines ever received uniforms, and so most, especially enlisted men, went to sea in clothes similar to those of the sailors. Marines also performed many of the same maintenance duties as the sailors, but the two groups were far from a happy "band of brothers." At sea, the marine detachment aboard ship provided an armed guard to the captain and his officers to enforce discipline. The traditional rivalry between marine and sailor that continues today began in the early days of the Revolution.

The daily life of Black soldiers, sailors, and marines in the Revolution differed little from that of their white comrades. Though prejudice and discrimination did not evaporate with the first shots at Lexington, Black servicemen in the Revolution certainly experienced a marked increase in equality throughout the war. Ultimately, as in every armed conflict, soldiers in the trenches and sailors and marines in the forecastle judged men by their performance rather than the color of their skin as they fought for their country's liberty, their unit's pride, and their mutual survival.

10

Behind the Lines

AFRICAN AMERICANS CONTRIBUTED to the success of the Revolution in roles other than those of soldiers, sailors, and marines. Black men and women built fortifications, laid roads, constructed bridges, and performed many other engineering functions necessary for the defense and mobility of the Continental army. In camp they cooked, cleaned, and mended uniforms. On the march they loaded and drove wagons and tended livestock. At coastal shipyards Black men built or repaired war vessels and their weapons. Black miners produced much of the lead to make musket balls for the rebel army. In fields and on plantations all across the new United States, Black farmworkers produced the meat, grain, and produce that fed the front-line troops. In towns and villages African Americans cleaned the streets and even served as community firefighters. Still others performed the dangerous military missions of spies, guides, and messengers.

Black Americans functioned in these behind-the-lines positions throughout the war, coming to their roles via a variety of avenues. Some served as the result of official levies; others, through owners who leased them to the military in exchange for their pay; still others—the freemen—worked for wages. Escaped slaves and those Black men captured or confiscated from Loyalists also worked to help the American army and navy.

The use of Black laborers to support rebel American military operations did not originate with the Revolution. Colonial militias, particularly those that did not permit Black enlistments, often required owners to provide a percentage of their slaves to bolster local defenses. Throughout the colonies, and certainly in the South, white Americans did not see the Black man with a shovel as threatening as one with a musket.

Black laborers became even more necessary after the Continental Congress placed levies on the states to provide regiments in proportion with their population. All of the states had difficulties filling their quotas, and the number of whites joining the army left few able-bodied men to provide direct support to the military or to perform the other day-to-day functions in towns, communities, and farms.

While Black laborers supported all kinds of military operations and performed much of the work that supplied ammunition, food, shelter, and clothing for soldiers and sailors, their most important impact on Revolutionary battles was their assistance in building fortifications. From New York City to Yorktown, Black men, wielding picks and shovels, ensured the survival of the army and thus the existence of the country.

In fact, in the first major battle between the rebels and the British at Bunker Hill on June 17, 1775, much of the initial success of the American infantry resulted from the earthen breastworks hastily dug before the British attacked. Black and white soldiers, who stood behind these redoubts during the battle, had prepared them with the help of other African Americans. One of the few laborers identified by name was a Connecticut slave named Seymour Burr, who subsequently served as a soldier in various Massachusetts regiments for the duration of the war.

After the British evacuated Boston, the Americans correctly assumed that they would then attempt to occupy New York City. Months before the actual attack, Gen. William Alexander began preparing fortifications to repel an invasion. On March 14, 1776, the New York legislature resolved to allow each corps commander within the state authority to order Black Americans to make themselves available for duty with "all the shovels, spades, pick-axes, and hoes they can provide." The act required slaves to report each day until local commanders determined they had prepared "a proper posture of defense." Free Black Americans, also included in the orders, worked only every other day.

Fortifications to bolster defenses did not begin with the American Revolution. From the beginning of warfare, soldiers had dug trenches and used logs and rocks to reinforce their defenses. However, not until the seventeenth century did commanders recognize the importance of combat engineers in designing fortifications that integrated natural and man-made objects with troop concentrations and artillery positions. Before he retired in 1702, French marshal Sébastien Le Prestre de Vauban introduced methods of building mutually supporting fortresses and of strategically trenching sites. He also developed maneuver techniques to breach enemy defenses. Although his writings on combat engineering focused on the huge forts and castles that dominated Europe, Vauban's designs of earthen trench works and parapets influenced military commanders, including Washington and other Americans, for the next 100 years.

Shortly after the Battle of New York, Washington noted in his journal the importance of digging fighting positions and their impact on stopping an enemy attack. Washington concluded, "I have never spared the spade and pickaxe."

Construction of field fortifications began with the digging of a ditch about four to five feet deep and about the same in width. The dirt from the excavation piled on the side facing the enemy produced a parapet about as high as the hole was deep. At the base of the parapet, soldiers prepared an earthen step on which to stand to fire their muskets. The trench provided protection from enemy artillery, while the parapet stopped musket fire and slowed a bayonet charge.

These dirt defenses were never totally complete. Soldiers and laborers continued to improve the earthworks as long as the unit remained in place. Because rain eroded the dirt mounds, the builders of fortifications lined the trenches with logs or, more commonly, with stout sticks bound together into "fascines." These fascines, tied together, formed a wall-like structure directly against the dirt mound and the sides of the trench. Time permitting, soldiers added sharpened wooden stakes facing toward the enemy as well as rocks and any other material that strengthened the defense.

Soldiers and laborers also chopped down trees along approaches to their positions as obstacles to slow an attack and disrupt unit formations. Because the Americans' tactic was to withdraw rather than stand in sustained combat against the superior British numbers, laborers with axes and saws also aided in retreats by downing trees across roads and destroying bridges to hinder the pursuing enemy army.

The Continental army provided its soldiers with shovels, picks, and axes purchased in quantity. Early in the rebellion, Washington ordered the tools marked "CXIII"[1] to note they were government property. On January 30, 1777, the Continental army issued orders that all property be marked "U.S.," "U. States," or "United States."

Few of the entrenching and cutting tools of the period have survived, and there is little uniformity among those in today's museums and collections. Shovel blades vary from seven to eight inches in width and seven to thirteen inches in length. Handles are about three feet long, with a six-inch "T" bar on the end of some. Picks and axes from the Continental army period are similar in construction to today's tools.

The problem for the United States was neither the availability nor uniformity of implements but rather the labor force needed to use the equip-

---

[1]The CXIII marking instructions originated from Washington's headquarters on June 18, 1776, but no definitive explanation exists. One guess is that the "C" stood for Continental; the Roman numerals "XIII," for the thirteen states.

ment. Since most able-bodied white men were occupied with military service, the obvious source for the rebels to turn to was the Black population. However, here they faced two immense obstacles. First, the majority of Black Americans were officially the property of individual white owners who completely controlled their slaves' activities; indeed, they owned them for the very purpose of having their own private workforce. Hence, owners were reluctant to diminish their own labor pools. The second obstacle for the rebels in securing laborers was that fully one-third of slaveholders were loyal to the British Crown—a fact that drastically reduced the number of slaves whose work the rebels could influence.

During emergencies commanders impressed whatever laborers they could quickly round up. Early in the war, including the defense of New York, the army and the states provided little or no pay for this labor. The passage of time and the movement of the war into the southern states, with their large Black populations, however, required more regulated use of Black labor and compensation for their work.

Owners looked upon time spent by their slaves digging trenches and felling trees for the army as periods of lost productivity. Considerations of individual profit generally took precedence over patriotism and support of the rebellion. As a result, southern states approached the use of Black labor to support the military in a number of ways; each, however, focused on the rights of owners and fair compensation for services rendered. Members of state legislatures, especially those in the South, were mostly slaveholders themselves and well aware that other slaveholders were the voters who decided elections.

Georgia was one of the first states to formalize regulations concerning the use of slaves as government and military laborers. On November 4, 1775, the Georgia Council of Safety ordered the impressment of 100 Black men to bolster the defenses around military storehouses in Savannah.

Owners immediately protested the use of their slaves in what they considered dangerous tasks that risked their safety and reduced their profitability. Legislators and military leaders had to take measures to appease slaveholders while still acquiring an adequate number of laborers. On October 15, 1776, the Georgia legislature passed a resolution that promised that any slave who became ill while in state service would be "conveyed to a proper hospital, and there supplied with necessary sustenance, medicines, and attendance." It also provided for payment to owners for any slave maimed or killed while working for the state.

Despite these promises, Georgians remained reluctant to provide their slaves for state or military employment. In September 1777 the legislature once again mandated that owners provide their slaves to repair and improve several forts, shore batteries, and public facilities. To ensure compliance, government officials ordered that owners provide a list of their male slaves between the ages of sixteen and sixty, 10 percent of whom would then be selected as state laborers.

The legislators did their best to minimize the concerns of owners by again promising to provide medical care for slaves who became ill while working for the state and to reimburse owners for any who died while serving the government. They also limited the period of service to no longer than three weeks and promised to pay owners three shillings per day for each slave's work. The legislature further authorized fines for owners who did not provide a list of their slaves. Some owners still refused to comply, and others submitted only partial lists.

The Georgia Slave Labor Act expired on February 1, 1778, but the need for laborers continued. In June 1778 legislators authorized a more direct means of acquiring laborers. When roads in the state became nearly impassable for either military or civilian traffic, the legislature instructed Col. Andrew Williams to hire slaves to make repairs. If owners did not willingly provide them, Williams could impress as many as he needed to complete the work. Still reluctant, however, to totally ignore or supersede property rights, the officials directed that no slave could be removed from his home county, nor could any be taken away from his owner for more than ten days.

South Carolina also hired or impressed slaves to support its military operations and to maintain public facilities and roads. The state hired slaves from the beginning of the war as dockworkers and shipbuilders. In addition, slaves on loan from their owners served as hospital orderlies and firefighters to fill positions vacated by white men who had enlisted.

On November 10, 1775, the South Carolina legislature directed the hiring of "a sufficient number of negroes to give all possible dispatch to the completing of the redoubt erecting upon James Island, to the westward of Fort Johnson."

Slaves and free Black Americans hired by the state also built double-walled defenses of palmetto logs around guns defending Sullivan Island, at the north entrance to Charleston Harbor. These defenses played a direct role in turning back the British seaborne attack against the city on June 28, 1776.

In South Carolina, as in Georgia, many slaveholders were reluctant to provide the enslaved for state labor even in exchange for their wages. On November 20, 1775, the South Carolina legislature, forced to take action, resolved "that the colonels of the several regiments of militia throughout the colony have leave to enroll such a number of able male slaves, to be employed as pioneers and laborers, as public exigencies may require." The resolution provided payment "for the service of each such slave while actually employed" but made it clear that providing that labor was at the will of the local military commander, not the owners.

A year later, the South Carolina legislature extended these provisions to impress slaves for civic functions, such as roadbuilding and mainte-nance, in addition to military support duties. Some South Carolina owners continued to resist providing their slaves for state or military duties in the same manner as their Georgia neighbors. South Carolina, however, was less willing to withhold slaves. When the British once again prepared to attack Charleston in the spring of 1777, American commanders sent mili-tary units into the city and countryside with orders to gather up every slave they encountered to work on the city's defenses. Exception from slave impressment required written permission from the governor.

Rebel commanders also expanded the state resolution on slave im-pressment to temporarily confiscate as many slaves as they needed to ac-complish their mission. On June 7, 1781, John Burnet wrote partisan leader Andrew Pickens, "All the negroes not claimed by the inhabitants who you think fit for the pioneer or wagon service you will please send to headquarters." Two days later, Gen. Nathanael Greene instructed Joseph Clay "to repair to Augusta and collect as many of the militia and negroes as you can and employ them in demolishing the works upon the Savan-nah River." When South Carolina regiments captured substantial goods and supplies from the British at Georgetown sixty miles up the coast from Charleston, on July 25, 1781, Gen. Thomas Sumter told Capt. W. R. Davis to impress as many slaves, as well as wagons and teams, as needed to evac-uate the provisions.

In March 1782, Gen. Francis Marion ordered Col. Peter Horry to build a fortification on the Santee River using Black laborers. Marion instructed Horry to request that local owners provide a percentage of their slaves; if they were uncooperative, he was to make his own estimate of an owner's number of slaves and impress proportionately, using force if necessary.

Virginia also hired slaves from the war's first days, but Lord Dunmore's offer of protection to escaped slaves reduced the number available. As in South Carolina and Georgia, many owners were reluctant to part with their slaves, preferring to keep their valuable property on their planta-tions. The Virginia legislature, dominated by slaveholders, supported the hiring of Black Americans from willing proprietors but did not approve of the military or the state impressing slaves without permission.

Volunteerism, rather than impressment failed to produce large num-bers of slaves for state service in Virginia, especially during the latter years of the conflict. In February 1781 the Continental army requested that the state provide forty slaves to construct an important fortification in Prince George County. The state was only able to produce half the requested number.

Small numbers of contracted slaves, usually fewer than a dozen at a time, did serve as wagoners in the Virginia quartermaster department and as foundry workers in the Fredericksburg gun factory. The state hired a few slaves, including women, from owners to work in civilian and military hospitals.

North Carolina and Maryland followed policies on slave laborers similar to those of Virginia. Both states relied on owners to voluntarily provide their slaves in exchange for their wages. During 1781 and 1782, slaves belonging to North Carolinian Robert Burton moved the majority of the supplies from wharves to the army in the field in Granville County. Slaves belonging to John Walker performed similar work at Wilmington, but at least five escaped, never to be found again. Walker was still unsuccessfully petitioning the North Carolina legislature as late as 1785 for reimbursement for his lost property.

State officials sent recruiters into the villages and countryside to seek willing owners. They placed notices in newspapers, like the one that appeared in the *Maryland Gazette* on August 15, 1776, requesting "a number of slaves or freemen laborers, for the purpose of carrying on a cannon foundry at Antietam in Frederick County." The state also authorized county sheriffs to provide local governments with Black Americans confiscated from Loyalists or captured as runaways and to collect their wages.

Those states which directly impressed slaves from their owners proved to be much more successful in securing laborers than those that depended on volunteer participation. Profit often won out over patriotism when owners believed that they needed their slaves more on their plantations than in the service of the state or nation. This did not mean, however, that slaves whom owners refused to provide to the state or the military as laborers did not contribute to the success of the Revolution. Whatever a slave's occupation—whether field hand, factory worker, or craftsman— he or she contributed to the production of food, clothing, and other supplies that sustained white and Black American soldiers in the field and sailors at sea.

Black people under the control of Americans who supported the Revolution were not the only source of slave laborers. In the end, the rebel American military and civilian government viewed all slaves as potential laborers.

The Continental army and the state militias generally returned captured runaways if their owners supported the rebellion, charging a recovery fee that went to regimental or state treasuries to fund additional labor. While owners were in the process of establishing ownership, unit commanders used the slaves as they saw fit.

The rebels considered slaves confiscated from Loyalists as spoils of war, and those people became the property of their captors. Some of the confiscated slaves helped the military build defenses, while others worked for the states as laborers. The states also sold slaves from captured Loyalists to American rebel patriots and gave the proceeds to the regiment or the unit's soldiers.

Slaves hired or impressed from rebel Americans or confiscated from Loyalists performed much of the labor that supported the army in the field as well as on the home front. Black Americans not only contributed their physical strength to the American Revolution; they also proved valuable as messengers, guides, and spies. Because the first battles of the Revolution took place in New England, where the local militia units were familiar with their areas of operations, navigating the terrain was not a problem for the rebel military units. However, when the war shifted to New York and later to the southern states, Continental army regiments, far from their homes, sought residents familiar with the local countryside as guides. Slaves, either hired from their owners or captured as runaways, often provided needed information on routes through forests and swamps and on the locations of river and stream fords.

On July 15, 1779, Gen. Anthony Wayne assembled his army in preparation for an attack against a British strongpoint on the Hudson River, at Stony Point, New York. About a mile from his objective, Wayne issued orders for a predawn bayonet attack. After a thirty-minute fight on the sixteenth, Wayne proved victorious in capturing the British garrison and gained the nickname "Mad Anthony" for his bold night assault.

The Continental Congress extended an official vote of appreciation to Wayne, and every written history since the Revolution mentions his great victory at Stony Point. Few note that the success of the attack resulted from a local slave named Pompey Lamb, who guided Wayne's army for the last mile through the darkness to the fort. According to Washington Irving in his 1859 *Life of George Washington*, "About half-past eleven, the whole army moved forward, guided by a negro of the neighborhood who had frequently carried fruit to the [British] garrison."

Some guides did more than just lead the way to an objective. On July 9, 1777, Lt. Col. William Barton of Warren, Rhode Island, gathered forty volunteers for the purpose of kidnapping Gen. Richard Prescott, the British commander at Newport, in order to exchange the officer for American general Charles Lee, whom the British had recently captured. Among the volunteers was Jack Sisson,[2] a local Black man who steered one of the five boats carrying Barton's force across the bay to Overing House, near Warwick Neck, where Prescott had made his headquarters.

After steering his boat through waters filled with British vessels, Sisson assisted Barton in subduing a sentry at the general's quarters. According to an article in the August 7, 1777, edition of the *Pennsylvania Evening Post,* "The colonel went foremost, with a stout, active negro close behind him." The article, credited to "a gentleman from Rhode Island," further explained that upon finding Prescott's door locked, "the negro, with his head, at the second stroke forced a passage" into the British general's quarters.

The kidnapping of Prescott and his eventual exchange for Lee provided a great morale boost for the rebellious Americans. A ballad about the event quickly spread from camp to camp and ship to ship:

> A tawny son of Africa's race Them through the ravine led,
> And entering then the Overing House, They found him in his bed.
> But to get in they had no means Except poor Cuffee's head,
> Who beat the door down, then rushed in, And seized him in his bed.

In addition to their role as guides, Black people, because of their familiarity with local roads and trails, frequently served as messengers. These messengers generally conveyed private correspondence, but a few carried official military dispatches.

African Americans also proved valuable in providing rebel commanders information on British fortifications and movements. Black spies, posing as laborers or runaways, were able to gather intelligence on enemy locations and intentions and deliver this information to the American military leaders. Because of the secret nature of their business, spies received little recognition for their work. Despite this protection of sources, some state legislatures did note Black involvement in intelligence activities.

In 1778 a Rhode Island Loyalist sold a slave named Quaco Honeyman

---

[2]Some accounts use the name Tack Sisson. Others call him Prince and confuse him with Prince Whipple, who rowed Washington across the Delaware. Jack Sisson is the most accepted name, and he apparently later enlisted for the duration of the war in Col. Christopher Greene's First Rhode Island Regiment. His obituary in the *Providence Gazette* on November 3, 1821, lists his age as seventy-eight and describes him as "a negro man" and as "one of the forty brave volunteers" who captured Prescott.

to a British officer serving in the occupation force at Newport. After working for his new owner long enough to view the British defenses of the city and port, Honeyman escaped to the American rebel lines to report his observations. In the state records there appears a brief notation that the Rhode Island General Assembly recognized Honeyman in January 1782: "The information he then gave rendered great and essential service to this state and the public in general."

On March 12, 1783, the South Carolina legislature recognized yet another Black spy, proclaiming:

> Whereas, a negro man named Antigua, a slave, lately belonging to Mr. John Harleston, deceased, was employed for the purposes of procuring information of the enemy's movements and designs by John Rutledge, Esquire, late governor of the state; and whereas, the said negro man, Antigua, always executed the commissions with which he was intrusted with diligence and fidelity, and obtained very considerable and important information from within the enemy's lines, frequently at the risk of his life.

As a reward for Antigua's service, the state legislature directed that his wife, Hagar, and their child be freed. The ordinance does not mention the ownership status of Antigua, but the presumption is that he had previously been granted his freedom.

Two more slave spies contributed to the final American victory over the British at Yorktown. In the spring of 1781, Virginia militia colonel Josiah Parker sent Saul Matthews, a slave held by Thomas Matthews, into Portsmouth to gather intelligence on the British force and its movements on the James River.

Saul Matthews did not immediately receive a reward for this dangerous mission; in fact, he found himself sold to another owner after the war. It was not until a decade later, in November 1792, that he successfully petitioned the Virginia legislature for his freedom "in consideration of many very essential services rendered to this Commonwealth during the late war."

The second African American at Yorktown served the American army as spy, guide, messenger, and even double agent. In March 1781 a slave named James,[3] in New Kent County, Virginia, received permission from his owner, William Armistead, to join the army under command of Gen. Marquis de Lafayette. Because of James's knowledge of the area around

---

[3]During his enlistment in the Continental army the slave spy was known as James Armistead; following the war, he assumed the name James Lafayette.

Portsmouth, Lafayette used the slave to deliver messages to spies already operating in the city.

British officials became so accustomed to James's being in their camps that Lord Cornwallis offered him payment to spy on the Americans. James was soon delivering accurate information to Lafayette on the British while providing Cornwallis inflated estimates on the strength of the Americans. James hid his real loyalties well. After the British surrendered at Yorktown, the defeated Cornwallis, at a meeting with Lafayette, was extremely surprised to see James, whom he had thought was an agent in his payment, as obviously a soldier in the American army.

Shortly after the war concluded, Lafayette expressed his personal appreciation for James during a visit to Richmond. In a certificate dated November 21, 1784, Lafayette wrote that James "properly acquitted himself with some important communication I gave him" and further noted that "his intelligence from the enemy's camp were industriously collected and more faithfully delivered."

Two years later, the Virginia General Assembly voted to free James and to compensate his owner for his value. The act stated that James entered "into the service of Marquis Lafayette, and at the peril of his life found means to frequent the British camp, and thereby faithfully executed important commissions entrusted to him by the marquis." It concluded that James had "kept open a channel of the most useful information to the army of the state." Nearly thirty years after his dangerous and faithful service, the Virginia legislature again recognized James with an award of $100 and an annual pension of $40.

Not all African American laborers, guides, messengers, and spies were so fortunate. Whether they served willingly or unwillingly, most Black noncombatants received neither their wages nor their freedom for their behind-the-lines support of the Revolution. Owners took their pay as well as returning them to slavery upon completion of their labor. Little recognized or rewarded for their service, these African Americans nevertheless played an important role in the success of the Revolution.

11

Great Britain and African Americans

AT THE START OF THE REVOLUTION, African Americans accounted for 20 percent of the total population of the thirteen colonies. The British realized that the half million Black population would play a critical role in the war's outcome, and they, like the American rebels, understood the advantages of having Black soldiers and laborers. Yet the British, too, were reluctant to arm Black people against whites.

In fact, for the British the issue of slavery remained unresolved. Because slavery was not integral to the local economy, only about 14,000 Black slaves lived in the British Isles in the 1770s. Slavery, however, did play an important role in the British colonies around the world, and English ship captains prospered in the slave trade with North America and the Caribbean.

Despite Great Britain's commercial interest in slavery, many African Americans at the time of the Revolution viewed the English as protectors and liberators. This resulted from a London court decision on June 22, 1772, which freed James Somerset because his Boston owner had transported him illegally to London.

While the Somerset decision did not free slaves throughout the British Empire, it did not take long for the word to reach the American colonies that slaves entering the British Isles would be freed. While colonial officials in America ignored the ruling, many slaves who heard about the court decision saw getting to England as a path to freedom. Few, of course, could escape their owners, much less manage to steal aboard ships to make the transatlantic voyage. At least two slaveholders placed advertisements in southern newspapers to solicit help in finding runaways they thought were seeking transport to England, but it is doubtful that slaves were successful in gaining their freedom in this manner. The British court ruling did, however, provide a glimmer of hope to the hundreds of thousands of African Americans in shackles who dreamed of freedom.

The expanding British Empire of the eighteenth century required large numbers of soldiers and sailors and an immense budget to support a worldwide army and navy. To fill the ranks, Britain offered enlistment bonuses and even pardoned criminals who were willing to enlist. The harsh discipline and low pay in the British army and navy, combined with long and often hazardous tours of duty far away from home, did little to encourage volunteers. At the time of the American Revolution, service in the British military was unpopular with the lower classes, who had traditionally filled the ranks. The upper classes, whose taxes largely paid for the military force, also expressed little enthusiasm for the life of the professional soldier and sailor.

Britain's population, neither in numbers nor by attitude, could support the worldwide commitments of the vast empire. Even the hiring of mercenaries from Germany, India, and other countries failed at times to produce sufficient personnel.

British commanders in North America, well aware of these problems, saw from the beginning of the Revolution that the abundant number of Black residents could support military operations. On June 12, 1775, Gen. Thomas Gage wrote from Boston to Lord Barrington, the colonial secretary, in London, "Things are now come to that crisis, that we must avail ourselves of every resource, even to raise the negroes, in our cause."

Many British officials both at home and in the colonies did not share Gage's support for the use of African Americans. On August 9, 1775, Lord William Campbell, the royal governor of South Carolina, wrote to Gage warning him not to "fall prey to the negroes." The following October, a group in London who identified themselves as "Gentlemen, Merchants, and Traders" addressed a petition to King George expressing their opposition to arming Black men against "our American brethren."

Gage, besieged at Boston by Washington's army and bereft of the opportunity to recruit Black men, heeded the advice. Meanwhile, Lord Dunmore in Virginia, facing the loss of his governorship and his property to the rebels, took action. Dunmore corresponded with his superiors and friends in London even before the battles at Lexington and Concord about his intentions to arm Black men to maintain British control in Virginia.

Dunmore did receive some encouragement, including a letter from Lord Dartmouth, the British secretary of state for the American Department, dated May 1, 1777, that acknowledged the possibility of providing arms and ammunition. Even though he received no official approval from London, Dunmore took it upon himself to begin arming slaves. At the same time that Gage supported using slaves to defend the Crown's interest, he informed Dunmore that he could not provide arms or equipment, nor could he reimburse any of the governor's expenses.

Dunmore began to recruit runaway slaves months before his official November 7 declaration that he would free those who joined his army. British officials in London did not condemn Dunmore's actions, nor did they support them or provide needed supplies. They simply left Dunmore on his own. The proclamation on freeing and arming slaves provided London with the opportunity to observe the consequence and reactions from the Americans without taking an official stance.

The thorough defeat of Dunmore and his slaves by the rebel Virginians made the lack of support from London appear to be a sound political decision. The reasonably easy British victory over Washington's army in New York in September 1776 also reinforced the belief that the British could crush the rebellion without the use of African Americans.

This view changed the following year with the American victory at Saratoga and the subsequent alliance between the rebels and the French. The British, unsuccessful in defeating the rebellion in the North, now turned to the South, where they hoped the large number of Loyalists would influence the war's outcome. This expansion of the conflict also increased the numbers of soldiers and support personnel required, and the British began to accept the fact that they needed African Americans if they were to achieve victory. As with the American army, the need for manpower ultimately proved the strongest reason for the British to accept Black soldiers.

African Americans were ready to meet the British manpower needs and were more than willing to exchange loyalty for liberty. From the beginning of the war, African Americans escaped from their rebel owners and crossed the lines to offer their services to the British.

When the war expanded into the Carolinas and Georgia, new opportunities arose for slaves to join the British. Previously, the slaves' only avenues of escape had been to reach ships along the coast or to undertake long overland treks to find the British lines. Now the British not only occupied the major southern ports, their army swept across the countryside. Opportunities to escape also increased as owners and overseers joined the rebel or Loyalist forces.

Slaves were the key to British strategy in the South. The initial objectives were the ports and coastal areas, since they contained the majority of the slaves. Capturing these areas denied the rebel army food and other supplies while providing the British important labor and military resources. Each slave who escaped to the British lines reduced the rebel support force by one man and added the same number to his liberators' efforts, thus at once easing the British manpower crisis and reducing the capabilities of the enemy.

Since Black men were now serving throughout the Continental army and Rhode Island had fielded an African American regiment, the British no longer had any qualms about arming Black soldiers to fight. By the summer of 1779, almost four years after Dunmore, they were prepared to formalize their offer of freedom to runaway slaves. On June 30 the British commander in chief, Henry Clinton, issued a proclamation from his headquarters at Philipsburg, New York. Clinton, a politician himself, began his statement with an explanation that he was taking action in response to the American policy of enlisting Black men as soldiers. He then announced that the British would purchase any African American soldiers captured while serving with the rebels.

Clinton then declared that any Black slave considered property of a rebel could cross the lines without fear of re-enslavement. He stated, "I do promise to every negro who shall desert the rebel standard full security to follow within these lines any occupation which he shall think proper."

Clinton's complex proclamation itself[1] was all but incomprehensible to slaves denied education. Its real meaning, however—freedom for slaves who joined the British—was clear, and that word spread quickly throughout the states.

The British offer of freedom to runaways had its limitations. Clinton's proclamation clearly extended freedom only to those Black Americans who were "the property of rebels." It excluded slaves belonging to Loyalists; in fact, the British army and navy often returned runaways or captured slaves to their Loyalist owners.

Despite this limitation, the pre-proclamation trickle of slaves who had crossed the lines to join the British quickly turned into a flood. By ones and twos slaves slipped away by land and sea to seek freedom with the British. Slaveholders at all levels, including signers of the Declaration of Independence, suffered the loss. They included Benjamin Harrison of Virginia, who reported losing thirty of "my finest slaves," and Arthur Middleton of South Carolina, who lost fifty of his Black chattel.

Other slaves, willing or not, came under British jurisdiction when the army occupied rebel-controlled villages and plantations. The liberation of rebel-owned slaves usually occurred as the British army maneuvered against its opponent or seized territory amenable for future operations. At other times, the British deliberately raided rebel-held areas to "liberate" slaves with skills needed to support their army, including carpenters, smiths, wheelwrights, coopers, wagoners, and cooks.

The British offer of freedom for slaves, along with their direct effort to remove slaves from their rebel American owners in contested areas,

---

[1]See Appendix J for the complete proclamation.

would seem to have created an environment in which most, if not all, slaves could take advantage of the chance for liberty. Such was not the case. While the numbers of slaves crossing the lines greatly increased immediately following Dunmore's proclamation in 1775 and Clinton's in 1779, proportionately few African Americans sought freedom by joining the British.

Reliable estimates of the number of rebel-owned slaves who escaped to the British in pursuit of freedom vary from 10,000 to 20,000.[2] Considering the fact that 500,000 slaves were in the colonies at the time and subtracting the ineligible third that belonged to Loyalists, one can conclude that only about 5 percent of African Americans during the Revolution gained or sought freedom by joining the British.

The reasons for this low number included perceptions, fears, and most important, opportunity experienced by slaves. African Americans were well aware of British inconsistencies about slavery: Loyalists supported it, British ship captains supplied it, and British individuals profited from it. American rebel leaders capitalized on these inconsistencies and did their best to convince their slaves that they were more likely to face sale to the West Indies than freedom if they ran away to the enemy.

Other slaves did not take advantage of opportunities to join the British in the belief that they might share in the future benefits of the country's liberty. Some had already fought alongside whites in colonial militias against Native Americans and believed that they were a part of the new nation. Slaves, particularly in the northern states, were also aware of the abolitionist movement that was encouraging emancipation. Still others accepted the offer of securing their freedom by fighting in the Continental army.

For the vast majority of Black Americans, however, neither mistrust of the Crown nor loyalty to the United States kept them in slavery. Rather, they remained under the control of their owners and overseers because of the lack of opportunity, which, in many cases, resulted from lack of information. White slaveholders did their best to prevent the news of the British freedom offer from reaching their slaves, and many Black Americans, enslaved on remote farms and plantations, were never aware of the opportunity.

---

[2]Some writers claim that more than 100,000 African Americans crossed the lines to join the British. This number is improbable in that it includes Black Americans belonging to Loyalists and those rebel-owned slaves who fell under British control as the result of military operations. While these Black Americans may have supported the British, they did not gain their freedom in exchange for their service.

In addition to denying their slaves information about the British offer, rebel slaveholders took more direct measures to prevent escapes and to capture and punish runaways who attempted to reach enemy lines. Slaveholders increased their inspections of slave quarters to search for clothing and food hoarded for a flight to eventual freedom. Owners began locking slaves in their cabins at night and chained "troublemakers" and others they thought might attempt to escape. In some cases, owners of property close to the fighting transferred their slaves to more remote locations or temporarily loaned them to family or friends more distant from the British lines. This movement of slaves from the proximity of the British became so common that the Virginia legislature, on May 4, 1780, enacted laws permitting owners from other states to take or send their slaves across its borders for protection. Pennsylvania, although a center of the abolitionist movement, passed a similar act on October 1, 1781.

Moving slaves both impeded their chance of escape and limited the success of British raids to find and impress them as laborers. Gen. Alexander Leslie reported to his superiors at British headquarters in Charleston, South Carolina, on March 27, 1782, that his efforts to gather slaves had been unsuccessful because the rebel owners had "taken the precaution of sending their valuable slaves across the river" into more secure territory.

Some slaveholders claimed during and after the war that their slaves stayed for other reasons. In a letter dated April 11, 1781, Chesapeake Bay plantation owner Charles Carroll wrote to his father from Annapolis, "I think our negroes on the island have given proof of their attachment. They might have gone off if they had been so disposed."

South Carolina plantation owner Gen. William Moultrie also boasted of the loyalty of his slaves in his postwar memoirs. Moultrie wrote that he owned about 200 slaves "and not one of them left me during the war, although they had great offers." The general even added that his slaves welcomed him home with shouts of "God Bless you, massa."

Perhaps the loyalty exhibited by slaves belonging to Carroll and Moultrie came as a result of good treatment. What is more likely, however, is that they did not flee because their owners had taught them to fear both the British and the reprisals of a failed escaped attempt. In later years, whites romanticized these "good master" and "loyal darky" ideals, but it takes little thought to realize that no man or woman voluntarily chose slavery over freedom.

County and state law-enforcement officials assisted owners in pursuing slaves who attempted to escape to the British. Groups patrolled the roads, checked waterways, and boarded merchant ships to search for escaped slaves. They rigidly enforced slave codes that required written passes for travel. In some instances, local militia captains patrolled forests and swamps in search of runaways. At one time in 1778 the state of Georgia had fully one-third of its militia assigned to securing or pursuing slaves rather than fighting the British. This, of course, in itself helped the British war effort, as it removed rebel soldiers from the fight.

Slaveholders, anxious to protect their property, actively sought assistance from state officials. On March 25, 1781, plantation owner Richard Barnes of Leonard Town, Maryland, wrote Gov. Thomas Lee describing the behavior of his slaves when the British forces neared his land. Barnes recommended:

> It would be advisable, while the enemy is in the Bay, to keep about sixty more men constantly patrolling from one part of the county to the other in order to prevent dissatisfaction and the negroes going to the enemy. . . . I am well informed upwards of twenty-five offered themselves to those ships the night they were in St. Marys.

Official punishment of slaves captured attempting to escape to the British varied from region to region. The northern states, with fewer slaves and more opportunities for freedom through service in the rebel militias or the Continental army, were more lenient than the southern. Always fearful of defection and rebellion, southerners imposed levels of punishment that would serve as deterrents. Virginia and South Carolina went so far as to legislate the death penalty.

Captured runaways, however, were valuable, and owners were reluctant to sacrifice their slaves as examples to others. Usually, the state imposed the death penalty only in the most severe cases, such as on leaders who encouraged other slaves to leave and those who committed robbery or other crimes during their flight.

Few of the apprehended paid with their lives. Some owners whipped or branded returned slaves, but this punishment often damaged their property and limited their ability to work without ending the slave's dream of liberty. As a result, most owners simply sold a returned slave, usually to the West Indies. This action served as a deterrent, since the West Indian plantations were notorious for harsh working conditions and general abuse of slaves. More important to the owner, of course, was that he received fair payment for his property while eliminating an escape risk.

Slaveholders and local law-enforcement officials were not alone in their efforts to prevent slaves from joining the British. Commanders in the state militia and in the Continental army knew that every escaped slave reduced their support base by one man while increasing that of the British by the same number. Military commanders in Virginia actively took measures to prevent slaves from joining the British. On April 23, 1776, Gen. Charles Lee ordered that all Black people capable of bearing arms be "secured immediately and sent up to Norfolk," where they could be protected.

Col. Isaac Read, one of Lee's subordinates, sent twenty-five of his men to patrol the banks of the Chuckatuck and Nansemond Rivers for runaways and to confiscate all watercraft that might assist in an escape. Read authorized his men to destroy the boat of any owner who refused to turn it over to the army. Another officer, Capt. John Weems, of the Anne Arundel County militia, reported to state officials on March 21, 1781, "I have posted guards at the most convenient places to prevent the negroes from going to the enemy and have secured all boats and canoes."

The Virginia navy also assisted when, in February 1777, it provided four galleys to patrol inland rivers and Chesapeake Bay to apprehend runaways. This was a significant action, because it removed the galleys from the pursuit of enemy merchant ships, the prizes of which provided financial rewards for their crews and the state government.

In South Carolina, military commanders took actions that superseded local slave codes in regulating movements of Black Americans. In March 1781, Gen. Francis Marion ordered his command to apprehend any Black man who did not have a pass authorized by a military officer, even if he possessed one signed by his owner.

By December 1781 officials in South Carolina became worried that even Black Americans directly supporting the Continental army and the state militia were potential runaways. On December 7, Gov. Otho H. Williams ordered his road-maintenance supervisors at Ferguson's Mill to expedite repairs and to then return the slaves under military guard to their owners as soon as possible to limit escape opportunities. At other locations, including the military-fortification construction efforts at Camp Howe, Georgia, officers held roll calls of slaves three times a day and assigned additional guards to watch the workers.

These rebel military efforts on land and water discouraged slaves from fleeing to the British but never completely stopped their efforts to gain freedom by crossing the lines. African Americans continued throughout the war to join whichever side they thought offered the best opportunity for liberty.

12

Black Men in Red Coats

AFRICAN AMERICANS WHO JOINED THE BRITISH served with them in the same capacities as those who served with the rebels. Freemen, slaves belonging to Loyalists, and runaways saw action with the British as soldiers, sailors, spies, guides, and laborers. As in the rebel armed forces, need proved to be the primary motivation for the numbers of Black Americans the British employed and the extent to which they used them.

Initially, the British hired them only as support personnel both because that was the extent of their needs and because of their early reluctance to arm Black men against white ones. From the rebel siege of Boston to the battle at the Yorktown breastworks and the final skirmishes in the Deep South, African Americans served the British as cooks, carpenters, teamsters, coopers, blacksmiths, orderlies, laborers, and in every other rear-echelon position.

Many of these Black workers served informally as assistants to individual soldiers or as company or regiment support personnel. In some instances, the British organized them into their own units to provide general services to a large unit or to an area of occupation. The earliest account of a Black unit in British service is in a population survey of Boston on June 24, 1775, ordered by General Gage, which mentions a "Company of Negroes." This same unit appears again on the list of British forces evacuated from Boston to Nova Scotia the following March.

The British again looked to Black people for support when they occupied New York in the fall of 1776. Some of these laborers continued to work for the British until their final evacuation of that city on November 25, 1783. This period of more than seven years marks the longest service by African Americans with the British in the Revolution.

During the British occupation of New York, runaway slaves and freemen constituted much of the city's and the army's support structure. Most of the town's wagon drivers and street-maintenance crews were African Americans. Others worked directly for the army, filling 10 percent of the food procurement and distribution positions. Military units also hired Black support personnel, often in great numbers. A 1781 payroll for the Seventeenth Regiment of Light Dragoons lists sixty-three men identified as "negroes."

When the British occupied Philadelphia in September 1777, they replicated their procedures used in New York by employing Black Philadelphians to maintain the city and to support their army. The core group of Black municipal workers, organized into the "Company of Black Pioneers," contained seventy-two men listed as privates, fifteen women, and eight children, according to a report dated July 13, 1777. The company's duties included cleaning the streets and removing abandoned property.

When the British evacuated Philadelphia less than a year later, they took along the Black Pioneers. Apparently they accompanied the British army to New York, although only one additional document verifies their existence. On September 17, 1778, each member of the unit, now listed as Capt. Allen Stewart's Company of Black Pioneers, received a clothing issue consisting of a greatcoat, winter trousers, a hat, a shirt, and a "sailor's jacket." Except for the last item, all garments were civilian clothes because the pioneer company was not an armed military unit. The sailors' jackets were probably issued because they were surplus from some naval unit.

The only limit to British use of African Americans in the northern cities was availability. Black Americans were in demand by both the rebels and the Crown, and although the British offered a fair wage in exchange for work and did not ask if a man was free or a runaway, the African American population in New England was not sufficient to provide large numbers of workers. This changed dramatically as the British shifted their campaign to the South, which contained huge numbers of slaves.

When the British captured Savannah, Georgia, on December 29, 1778, as a base of operations for their southern campaign, they knew the rebels would attempt to retake the port. British general Augustine Prevost immediately began bolstering the town's defenses. In early 1779 he ordered a subordinate to gather all of the runaways and other slaves belonging to rebels he could find to build infantry and artillery fortifications along the city's primary land and sea approaches. Slaves belonging to Loyalists also worked on the port's defenses.

Newspaper reports of the time, along with correspondence from residents, very greatly in estimates of the number of Black laborers in the city and range from 200 to 4,000. A realistic figure, considering the numbers available and the amount of work accomplished, is about 500.

In September and October of 1779 the Americans and their French allies unsuccessfully attempted to retake Savannah. The British commander, Gen. Henry Clinton, attributed the victory to the well-built defenses. An account of the battle in a rebel newspaper, the *New Jersey Gazette*, on December 8, 1779, also credited the successful British defense to its "strength and number of works" built by "upwards of 2,000 negroes."

The British used Black labor to build defenses at other seaports, including St. Augustine, Florida. Military reports from that port's commander, Col. Lewis von Fuser, to General Clinton accounted for 130 Black workers on October 2, 1779. A subsequent report on October 24 showed that this number had increased to 300.

British commanders in Savannah, while successful in their initial defense of the city, anticipated that the American rebels would try again, and for that attack they needed to further fortify the city. With more and more British units campaigning across the South and increasing their use of Black laborers and craftsmen, too few runaways or confiscated slaves were available to meet all of the city's building requirements.

In December 1780 the Loyalist governor of Georgia, James Wright, wrote to British secretary of state Lord George Germain explaining that in accordance with authorization granted in previous correspondence, he had issued orders that permitted commanders to impress Black people, regardless of ownership, into the Savannah workforce. Wright also provided an excellent description of the city's defenses as well as stating that he was also considering using Black men as soldiers.[1]

On May 12, 1780, the British, under the command of General Clinton, succeeded in capturing the major port of Charleston, South Carolina, and immediately employed Black Americans to clear battle debris and rebuild the city's defenses. They had no trouble finding volunteers, for the British victory had brought a flood of runaways from both rebel and Loyalist plantations.

General Clinton consolidated his army at Charleston and then sent out columns, with the largest force under Lord Cornwallis, to subdue the rebels in the remainder of South Carolina. Cornwallis's movement northward brought more and more African Americans under British control. Charles Steadman, Cornwallis's commissary officer, later concluded in his writings on the war: "The negroes generally followed the British army."

---

[1]Governor Wright's letter appears in Appendix K.

Cornwallis used as many Black Americans as possible, but so many joined his force that he soon had problems feeding, clothing, and controlling them. On May 17, less than a week after the fall of Charleston, Cornwallis addressed a note to Clinton expressing his concerns about the number of Black Americans seeking his protection. Three days later, Clinton responded:

> As to the negroes, I will leave such orders as I hope will prevent the confusion that would arise from a further desertion of them to us, and I will consider of some scheme for placing those we have on abandoned plantations on which they may subsist. In the mean time Your Lordship can make such arrangements as will discourage their joining us.

While Cornwallis led the major portion of the British army, other commanders with smaller forces had similar experiences with the Black population of the South. Nisbet Balfour, in charge of the British column charged with seizing Ninety Six, an American outpost in western South Carolina, found that Loyalists in the region readily provided their slaves to support the army. Balfour also put to work slaves that had escaped from their rebel owners. In a June 24, 1780, letter to Cornwallis he wrote, "Many negroes captured from people who have left the country are brought in here. I mean to make use of some of them on the public works."

Three weeks earlier, on June 3, Clinton had taken measures to safeguard those Black Americans who had already sought British protection. In a memorandum to Cornwallis and the commandant of Charleston, Clinton announced that slaves running away from rebel owners now belonged "to the public" and would receive their freedom if they loyally supported British war efforts. Meanwhile, the British would provide food, clothing, and adequate wages in exchange for their labor.

Clinton also recognized that the runaways owned by the Loyalists desired freedom just as much as slaves belonging to rebels. However, the British commander, unwilling to anger Americans Loyalists, did not extend an offer of liberty to these slaves. Instead, he promised Loyalists that their runaways would return to their control. Clinton's only compensation to the Loyalists' slaves was a promise that owners would not punish them.

On August 16, Lord Cornwallis defeated the rebel army at Camden and advanced into North Carolina, attracting still more runaways to his force. By September, so many Black Americans were accompanying Cornwallis's army that he and Clinton agreed to appoint John Cruden, a North Carolina Loyalist and merchant from Wilmington, as the commissioner of sequestered estates, to take control of those runaways not needed to directly support the army.

Cruden's mission was to provide the British army with food and supplies produced by runaway slaves on confiscated rebel plantations and other properties. His initial area of responsibility for management of former rebel-owned lands included only South Carolina but expanded into North Carolina a year later. On August 22, Balfour wrote Cruden:

> Whereas it has been represented to me that there are many negroes the property of the enemy within our lines in North Carolina, which are now unemployed; in order therefore to prevent the said negroes from becoming a burden to Government or nuisance to the community I do hereby authorize and empower you to take the same into your custody and possession, and employ them to the best advantage, either sawing lumber for the use of Colonel [James] Moncrieff in making naval stores, or in any other manner that may seem to you most advantageous to Government.

Cruden, working on a commission basis for goods produced, was motivated to consolidate captured rebels' slaves, land, and other assets to provide supplies and services for the British army. His greatest success occurred within Charleston, where he placed Black workers with the army, navy, and the city as drivers, laborers, and hospital workers.

Cruden was not as successful in the countryside. Even though some of the Black Americans were willing workers, many suffered from malnutrition, lack of clothing, and diseases such as smallpox. Although he had no difficulty securing 100 white overseers to manage more than 5,000 Black farmworkers, the captured plantations were run-down and battle-damaged. Before the farms had made any great contributions to the British or to Cruden's pocketbook, the rebels gained the upper hand in the southern campaign, forcing the British to abandon rebel properties in 1781.

Despite Cruden's lack of success on the farms, African Americans provided significant direct support to British commands in the field. Charles Steadman placed them in captured sawmills and gristmills to produce lumber and flour for the army. More important, however, was that he used Black Americans as foragers. Whereas Cruden's plans to produce food and other staples on captured plantations simply took too long, Cornwallis and other field commanders employed a much more direct and faster supply system by sending Black Americans into the countryside to confiscate or steal anything his army needed.

Hundreds of Black foragers seized livestock, grain stores, and crops and delivered them to regimental quartermasters, who also employed Black laborers and clerks. Foraging was not indiscriminate, nor was it unorganized. Cornwallis assigned foragers to units and required them to wear their regiment's markings. He also issued orders to flog any Black forager without identification and "to execute on the spot any negro who is found quitting the line of march in search of plunder" for himself rather than the regiment. On February 5, 1781, Cornwallis issued additional orders to control his foragers, including formally stating that they were not to carry firearms under any circumstances.

Some of the Black foragers and laborers for the British army realized that they had escaped one master only to be placed under the control of another. Some runaways escaped once again to seek freedom deep in the forests or in the Spanish territory of Florida. By early 1781 defections were so common that Cornwallis prohibited his foragers from using horses in their official duties as a means to impede escape attempts.

Most Black Americans, however, believed they could improve their lot by joining the British. Promises of immediate wages for labor and the possibility of postwar freedom encouraged them to leave their rebel master and join the British right up to the final days of the war. By 1781 so many Black Americans were working for the British that the army command in South Carolina issued formal instructions to standardize employment practices, wages, clothing allowances, and accountability.[2] In addition to reflecting the extreme bureaucracy of the British army, the instructions also betray the opinion of the English commanders concerning the worth of women. Paragraphs two and five both note that two women equaled only one male laborer, and females were to receive only half the pay of their male counterparts.

Large numbers of Black laborers and servants accompanied Cornwallis's army as it advanced into North Carolina. In the spring of 1781, Capt. Johann Ewald, a company commander in the Hessian Jager (Light Infantry) Corps, joined the British army as it marched northward. In his journal, Ewald recorded his impressions: "I cannot deny that the enormous train of the army astonished me considerably. Not being accustomed to it as yet, the army looked to me like a migrating Arabian or Tartar horde."

Ewald noted that each officer had several Black servants and, probably with some exaggeration, stated, "Indeed, I can say that each soldier had his negro to carry his food and his bundle."

[2]The complete instructions appear in Appendix L.

Cornwallis continued to employ Black foragers to supply his army during their march toward Yorktown. In addition to food, the foragers secured horses for the British cavalry so successfully that the Americans had difficulty finding sufficient mounts for their soldiers. In a letter to Washington on July 20, 1781, General Lafayette complained about the lack of horses and credited the shortage to Cornwallis's Black foragers. Lafayette concluded, "It is by this means the enemy have so formidable a cavalry."

Black laborers built most of the defenses during the siege of Yorktown and continued to work for the British after the surrender. Little combat occurred following Yorktown, and the rebel Americans' control of the countryside limited foraging. Black workers, however, continued to aid the British as laborers and servants.

Not all of the African American support of the British was typical. In January 1782 the British held an "Ethiopian Ball" to which officers escorted Black women dressed in the finest clothing of the time. An angry American prisoner, Daniel Stevens, wrote to a friend on February 20, "The ball was held at a very capital private house in Charleston and the supper cost not less than 80 pounds sterling, and these tyrants danced with these slaves until four o'clock in the morning."

While the British readily employed African Americans as laborers, skilled workers, foragers, and even dance escorts, they remained reluctant to place muskets in the hands of Black men for fear of slave rebellions. They saw the Black population as a source of cheap labor rather than a pool of potential soldiers. Except for those who joined Lord Dunmore in Virginia in 1775, only a few African Americans served in the British army while the war's main focus remained in the northern states. The regular regiments, recruited and trained in Britain, did not seek Black volunteers. Overall, the British and their American Loyalist allies did not look to Black men to fill their military ranks until the final months of the war, when need for manpower outweighed any other consideration.

Loyalist militia units in the northern states generally followed the same exclusionary regulations practiced by the colonies prior to the Revolution. In the same manner as the rebel militias, however, local commanders often made their own rules and recruited anyone capable of carrying a musket. An article in the November 29, 1776, edition of the *Virginia Gazette* states that one-fourth of the twenty-four Loyalist prisoners captured by a rebel Rhode Island unit in a skirmish near New York were Black.

Rumors were widespread on both sides in July 1776 that the Loyalists were recruiting a regiment of 800 Black men, but there is no evidence that such a unit ever existed. There are verifiable reports from the Battles of Stony Point and Newtown, in New York, in 1779 that the Americans captured several Black soldiers serving in Loyalist units, though nothing supports the contention that they were from a segregated unit.

British commanders tolerated Black men in the Loyalist units, but, for their part, they preferred that Black recruits serve as laborers rather than soldiers. Some senior Loyalist commanders, exercising their own prejudices and seeking British favor, lobbied to exclude Black enlistments. In 1779, Alexander Innes, the British-appointed inspector general of Loyalist forces, issued orders that limited recruitment of Black men and encouraged the discharge of those already in uniform.

After the war shifted to the South and manpower needs increased, both the Loyalists and the British Regular Army relaxed their enlistment standards and accepted limited numbers of Black men as soldiers; even so, the vast majority continued to serve in support positions.

In addition to their own objections to arming Black men, the British and Loyalists knew that sending Black soldiers against the white rebels often made those Americans fight all that much harder. In a letter dated February 20, 1781, to rebel leader Francis Marion, Gen. Thomas Sumter of South Carolina explained that the use of Black soldiers by the British was "sufficient to rouse and fix resentment and detestation of every American who possesses common feelings."

Despite such reactions from the rebels, the British armed Black men to meet their personnel requirements. Once again, need rather than philosophy or regulations ruled their decisions. In Savannah, Augusta, Charleston, and other places threatened by rebel attack, the British relaxed their regulations and filled gaps in their lines with Black soldiers.

In Savannah on October 20, 1779, about 200 Black soldiers assisted in the successful defense of the city against a joint French and rebel American attack. Even the rebels acknowledged the contributions made by the African Americans. A description of the battle in the December 8, 1779, issue of the *New Jersey Gazette* credited the British victory to their strong defenses, manned by 1,700 regular troops and reinforced by "a great number of sailors, marines, militia, and armed blacks." More than a year later, the British muster roll of Savannah defenders mentions a corps of 150 Black infantrymen. Another 200 Black soldiers assisted in the defense of Augusta in June 1781.

Black men also served with Loyalist units in the South and accounted well for themselves. During a skirmish at Hanging Rock, North Carolina, in August 1780, Samuel Burke, a Black Loyalist, killed ten rebel soldiers.

After the fall of Yorktown and the surrender of Cornwallis on October 19, 1781, most combat between the British and Americans ceased. For the next two years the British occupied major ports, including New York, Savannah, and Charleston, not yet willing to totally abandon their colonies. The stalemate caused a few British commanders to express interest in arming large numbers of Black men and resuming active combat. The most vocal of this group was Lord Dunmore, who arrived in Charleston on December 31, 1781, after several years of leisure in England. Dunmore met with John Cruden, and the two devised plans to recruit an army of 10,000 Black men led by Loyalist officers. According to the plan, Black soldiers would act as sergeants and eventually work their way into officer positions. In a letter to General Clinton on February 2, Dunmore modestly offered to act as commander of the Black legion.[3]

Neither Clinton nor officials in London endorsed Dunmore's plan to arm large numbers of Black men, in part because support for the war in general was waning and plans for withdrawal had begun. By June, Dunmore accepted the lack of support for his plan and returned to Great Britain.

From Yorktown until their final withdrawal, the British, always short of manpower, continued, on a limited basis, to arm Black men as the need arose. When the Americans once again threatened to attack Charleston in 1782, British general Alexander Leslie requested permission from his superiors to arm additional Black men. On March 12, Leslie wrote Clinton, "The necessity I shall in all probability be under of putting arms into the hands of negroes . . . appears to me a measure that will soon become indispensably necessary should the war continue to be carried on in this part of America."

Leslie did enlist a small number of Black soldiers, most of whom were assigned to the infantry. However, in at least one instance they served as British cavalrymen. About 100 Black horsemen formed a cavalry unit that had the responsibility of apprehending British deserters on the outskirts of Charleston. The Black cavalrymen encountered the rebels on at least one occasion and, in a brief fight, suffered two casualties in April 1782.

While the British were generally reluctant to arm Black men as redcoats in their regular army throughout the war, their German Hessian[4]

---

[3]Dunmore's letter can be found in Appendix M.
[4]The German mercenaries acquired their name from their first three commanders in chief, von Heister, von Knyphausen, and von Lossberg, who were Hessians.

mercenaries were not. Nearly 30,000 Hessians in the pay of the British fought against the Americans in every major campaign of the war. Always suffering a shortage of replacements for soldiers absent from battle because of wounds, injury, disease, and desertion and sharing few of the Anglo prejudices against Black people, the Germans welcomed African Americans as soldiers, musicians, and support personnel.

Except for being the object of Washington's successful attack against them at Trenton the day after Christmas, 1776, the Hessians have received little notice in the histories of the American Revolution. Even lesser known is their recruitment of Black soldiers and laborers.

For nearly two centuries there was a virtual gap in available information on Black men serving with the Hessians. Only rare diary entries, some brief mention in official reports, and a few obscure prints and paintings verified the roles Black people played in the activities of the German mercenaries. One of the first references to the Germans' enlistment of Black men appears in the official documents of the Hessian headquarters, written by Adj. Gen. Carol Baurmeister. In New York in 1777, Baurmeister recorded that officers in the Erbprinz Regiment were recruiting Black infantrymen to fill vacancies in their units. Capt. Johann Ewald wrote in his journal about the large number of Black personnel accompanying Cornwallis's army as it advanced into North Carolina in 1781. He also noted that he used African Americans as scouts and lookouts in his company.

An engraving from about 1784 by J. C. Muller of a drawing by J. H. Clark, currently in the Anne S. K. Brown Military Collection at Brown University, shows two white pikemen, two white musketeers, and a Black drummer. All of the soldiers in the painting, identified as "Hessian Third Guard Regiment," are in uniform. Still another print in the private collection of Dr. Hans Bleckwenn displays a Hessian squad with a Black drummer and regimental flags.[5]

It was not until 1972 that details about Black participation with the Hessians became widely available. The state archives in Marburg, Germany, began publishing a series of five books over a period of four years about Hessian service in the American Revolution. In *Hessian Troops in the American Revolution (HETRINA)* the archive listed the military records

---

[5]The print is thought to have been made in 1789 in Hessia after the unit had returned to Germany from America. The presence of the drummer of the postwar print supports claims that Black Hessians returned home with their German comrades.

of all soldiers who enlisted in the mercenary force from Hesse-Cassel and Waldeck[6] as well as Black men who joined the unit in the United States.

The *HETRINA* publications list 131 soldiers who are identifiable as Black. Some of these entries are extremely limited and provide only a name common at the time to African Americans, such as Cato or Cuff. Other entries are substantial enough to provide excellent information on the military jobs they performed as well as their race, origin, and age.

Of the 131 Black Hessians listed in *HETRINA*, 94 enlisted as drummers; the others, as infantrymen. The reason so many Black members served as drummers was because few of them had experience with weapons and it was much easier to train them in the simple drum-beating repetitions than the complexities of firearms. Drummers, despite their role as musicians, carried swords and enjoyed the full status of being part of the combat force.

Another factor that influenced the number of drummers was that the Black Hessian volunteers were extremely young, mostly in their teens, with a few as young as ten or eleven. Armies of the period typically employed boys as drummers until they reached adulthood and then transferred them to the ranks of infantrymen. Indeed, the *HETRINA* study lists three Black drummers who later moved to other positions in their regiments.

Additional specific information about Black Hessians, despite the extensive records at Marburg, is neither easy to find nor simple to interpret. Germans at times translated African American names in the records and often omitted race. When they did list race, they referred to the Black Hessians as "neegers," "negroes," or "Moors." Some of the service records included only a first name and the date and place of enlistment.

Typical of the Marburg records of Black Hessians is that of Jack, no last name recorded, who enlisted in "Carolina" for the Fifth Company of the Knyphausen Regiment in August 1779. Sixteen-year-old Jack joined as a drummer and served until April 1782, when rebel Americans captured him and the Hessians subsequently dropped him from his regiment's rolls.

Most of the Black Hessians were former slaves who had escaped from rebel owners. A few, however, were runaways from Loyalists. Several records of their discovery and return to their owners demonstrate that this was a legal issue with the Hessian officers rather than a prejudicial

[6]The work excluded about one-third of the Hessian force—those who enlisted from the provinces of Hesse-Hanau, Anspach-Bayreuth, Anhalt-Zerbst, and Brunswick.

one. Regulations required them to return property to Loyalists, and they did so when necessary.

Hessian officers and enlisted men had extremely limited contact with Black people before their arrival in America, and slavery was little known in the German provinces. Regimental records and the letters and reports by Hessian officers contain no condescending or derogatory references to Black people. Hessian officers and enlisted men alike evaluated Black soldiers by their performance rather than the color of their skin. Black Hessians shared the same duties and responsibilities and received rations and clothing equal to those of their white counterparts.

In addition to their roles as soldiers and support personnel, African Americans also aided the British, Hessians, and Loyalists as spies, messengers, and guides. Like the rebel Americans, the British and their allies relied on their Black members' knowledge of the countryside and abilities to gather and pass along information.

The British did not establish a formal spy network of Black people, but they did listen to them when they shared their knowledge of back roads and waterways, especially useful in the more rural southern states, and provided information about the American armed forces. Runaways who had fled plantations and villages only days earlier could report to the British about the morale of the population as well as the amount of food and other supplies available. Escaped slaves who had recently been working as laborers for the rebel army could provide information on the enemy's numbers, capabilities, and occasionally their intentions.

One of the more successful British uses of Black informants was that of Lord Francis Rawdon, commander of the Royal Forces at Camden, South Carolina. In a dispatch dated November 13, 1780, to Cornwallis, Rawdon reported:

> A negro who came in this afternoon says that he was carried prisoner to Morgan and Washington at Hanging Rock, and escaped from them last night. He reports that in concert with Morgan they were to have attacked this post; and he mentions the point at which the assault was to have been divested, which is indeed the weakest in the line. The dispersion of Morgan's force overturned this plan.

In another dispatch to Cornwallis on December 28, Rawdon made a typical report based on information gleaned from Black informants: "A negro asserts that a party of rebel cavalry under the command of Major Marshall lay last night at Murphy's beyond Lynches Creek; 25 miles from hence."

Information such as this was often too old to be useful. On other occasions, commanders simply did not believe their informants, who they perceived might make up a "good story" in exchange for food, shelter, or other aid in their quest for freedom. British commanders were also aware that at times rebel Americans sent Black people into their camps to deliberately spread rumors and inflate accounts of numbers and capabilities.

During the Revolutionary War, intelligence from spies and espionage was mostly worthless to both sides. Commanders could place little trust in their limited intelligence assets, and both sides were suspicious of any information from nonmilitary sources.

Black guides, however, proved extremely useful to the British in traversing the countryside and inland waterways. Usually, these guides merely eased the movement of the British army by showing them better routes and stream fords, but on occasion they directly influenced the outcome of battles.

In December 1778, British general Archibald Campbell's attack against the rebel defenses of Savannah probably would not have been successful if not for the assistance of Quamino Dolly. In a written report to his superiors on January 16, 1779, Campbell explained that he was preparing for a frontal assault when Dolly entered his camp and volunteered to guide the British through a swamp to attack the American rear. Campbell sent his light infantry with the Black guide, and the combined attacks against the American rear and front yielded a quick and decisive victory.

Black guides also played an important role in the British defense against the American and French efforts to retake Savannah. As the enemy land and naval force closed on the port in September 1779, British forces in South Carolina moved to reinforce the city. Col. John Maitland relied on Black personnel to guide his regiment from Beaufort to Savannah on a route through a swamp along the Dawfuise River, an alternative that allowed the British to bypass the rebel army.

African Americans also served the British navy in the same capacities as they supported the rebels—as pilots along the coast and as seamen aboard British men-of-war and support vessels. Although few in number, Black pilots made significant contributions by guiding British ships through the many channels, rivers, and waterways along the extensive Atlantic coast. Their navigational skills allowed the British ships to avoid American strongpoints as well as shallow waters and reefs that might wreck their vessels. Many of the Black pilots in service to the British were runaways from rebel owners, while some were slaves provided by their Loyalist owners.

British naval captains, always short of manpower, also welcomed Black crewmen. Runaways and freeman volunteered for the British navy and received pay equal to that of white sailors. According to the surviving British ship rosters of the period, nearly every vessel had several sailors listed under a single name and identified as "negro" or "Black."

Little other information about these Black British sailors exists. One of the few accounts is a brief biography of John Marrant written by William Aldridge, "from the lips of Marrant himself," shortly after the war ended. According to Aldridge, Marrant was born free in New York and worked as a musician and preacher before the Revolution. Shortly after the war began, Marrant joined the crew of the British man-of-war *Princess Amelia* and served in the Royal Navy for the next seven years.

In 1781, Marrant participated in a sea battle which he later recalled for Aldridge:

> We had a great number killed and wounded, the deck was running with blood. Six men were killed and three wounded at the same gun with me. My head and face were covered with blood and brains of the slain. I was wounded but did not fall until a quarter of an hour before the engagement ended and was happy during the whole of it.

Black soldiers, sailors, and support personnel served with the British in every major battle and in most skirmishes of the Revolution. Across the lines they often faced other Black soldiers who may have hailed from the same plantation or town, or even the same region of Africa, before their enslavement. While they may have stood on opposite sides, they shared the motivation of seeking personal liberty and attached themselves to whichever army or navy seemed to provide the most potential of freedom.

13

The Fate of the Black Loyalists

THE SURRENDER OF CORNWALLIS TO WASHINGTON at Yorktown meant victory for the Americans and the independence of the United States. With the liberty of their country assured, Americans immediately began reclaiming their possessions seized by the British in accordance with the articles of the Yorktown surrender agreement, which stated that all property owned by Americans in British hands was to be returned.

Recovering land, homes, and businesses, however, was not the victorious Americans' highest priority. Their major concern was their most valuable and mobile property—their slaves. Within hours of the British surrender, American military commanders posted guards along the beaches near Yorktown to prevent runaway slaves from boarding British vessels. On October 25, 1781, only six days after the surrender, Washington issued orders that further limited the movement of African Americans and established a board to determine ownership of Black Americans.

Washington's actions were timely in that the rebels, their French allies, and the British and their Loyalist supporters all looked upon slaves as spoils of war. Owners attempted to reclaim them; French officers, who had acquired Black captives by catching runaways and by confiscating the property of the Loyalists, tried to protect what they now considered their personal property; British commanders wanted either to honor their promise of freedom to runaways who had supported their army or to exploit them for personal financial gain; and profiteers gathered them for resale.

During the months following Yorktown, the British withdrew into the port cities of New York, Charleston, and Savannah. A few Loyalist militia units continued to fight, but for all practical purposes, the Revolution was over. Although defeated, the British were not ready to abandon the colonies, but neither were they strong enough to resume combat. The Americans, while not happy with British soldiers still on their soil, were too weak to mount a military operation to oust the redcoats. They also did not have a navy strong enough to prevent British naval resupply of the ports they controlled.

For more than two years after Yorktown, the British and the Americans remained stalemated. Although they no longer fought for territory, the battle for the possession of Black Americans continued. Large numbers of African Americans lived in New York, Savannah, and Charleston; they included slaves who belonged to Loyalists, slaves whom the British had captured or confiscated from rebels, and slaves who had joined the British in exchange for the promise of freedom.

Of these groups, the fate of slaves belonging to Loyalists was the most straightforward because no one had ever promised freedom to them. After Yorktown, some Loyalists expected the British to evacuate them and their slaves to Florida or the British West Indies so that they could rebuild their fortunes with cheap labor. Other Loyalists opted for evacuation to Canada or Great Britain, where they could not take their slaves, so they sold them to those relocating to areas where slavery remained legal. Some Loyalists even took their slaves across the lines to sell them to the rebels.

Negotiations between the Americans and British following Yorktown were fairly amiable. The British allowed some rebel slaveholders into their sectors to search for their property. Loyalists supported these searches and lobbied for the total return of slaves belonging to the rebels. Their reasons were not benevolent; they were negotiating for recompense for their land, homes, and businesses now in the hands of the victors and did not want to antagonize their enemies. U.S. and state political leaders added their influence by demanding that the British return all rebel-owned slaves, threatening that if they did not, the Americans would make it impossible for British and Loyalist creditors to collect debts within their borders.

Two British officers took the lead in determining the fate of the Black residents in the three occupied cities. Gen. Alexander Leslie, commander of the British forces in the South, and Gen. Guy Carleton, commander of New York and senior royal officer in the Americas, corresponded to determine their course of action.

Carleton, the former commander of British forces in Canada and one of Britain's ablest officers, had assumed his command on May 5, 1782, and immediately began efforts to conclude all hostilities and to make political arrangements for peace. Although he was aware of the issue in general and the ownership of runaway rebel slaves in particular would be at the heart of negotiations, Carleton had a strong sense of responsibility to do what he thought was right. Instead of taking the easy route of appeasing the Americans, Carleton expressed his support for Leslie and re-

fused to surrender any Black Americans who had joined the British in response to their promised freedom.

Leslie, too, considered the British promise of freedom for runaways
an obligation they must honor. On June 27 and August 10, 1782, he
wrote Carleton from his Charleston headquarters to request instructions
for the disposition of Black people. He included his opinion by stating:
"There are many negroes who have been very useful, both at the siege of
Savannah and here. Some of them have been guides, and for their loyalty
have been promised their freedom." Leslie concluded that there would
be no justice if they abandoned the slaves to "the merciless resentment of
their former masters."

While Leslie and Carleton were corresponding, the British garrison
and their Loyalist supporters began evacuating Savannah on July 6.
Leslie, without specific orders from Carleton, ordered the Royal Navy to
transport all who desired to leave the city. By the time the final British
ship left Savannah on July 21, more than 5,000 African Americans had
departed for Jamaica or St. Augustine. Most, however, went as the property of Loyalists and British officers; few gained their freedom.

Some of the Black people in Savannah chose not to join the evacuation and risk re-enslavement. Instead, a group of 300, many of whom had
learned how to use firearms as soldiers in the British army, slipped
through the American lines around the city and established a colony in
the swamps along the Savannah River. This group lived off the land and
occasionally raided nearby farms for several years before Georgia and
South Carolina militiamen destroyed their primary camp at Bear Creek
in May 1786. Those Black Americans not killed in the fight found themselves back in bondage.

Leslie remained in Charleston and continued his correspondence with
his superior in New York. Both Carleton and Leslie recognized the need
to end the war as peacefully as possible and to not jeopardize future business and commerce between the two countries. Leslie contacted South
Carolina governor John Mathews and proposed that the two leaders appoint a board of commissioners to determine the fate of the more than
5,000 African Americans residing within the British lines in Charleston.

Lengthy negotiations between two British commissioners and an
equal number of Americans finally resulted in a compromise signed on
October 10, 1782. The two sides agreed that all slaves belonging to South
Carolinians then in the hands of the British would return to their original owners "as far as is practicable." The agreement, though, did recognize Clinton's offer to Black Americans who willingly joined the British
during the war. Provisions exempted all former rebel slaves who had

crossed the lines to serve in the British army or who had otherwise received a promise of freedom.

The joint commission was to assess the value of each slave exempted from return to his former South Carolinian owner and determine the amount the owner would receive within six months. A final portion of the compromise prohibited punishment of any slaves returned to their owners.

It took only a few days after its signing for the agreement to fall apart. Some British ship captains and unit commanders would not allow the American commissioners to inspect their areas for runaways, and representatives disagreed about the status of Black Americans identified for return to their former owners. Of the first 150 claimed by the Americans, the British disagreed with fully one-half of the cases and refused to turn over the former slaves.

Actions outside of Charleston also influenced the commission's work. Less than a week after the agreement, American forces, which were surrounding the city under the command of Gen. Nathanael Greene, captured three British soldiers at a remote outpost. Leslie immediately sent a letter to the American commissioners demanding the soldiers' release and stated that the entire slave-exchange program would end if the Americans did not return them.

The commissioners forwarded Leslie's letter to Governor Mathews, who, already unhappy with the lack of access given his commissioners to ships and units, replied by writing a letter accusing the British of bad faith. With no additional debate, he concluded his correspondence by declaring the agreement void and ordering his commissioners to return home.

In a November 18 letter to Carleton, Leslie placed the blame for the failure of the agreement on "the behavior of Mr. Mathews the Rebel Governor and General Greene in insulting the outposts at the very time I was acting with the utmost moderation and forbearance."

Even with his "moderation and forbearance," Leslie took no further measures to appease the South Carolinians or to return their slaves. In December the British began evacuating Charleston. By the time their last ship set sail from the port on December 14, more than 5,000 Black residents had left the city. Over half, mostly slaves still in possession of Loyalists, went to British possessions in the West Indies. Another 500, again most still in bondage, went to east Florida.

Many of the former rebel-owned slaves sailed to New York, England, and Nova Scotia and to the freedom promised them by Clinton's original proclamation. Not all were so fortunate. Some British commanders took as many as 800 and placed them on ships bound for the West Indies, where they either sold them to Spanish plantation owners or put them to work on British-owned properties.

Leslie apparently played no role in this deception. Lt. Col. James Moncrieff, a British engineer who had designed and built the Savannah fortifications that saved the city from the rebels and who had later assumed responsibility for Charleston's defenses, was the likely leader of the larceny. Although there is no absolute proof of Moncrieff s taking the Black participants and returning them to slavery, he did own large properties in the West Indies, where the slave population markedly increased shortly after the Charleston evacuation.

With Savannah and Charleston now back in American hands, only New York remained a holdout of British occupation. Even before Leslie sailed from Charleston, the Americans and the British were working on a peace document to formally end hostilities. On November 30, 1782, the British and Americans signed a Provisional Peace Agreement. Article VII of the document stipulated:

> All hostilities both by sea and land shall henceforth cease, all prisoners on both sides shall be set at liberty, and His Britannic Majesty shall with all convenient speed and without causing any destruction or carrying away any negroes or other property of the American inhabitants withdraw all his armies, garrisons, and fleets, from the said United States.

Contents of the agreement spread quickly, and slaveholders flocked to New York to repossess runaways who had joined the British. Rumors also circulated within the city that officials would return all slaves to their owners.

Boston King, who had escaped from a plantation owned by Richard Waring, near Charleston, South Carolina, to join the British army and then sought their protection in New York, later wrote in his memoirs of the reaction of the city's African Americans to the rumors that they would be turned over to their former owners: "This dreadful rumor filled us with inexpressible anguish and terror." King described the panic that set in, "especially when we saw our old masters coming from Virginia, North Carolina, and other parts, and seizing upon their slaves in the streets of New York, or even dragging them out of their beds."

Carleton quickly put a stop to attempts by American owners to repossess their slaves when he announced his interpretation of Article VII of the Provisional Peace Agreement. According to Carleton, all previously rebel-owned Black Americans who had accepted Clinton's offer were free. The general's statement stopped the seizing of Black people in New

York, but it did not end the disagreement between the Americans and the British.

The two sides remained stalemated during the winter of 1782–1783. Still lacking a formal peace agreement, Carleton continued to occupy New York. The Americans, although unwilling to resume combat to purge the British from their shores, maintained a siege of the city and increased their demands for the return of their escaped slaves.

On April 15, 1783, Congress instructed General Washington to expedite the return of former slaves and other property held by the British. Washington wrote Carleton on April 22 requesting a meeting to resolve property issues. Carleton, still standing by his belief that it was morally wrong to break the promise of freedom made to runaway slaves, reluctantly agreed to the meeting in a letter to Washington on April 24. His response showed not only his hesitation but also respect for the American commander when he concluded, "I cannot decline the personal interview by your Excellency."

Carleton and Washington met at Orangetown, on the Hudson River, on May 6.[1] The British commander began by restating that he had a responsibility to honor Clinton's Philipsburg Proclamation, which promised freedom to slaves owned by rebels who crossed the lines. Carleton stated that he did not intend to return slaves who had sought British protection prior to the Provisional Peace Agreement of the previous November 30. He did agree, however, to return those slaves who had joined the British after that date or whom the British had confiscated from their owners.

Carleton's honorable stance was also audacious. He based his actions on his conscience rather than official policy. Clinton's proclamation had no legal sanction in either the United States or in Great Britain. The Americans had won the war, and their laws, not Britain's, now governed the United States. Nevertheless, Carleton remained firm and told Washington that delivering the runaways to their former owners would be placing them in danger of execution or extreme punishment, and he concluded that their return "would be a dishonorable violation of the public faith pledged to the negroes in the Proclamation."

Carleton's only concession regarding these slaves was to agree to maintain a registry of all freed Black Americans evacuated from New York, including names, descriptions, former owners, and the names and destinations of the vessels on which they sailed. If future agreements or

---

[1]The official report of the meeting appears in Appendix N.

treaties determined these actions to be invalid, then the list of names would be available to compensate owners for the loss of their property.

Washington, who had several runaway slaves of his own living in New York, openly expressed his dissatisfaction, saying that Carleton was not adhering to the spirit of the Provisional Peace Agreement and voicing his doubts as to the accuracy of the proposed "Book of Negroes."

Despite his anger, Washington had neither the military or the political power to challenge the British commander's decision. All he could do was propose a second meeting the next day in hopes of gaining a better resolution, but Carleton became ill, and the meeting never took place. It is doubtful that a second meeting would have changed anything had it occurred. Washington and his staff recognized Carleton's steadfastness in fulfilling what he considered his obligation to the Black Americans who served the British. Only a few hours after their first meeting, Washington wrote to Benjamin Harrison, "I have discovered enough to convince me that the slaves which have absconded from their masters will never be restored."

Carleton honored his request to create a registry of escaped slaves. From May through November, British commissioners, with American observers, held meetings every Wednesday from ten in the morning until two in the afternoon at the Queen's Head Tavern on the corner of Pearl and Broad Streets in lower Manhattan. They registered former slaves and recorded details of their enslavement, escape, and service to the British.

Those whose claims stood up to the scrutiny of the board of commissioners received a certificate entitling them to transport out of New York. The certificates, signed by Brig. Gen. Samuel Birch, stated:

> This is to certify to whomever it may concern that the bearer hereof, a negro, resorted to the British lines, in consequence of the Proclamations of Sir William Howe, and Sir Henry Clinton, late Commanders-in-Chiefs in America; and that the said negro has hereby his Excellency Sir Guy Carleton's permission to go to Nova Scotia, or wherever else he may think proper.

By the time the Book of Negroes closed, it contained the names of 1,336 men, 914 women, and 750 children who had received certificates signed by General Birch. The British offered the registrants transport to Nova Scotia, Florida, or the West Indies. None expressed any interest in traveling south, where they feared a return to slavery; all opted for resettlement in Nova Scotia.

On September 3, 1783, the United States and Great Britain signed the

Treaty of Paris, which formally ended the Revolution. Under terms of the agreement, the British recognized the independence of the United States and granted to the new country generous boundaries reaching west to the Mississippi River, north to the Great Lakes, and south to Florida. The Americans agreed to cease any persecution of Loyalists and to make efforts to return confiscated property. They also agreed to pay pre-war debts owed to the British and the Loyalists.

The only reference to African Americans in the Treaty of Paris was the inclusion of the clause from the Provisional Peace Agreement about the British not "carrying away any negroes or other property of American inhabitants." Carleton[2] began evacuating New York as soon as he received word about the treaty signing. In accordance with their promises, the British provided transport for the 3,000 former slaves registered in the Book of Negroes. Several hundred other runaway slaves not registered also departed aboard private vessels.

Not all the Black residents evacuated New York. Some became property of the victorious Americans when their Loyalist owners sold them. Several hundred sick, disabled, and aged slaves belonging to Loyalists were simply left behind.

On November 21, Washington and his army crossed into Manhattan and occupied Harlem Heights. The last British troops, Loyalists, and freed Black people sailed from the harbor on the morning of the twenty-fifth, and the American army triumphantly marched into the city. The Revolution was finally over.

Just how many Black Americans left the United States under British protection during the war is difficult to estimate. Other than the Book of Negroes maintained by Carleton in New York, the British kept no comprehensive records, and American inspectors had limited access to evacuation vessels that sailed from New York, Charleston, and Savannah. Estimates put the number of Black people evacuated from the three ports at about 15,000. This number in itself is probably low because Loyalists unofficially removed their slaves to the West Indies and other destinations throughout the war. In all likelihood no fewer than 30,000 and

[2]In a war in which African Americans had few allies to support their rights and promote their freedom, Carleton is deserving of high praise. Without his firm stance demanding that Britain honor its promises of freedom to rebel-owned slaves who crossed the lines, it is doubtful if many would have achieved their liberty. Carleton sailed for London from New York. He returned to Canada as the governor of Quebec in 1786 and retired to England ten years later. He died there on November 10, 1808.

no more than 50,000 Black people left the United States during the American Revolution.

Even these numbers are mostly meaningless because the vast majority of Black Americans evacuated by the British and Loyalists remained slaves and the life of bondage was no better in Florida or the West Indies than in New England or the South. In fact, the transfer was worse for most because it separated some slave families permanently.

The future of Black people freed by the British depended on where those African Americans located after the war. The only significant number of Black people freed by Great Britain as a result of the Revolution were the 3,000 former rebel-owned slaves evacuated from New York to Nova Scotia. About 1,000 other African Americans freed in Savannah and Charleston relocated to east Florida and remained there when the British ceded the territory to Spain in September 1783. About 200 or so former slaves made their way to London and freedom, while more than 100 gained liberty by returning to Europe with the Hessian regiments. Several hundred more relocated to the Bahamas and the West Indies, but they always faced the danger of seizure and re-enslavement.

Only the 3,000 that accepted passage to Nova Scotia, many of whom had accompanied the British to New York from Savannah and Charleston, remained a traceable group. They sailed from New York with the joyous promise of "freedom and a farm," only to soon discover that white Loyalists had already claimed all the land. While they were, in fact, free, the African Americans found that they had no choice but to work at extremely low wages for the landholding Loyalists on the cold, windswept, shallow soil that was not nearly as fertile or productive as that of the farms in the United States. Many of the former slaves lived in Birchtown, a shanty village named in honor of the British general who signed their certificates of freedom in New York. Although British officials provided food and some other supplies, many of the Black residents had to struggle against starvation and disease.

Several African American leaders arose in Nova Scotia to establish churches and to lobby for the promised farms. One of the most active was Thomas Peters, a former slave who had served as a British soldier. After many years of unsuccessful attempts to secure the promised farmland for himself and others, Peters sailed to England to present his case to higher authorities. Abolition leaders welcomed Peters to London and introduced him to the leaders of the "back to Africa movement."

Because Black people living in England after the Revolution were faring no better than those in Nova Scotia—enduring unemployment, poverty, and racism—abolitionist supporters had begun measures in 1786 to relocate Black people from England to Sierra Leone, a defunct Crown colony on Africa's west coast where a group of bankers and politicians had taken control. With personal profit and some degree of benevolence as motives, the group had formed the Sierra Leone Company.

With financial support from the British government, the company had begun transferring Black people and poor white people to Sierra Leone. By the time Peters arrived in London, the project was in jeopardy primarily because of the lack of available immigrants. Peters rushed back to Nova Scotia to recruit settlers for Sierra Leone. With dreams of wealth and their own independent country, nearly half of the Black population volunteered for the venture. On January 15, 1792, a fleet of fifteen ships carrying 1,193 Black people departed from Halifax Harbor for West Africa.

Sierra Leone proved much better for the former slaves. Its climate, land, and resources produced wealth for those who worked hard. It was not utopia, however. Black people from Nova Scotia divided into rival camps based primarily on religious affiliations. These groups also experienced some difficulties in getting along with the original Black settlers from England. Peters, whom many believed would become the first head of state of an independent Sierra Leone, was accused of theft and died in disgrace soon afterward.

Despite their difficulties, the Black occupants from Nova Scotia and England prospered, and the colony thrived. The Nova Scotians, as the majority, took the lead in administering the colony. Many became wealthy, some facing ridicule for their snobbery and the low wages they paid native African workers on their farms. The British were happy with the success of the Sierra Leone Company but were not willing to surrender the territory. In 1808 the British reclaimed the country as a Crown colony and levied taxes on its residents.

Today the descendants of slaves freed by the British from their rebel owners still live in Nova Scotia and Sierra Leone. This is because, even in defeat, the British—at the insistence of Carleton—fulfilled their promise of freedom. However, the 5,000 Black Americans who gained their freedom by joining the British were the exceptions to the rule of slavery in America, and they accounted for only 1 percent of the total enslaved Black people in the thirteen former colonies.

14

Abolition and the Revolution

THE ISSUE OF SLAVERY POLARIZED THE AMERICAN PEOPLE from the time the first slaves stepped ashore in Virginia until the practice ended with the Civil War. The earliest opponents voiced their concerns about human bondage based on religious beliefs and, by the time the Revolutionary War began, the objections had expanded to include the concept of inalienable rights of all humans. The movement to end slavery increased in momentum when Americans revolted against the British to secure independence for the newly declared United States. African Americans and their white supporters believed that liberty for the new nation should also mean freedom for all its inhabitants.

The difficulty with this argument was that the majority of white Americans saw the Revolution not as just a cause for political independence from Great Britain but, more important, as an opportunity for economic freedom. A critical motivator behind forming a new country was the potential for wealth from agriculture, industry, shipping, trade, and other occupations once British tariffs and taxes no longer existed. Essential to this nation and wealth building was cheap labor, and many colonists, especially in the agricultural South, believed that their own and their states' fortunes depended on the ownership and trade of Black slaves.

African Americans learned early on in the Revolution that the pursuit of national liberty did not include freedom for them and that slavery would not end with the war regardless of the outcome. Black Americans did not decide to support the rebels or the British based on political agendas but rather on which offered the best chance for individual freedom.

The Revolution provided the first large-scale opportunity for slaves to escape bondage, but it was not the first time they had tried. Despite the strict slave codes that denied Black people the right to publicly assemble, own weapons, or move freely about the countryside, African Americans had revolted against their white owners in New York, South Carolina, and other colonies prior to the outbreak of the Revolution.[1]

Black Americans were not alone in their fight for freedom. Some white religious and social leaders opposed slavery and initiated the abolitionist movement.[2] While the majority of white Americans supported slavery based on economic need and the supposed inferiority of the Black race, the abolitionist minority developed substantive arguments against the continuance of the practice.

The "Germantown Protest," published by Pennsylvania Quakers in 1688 as the first American antislavery document, opposed the practice because it violated their religious beliefs about the "basic rights of man." Samuel Sewell argued in his 1770 essay "The Selling of Joseph" that slavery was evil and detrimental to the white owners' morality. At about the same time, Quaker schoolmaster Anthony Benezet began republishing and distributing all material against slavery he could gather while at the same time writing to American and European leaders seeking support to end the practice. Benezet also strongly supported educating Black Americans to prepare them for freedom and founded a school in Philadelphia in 1770 to do so.

One of Benezet's early converts was Benjamin Rush, a prominent Philadelphia physician. Rush noted in a letter on May 1, 1773, to English Quaker Granville Sharp that only three years earlier few Americans had opposed slavery but that of late "a spirit of humanity and religion begins to awaken, in several of the colonies in favor of the poor negroes."

Rush demonstrated his support for emancipation financially as well as in his writings. He provided free medical services for indigent Black people and refused a lucrative offer to move to Charleston, South Carolina, because of the number of slaves in the city. In early 1775, Rush became one of the founders of the Society for the Relief of Free Negroes Unlawfully Held in Bondage. The society, formed in Philadelphia's Sun Tavern, was the first organization that included multiple religious and other groups that supported African Americans.

The Revolution's most eloquent spokesman arrived in the colonies from England in late 1774 and brought with him an affection for liberty

[1]Pre-Revolution slavery issues are covered in chapters 2 and 3. An example of early slave codes can be found in Appendix B.
[2]While the terms abolition and abolitionist were not common until shortly after the Revolution concluded, they now indicate any antislavery movement.

that had no race limitations. Thomas Paine is most famous for his 1776 *The American Crisis*, in which he wrote, "These are the times that try men's souls. The summer soldier and the sunshine patriot will, in this crisis, shrink from the service to their country; but he that stands it now deserves the love and thanks of man and woman."

Paine honored his personal duty and shouldered a musket in Washington's army. He was equally as steadfast in standing up for the rights of African Americans. On March 8, 1775, he published an article in the *Postscript to the Pennsylvania Journal and Weekly Advertiser* entitled "African Slavery in America." Paine, who a month later helped form the abolitionist society at the Sun Tavern, began his essay: "That some desperate wretches should be willing to steal and enslave men by violence and murder for gain, is rather lamentable than strange. But that many civilized, nay, Christian people should approve, and be concerned in the savage practice, is surprising."

Black Americans did not stand idly by while white abolitionists lobbied to end slavery. They continued to file court cases seeking individual freedom, and Black men, such as Felix Holbrook, in Massachusetts in 1773, petitioned colonial legislatures to take measures to end slavery altogether.

Black authors also contributed articles and letters to newspaper editors that expounded "liberty for all." In the February 10, 1774, edition of the *Massachusetts Spy* a writer identified only as "A Son of Africa" wrote of his joy in "that there is in this and the neighboring provinces such a spirit for liberty." He added that unfortunately the rays of freedom were being overshadowed by "a cloud" of slavery. He then asked, "Are not your hearts also hard, when you hold men in slavery who are entitled to liberty by the law of nature, equal as yourselves?"

When the first shots of the Revolution rang out at Lexington and Concord, the antislavery faction was small but unanimous about why an independent United States should not allow the ownership of human beings. These arguments, which would remain the mainstay of the abolition movements for the next three-quarters of a century, included multiple reasons to end slavery: religious and moral; social and political; and economic, emotional, philosophical, and racial.

The abolitionists proclaimed that there is a human brotherhood among all races before God and that slavery severely compromised the owner's morality. They also argued that the Scriptures did not warrant slavery and denied claims of some slaveholders that they were providing religion to pagans. In addition, the abolitionists emphasized that slavery produced a social ill in that the threat of an uprising was always possible and no that one denying freedom to others could truly enjoy it themselves.

Abolitionists also questioned the economic advantages of slavery and noted that the states with the most slaves had the least amount of industry. They pointed out that slaves, owned by the wealthy, took jobs away from poor whites. Abolitionists furthermore denounced the theories of racial inferiority and concluded that slavery was both cruel and unjust, stripping away from Black people certain inalienable rights that belonged to all humans.

The antislavery movement and the incongruity of trading in slaves while promoting independence for the country prompted the Continental Congress to take action. In October 1774, Congress discontinued the importation of slaves effective December 1. On April 6, 1776, Congress reaffirmed this stance with legislation which read: "That no slave be imported into any of the thirteen united colonies."

Representatives of the southern states joined those from the northern and middle regions in passing this bill. Their reasons, however, were not humanitarian but rather an expedient, temporary wartime measure. It is also noteworthy that by 1776 the 500,000 African Americans in the United States were reproducing at a rate that steadily increased their population, thus reducing the need for additional imports. Still another factor in passing the law was that backers knew that legislation would not stop the many ships that continued to smuggle slaves into the colonies.

The far greater impediment to bringing more slaves into the United States was the war itself. Warships and privateers of both sides preyed on unarmed merchant and slave ships flying the opposition's flag in order to capture and sell their cargoes as prizes for personal gain.

The end, or at least the slowing, of the importation of new slaves placed the focus on the emancipation of those already held in bondage in the former colonies. Slaves and abolitionists shared the revolutionary zeal for liberty and independence of the United States in hopes that individual freedom would follow. Although the Declaration of Independence made no mention of ending slavery, the proclamation that "all men are created equal" provided encouragement.

As the war progressed, more Americans realized the inconsistency of preserving slavery while seeking national independence. Some state governments took steps to end, or at least limit, slavery. These actions, however, continued to be the result of slavery economics rather than moral, humanitarian, or ideological reasoning. The northern states, which took the lead and did the most to end slavery within their borders, also had the smallest Black population and received the least monetary gain from slavery enterprises. The middle states generally avoided decisive stances on slavery. In the South, where in some states there were more Black slaves than free whites and where the tobacco, rice, and cotton industries depended on slave labor, whites viewed abolitionists as a worse enemy than the British or the Loyalists.

Despite the support for abolition in New England, the war stalled any actions to free the slaves. The battles of the Revolution, which often directly threatened state capitals and leaders, precluded most actions not directly involved in the continuation of the fight and the country.

Not everyone in New England favored emancipation. While the southern plantation system that produced fortunes was not practical in the North, slaves did provide valuable economic services for their owners as skilled and unskilled workers. Many New Englanders valued their slaves and benefitted economically from their labor. They were not interested in freeing their valuable property; in fact, the price of slaves continued to increase in New England throughout the war.

The majority of New Englanders, however, supported abolition and enacted legislation ending slavery within their borders. That is not to say, however, that the process took place quickly or completely.

Vermont took the first action to end slavery when its representatives met in June 1777 to adopt a constitution which declared:

All men are born equally free and independent Therefore, no male person born in this country or brought from over the sea, ought to be holden by law to serve any person as a servant, slave, or apprentice after he arrives to the age of twenty-one years, nor female in like manner after she arrives to the age of eighteen years, unless they are bound by their own consent after they arrive to such age, or bound by law for the payment of debts, damages, fines, cost or the like.

In 1786, Vermont again confirmed that "by the Constitution of this state the idea of slavery is expressly and totally exploded by our free government." Unfortunately, the Vermont Constitution was more symbolic than significant. Their constitution had no legal standing in that the state of Vermont did not exist. Legally, it was still a part of New York, which blocked its efforts to become the fourteenth state until 1791, based partly on its position on slavery. Furthermore, at no time during Vermont's movement to declare itself a state did it have more than fifty Black residents.

Pennsylvania Quakers, who led the prewar abolitionary movement, continued their efforts during the Revolution, but they did not achieve immediate success. Bills to end slavery brought before the Pennsylvania legislature in 1778 and 1779 met with defeat. After much debate, the assembly finally passed an "Act for the Gradual Abolition of Slavery" on March 1, 1780, providing Pennsylvania the distinction of being the first state to pass a law to put an end to slavery.

The 1780 act did not, however, immediately free all slaves in Pennsylvania. As its title noted, emancipation was to be gradual in that no future child "born a slave" would remain one; those currently in bondage would remain so. It was not until eight years later when the legislature passed another act, on March 29, 1788, that the state legally ended the slave trade. The act also provided measures to prevent owners from moving pregnant slaves farther south so that they could sell rather than free their offspring. These provisions proved successful because the number of slaves in the state dropped from 4,000 in 1790 to 200 in 1820.

The Massachusetts legislature made its first efforts to end slavery in June 1777 when it drafted a bill "preventing the practice of holding persons in slavery." The draft immediately created such controversy that the legislature appointed a committee to study whether the bill might cause. difficulties in relations with other states. After brief consideration by the committee, the Massachusetts legislature ordered the bill "to lie"—a move which placed it aside, with no action taken.

Massachusetts legislator and future U.S. president John Adams explained the action in a letter to his friend James Warren on June 22:

> We have had a bill before us for freeing the negroes, which is ordered to lie, lest if passed into an Act it should have a bad effect on the Union of the Colonies. A letter to Congress on the subject was proposed and reported, but I endeavored to divert that, supposing it would embarrass and perhaps be attended with worse consequences than passing the Act.

Two weeks later, Adams again wrote Warren: "The bill for freeing the negroes, I hope will sleep for a time. We have causes enough of jealousy, discord, and division, and this bill will certainly add to the number."

Three years later, the Massachusetts legislature adopted its constitution of 1780, which stated that "all men are born free and equal," but the representatives did not intend for the clause to apply to Black slaves. In April 1781 a series of court cases took place in which runaway slave Quock Walker sued his owner Nathaniel Jennison for his freedom. After two years and numerous trials and hearings, Massachusetts chief justice

William Cushing ruled in favor of Walker and referred to the Revolution and the recent state constitution when he stated:

> Sentiments more favorable to the natural rights of mankind . . . have prevailed since the glorious struggle for our rights began. And these sentiments led the framers of our constitution of government to declare that all men are born free and equal; and that every subject is entitled to liberty. In short, without resorting to implications in constructing the constitution, slavery is in my judgement as effectively abolished as it can be by granting the rights and privileges wholly incompatible and repugnant to its existence. The court are therefore fully of the opinion that perpetual servitude can no longer be tolerated.

The Walker decision did not immediately end slavery in Massachusetts. Slaves continued to be bought and sold for several more years, but additional court cases continued to find in favor of emancipation. Some slaves merely left their owners to seek life and employment elsewhere when they became aware that the courts would not return them to their owners. In some cases, owners shipped their slaves out of state and sold them farther south. By the time of the census of 1790, Massachusetts listed no slaves as residents.

In New Hampshire a group of nineteen slaves petitioned the state legislature in 1780 for their freedom. Their argument was that slave traders had forcibly removed them from their native Africa, where they had been born free, and brought them to a country where they were "compelled to drag on their lives in miserable servitude." Their petition urged the granting of the men's emancipation so "that the name of slave may not be heard in a land gloriously contending for the sweets of freedom." It further concluded with the statements that "the God of nature gave them their life and freedom" and "that freedom is an inherent right of the human species."

The New Hampshire assembly debated the petition in two separate sessions but on June 9 postponed the action "to a more convenient opportunity." Apparently the opportunity for official action remained inconvenient for some time. It was not until 1857 that New Hampshire formally banned slavery within its borders. In the meantime, the state legislature adopted a constitution in 1783 which included a bill of rights that many interpreted as ending slavery. By 1790 there were only 150 slaves in the state; the number had decreased to 8 by the census of 1800.

A group of slaves petitioned the Connecticut legislature the same year, as did their fellow Black people in New Hampshire. The Connecticut slaves wrote:

> Although our skins are different in color, from those whom we serve, yet reason and revelation join to declare, that we are all creatures of that God, who made of one blood, and kindred, all the nations of the Earth; we perceive by our own reflection, that we are endowed with the same facilities with our masters, and there is nothing that leads us to believe, or suspicion, that we are more obliged to serve them, than they us.

After brief debate, the Connecticut legislature "resolved in the negative" the petition. The Connecticut legislature received several other bills to end slavery during the war but responded negatively to each. It was not until January 1784 that the legislature adopted a statue that mandated that all children born after the first of March of an enslaved mother would become free on their twenty-fifth birthday. In 1797 the legislature reduced the age to the twenty-first birthday.

Quakers in Rhode Island began to lobby to end slavery in 1775, shortly after the Revolution began. The state's legislature took no action, explaining in 1779 that the time was not yet "favorable" for abolition. The service of the Rhode Island Black Regiment in the war persuaded some that the time had become more favorable. An even larger influence was the economic decision by the state's farmers to use hired rather than slave labor. By 1784 a bill that declared slavery a violation of the rights and privileges of African Americans and provided for the gradual emancipation of all slaves born after the first of March passed with little opposition. The bill also permitted owners to free their slaves, with no future financial responsibility for their care. The nearly 4,000 slaves in the state at the time of the legislation decreased to less than 1,000 by 1790.

In New York antislavery representatives obtained a clear majority in the state's legislature in 1777 and adopted a policy statement that "every human being who breathes the air of the state shall enjoy the privileges of a freeman." The resolution, which passed by a vote of thirty-one to five, took no direct action to end slavery but urged future legislative sessions "to take the most effective measures consistent with public safety for the abolishing of domestic slavery."

Apparently, the 1777 legislature, as well as those for the next eight years, did not believe that ending slavery was yet "consistent with public safety." Except to vote in 1781 to free slaves who were serving in the military, the New York legislature took no further action until 1785, two years after the last British soldiers had sailed for England.

The New York legislature of 1785 eventually adopted a plan of gradual emancipation that freed future children born of slave mothers. Much of the pressure for this action came from the New York Manumission Society, formed in January 1785. Interestingly, while the society supported ending slavery, many of its members were slaveholders. It was not until 1809 that the society amended its constitution to expel members who owned slaves.

Despite its flaws, the New York resolution reduced the number of slaves in the state—albeit gradually. Its total of more than 20,000 slaves, over 10 percent of the state's entire population during the decade before the Revolution, remained about the same through 1790. The number finally began to decline to 15,000 in 1810, 11,000 in 1820, and less than 100 in 1830. Once again, however, as in the other northern states that "freed" their slaves, there is no record of how many gained their freedom as opposed to how many were sold to new owners in the South. As many as half of them may have remained enslaved, not having gained the freedom promised by the state.

Quakers in New Jersey, led by John Cooper of Trenton, began a concentrated effort to end slavery in their state as soon as the Continental Congress adopted the Declaration of Independence. In 1778, Gov. William Livingston joined the abolitionists and called on the New Jersey legislature to recognize that slavery was "utterly inconsistent with the principles of Christianity and humanity; and in Americans who have almost idolized liberty, peculiarly odious and disgraceful."

The New Jersey legislature did not heed the recommendations of their governor. Over the next several years, the only action they took regarding slavery was to pass several laws that freed a few individual slaves confiscated from Loyalists.

Cooper continued to lobby for abolition directly with the legislators and through the press. In the September 20, 1780, edition of the *New Jersey Gazette*, he wrote:

> While we are spilling our blood and exhausting our treasures in defense of our own liberty, it would not perhaps be amiss to turn our eyes toward those of our fellowmen who are now groaning in bondage under us. We say, "all men are equally entitled to liberty, the pursuit of happiness;" but are we willing to grant this liberty to all men? If after we have made such a declaration to the world, we continue to hold our fellow creatures in slavery, our words must rise up in judgement against us; and by the breath of our own mouths we must stand condemned.

Cooper's eloquence did not sway the legislators, many of whom owned slaves themselves. In 1783, 1785, and 1794, bills to provide gradual freedom failed. New Jersey did not pass a law to begin freeing its slaves until 1804, twenty-eight years after the Declaration of Independence. Even this late action had its limitations. Although it proclaimed that all African American children born after July 4, 1804, in the state would be free, they were "bound to serve" their mothers' owners until age twenty-five if a male and until age twenty-one if female.

The 1790 census reported that New Jersey had 11,432 Black residents, only 220 of whom were free. The number of slaves in the state actually rose for the next twenty years, and their numbers did not substantially decrease until the 1820s. In 1860 the census noted that owners still denied eighteen slaves their liberty in New Jersey.

Other states also had their champions of abolition. John Dickson, the head of the Delaware legislature, freed six of his own slaves in 1781 and encouraged the assembly to adopt a gradual emancipation law. His efforts with his peers were fruitless.

An African American, identified as "Vox Africanorum," wrote in the *Maryland Gazette* on May 15, 1783:

> Liberty is our claim, reverence for our Great Creator, principles of humanity and the dictates of common sense, all convince us, that we have an indubitable right to liberty. Though our bodies differ in color from yours; yet our souls are similar in a desire for freedom. Disparity in color, we conceive, can never constitute a disparity in rights.

In Virginia, St. George Tucker, a William and Mary law professor, sent his state legislature a pamphlet entitled *A Dissertation on Slavery*. Tucker proposed a gradual emancipation and declared, "While America has been the land of promise to Europeans, and their descendants, it has been a vale of tears to millions of the wretched sons of Africa."

Tucker, aware that his proposal would not be well received, made efforts to placate his fellow southerners. While he recommended a plan of gradual freedom, he included provisions that prevented free Black people from holding public office, owning land, or bearing arms. Although Tucker made his proposal in 1795, more than a decade after the conclusion of the Revolution, neither house of the Virginia legislature acted upon it.

Throughout the South, whites continued to deny Black residents liberty. The prosperity of the states and of individuals continued to be based on slave labor. It would take nearly a century after the Declaration of Independence and another war, this time American against American, to finally emancipate all slaves in the United States.

While many Black Americans pursued their individual freedom in exchange for military service in the Revolution as well as assisting in the abolitionary movement, other African Americans directly participated in the advancement of science, literature, religion, trade, arts, and all other economic and social aspects of the new nation. Black Americans during the Revolution and the postwar period proved that they could contribute not only on the battlefield but also to social and technical innovations. When provided equal opportunity, African Americans clearly demonstrated that they could rise above slavery and become equal partners in the future of the United States.

Many of their accomplishments during and after the Revolution were continuations of achievements begun during the colonial period. Throughout the war, Phillis Wheatley, widely read on both sides of the Atlantic Ocean, continued to write and publish her poetry, much of which praised liberty and condemned tyranny. When she died at the young age of thirty-one, the *Massachusetts Centennial* stated in her obituary on December 8, 1784, that she was "known to the literary world by her celebrated miscellaneous poems."

Benjamin Banneker, born a slave in Maryland in 1731, designed and built, at age twenty-two, a wooden clock that was one of the first mechanical timepieces wholly made in America. As a mathematician and astronomer, respected both in the United States and Europe, Banneker began publishing a series of six almanacs in 1791. These almanacs included weather and astronomical information as well as studies on a wide range of subjects, such as beekeeping, insect reproduction, and the ability of Black people to perform complex intellectual tasks. Also in 1791, Banneker served as a member of the commission that surveyed and laid out the plan for the capital in Washington, D.C.

Another Black man, Jean Baptiste Point du Sable, supported the Revolution by expanding American claims westward. Born free in Haiti, du Sable established a trading post at the eventual site of Chicago, Illinois, in the early 1770s. Du Sable paid a price for supporting American independence. In July 1779, British forces arrested him, confiscated his trading goods, and destroyed several of his stores along Lake Michigan when he refused to pledge his loyalty to the Crown. After the war, du Sable returned to Chicago, where he was instrumental in the town's development over the next two decades.

Black businessmen also proved their abilities and made their fortunes during this period. Paul Cuffe, born free in Massachusetts, at age twenty-one petitioned his state's legislature in February 1780 for relief from paying property and poll taxes because he did not receive the same benefits and privileges as whites. Although Cuffe lost his court case, he was not defeated. Over the next three decades he assembled a fleet of twenty-five trading vessels and became a prosperous businessman. He built schools for Black children and paid for their teachers. Cuffe also became an advocate of the "back to Africa" movement.

Black sailor James Forten returned to Philadelphia after his service aboard an American privateer and capture by the British to work in a sail-making shop. He worked his way up to foreman of the Black and white workers and eventually took over the shop's ownership. His invention of a manufacturing process produced cheaper, better sails for military and merchant vessels and made him a fortune. Forten later assisted in the organization of Black Americans to defend Philadelphia in the War of 1812 and actively campaigned for equal rights until his death in 1842.

African Americans also took the lead in establishing religious organizations during and immediately after the Revolution. Lemuel Haynes, born a slave in Connecticut in 1753, grew up as the property of a church deacon who provided the young man an education. Haynes frequently read sermons to the white congregation before interrupting his religious training to participate as a soldier in the Revolution, including service in the Battle of Ticonderoga in 1775.

In 1785, Haynes completed his religious training and became the first Black minister of the Congregational church in America. He continued to preach to both white and Black people and served for thirty years as the pastor of the white Congregational church in Rutland, Vermont. His sermons were published and widely distributed even after his death in 1833.

Other Black clergymen believed in the necessity for separate places for Black Christians to worship and began their organizational efforts during the war. Richard Allen and Absalom Jones broke away from the white St. George's Methodist Episcopal Church in Philadelphia to form the Free African Society in 1787. This Black church eventually evolved into the St. Thomas African Episcopal Church and the Bethel African Methodist Church.

African American leaders in the South also formed Black churches. David George led the way by organizing the first Black Baptist church in America in Silver Bluff, South Carolina, in 1775. In 1778, George Liele began a Baptist church in British-occupied Savannah, Georgia. Andrew

Bryan, baptized by Liele, took over the leadership of the Black church in Georgia after the war.

Fraternal organizations, which would play an important role in the advancement of African Americans also had their beginnings during the Revolution. Prince Hall, born free in Barbados, came to America in 1765 to become a Boston property owner and religious leader. Two months before the Revolution began, British military personnel initiated Hall and fourteen other "free men of color" into a lodge of the Free and Accepted Masons.

Hall joined the militia against the British at Bunker Hill and enlisted in the Continental army in 1778. He resumed lodge meetings following the war and applied for a formal charter. Denied official sanction by American Masons, Hall secured recognition from the British in 1787 and formally organized African Lodge Number 459. The Prince Hall Masons became a leading African American social organization.

While individual Black people proved they could succeed in every area of American life, from the battlefield to the boardroom, they remained the minority. Most Black leaders were either born free or emancipated at a young age. The vast majority of African Americans did not have the opportunity to prove themselves, as they remained shackled in slavery. Although the United States had achieved its liberty, all its residents had not—and would not for many decades.

15

The Assessment: Numbers, Influence, Results

DECLARING INDEPENDENCE WAS A HIGH-STAKES GAMBLE for the white American colonists. While the odds favored the powerful, wealthy, and resourceful British, the Englishmen did not hold all the cards. In fact, advantages and disadvantages seemed fairly balanced. Black Americans were the wild card in the deck.

By participating in every major battle, Black soldiers and sailors were critical to the outcome of the war. Both the white rebels and the British needed them behind the lines as laborers, messengers, guides, and spies. Both also enlisted them as soldiers and sailors, even if reluctantly.

As many as 100,000 Black people joined the British during the Revolution. They escaped from rebel owners, involuntarily accompanied their Loyalist owners, or were displaced by the various campaigns and battles during the Revolution. Despite the promises of Lord Dunmore and General Clinton, only about 5,000 slaves received their freedom for their service to the British. The vast majority remained the property of their Loyalist owners and merely exchanged slavery in the American colonies for slavery in Florida or the West Indies. Rebel owners reclaimed or recaptured many of those remaining in the former colonies. Some died in direct combat as members of English or Hessian regiments, but far more succumbed to disease, starvation, and the other harsh conditions of refugee camps where they awaited disposition.

African Americans, as property of Loyalists and as runaways from rebel owners, played an important role in British operations to counter the Revolution. While their participation as frontline soldiers was minimal, they constructed defenses, provided food, and functioned in other rear-area occupations.

An even greater number of Black Americans provided support for the American rebels. Much of the food and materials that kept the rebel army in the field and its navy afloat came from the labors of slaves. These Black workers also assumed many positions on farms and in villages, which permitted whites to join the military with no downturn in production or services.

The American rebels employed African Americans as soldiers and sailors to a greater degree than the British. Throughout the war, Black men served in the militias and the Continental army directly as recruits to fill the constant need for manpower, as substitutes for whites, and as servants to their owners.

Detailed research into the surviving records of the war—both official and unofficial—has produced a general consensus that about 5,000 Black men served the revolutionary cause as soldiers. Since there is ample evidence that a total of about 300,000 Americans joined the rebels, it appears that only one in sixty, or fewer than 2 percent, of the rebel soldiers were Black.

These figures are true but misleading because the gross numbers do not consider the length of enlistments by Black men as compared to whites. White volunteers for state militias and the Continental army joined for periods of three to twelve months. Most spent an average of six months in the military and then returned to their civilian occupations. On the other hand, many Black men enlisted "for the duration" in exchange for their freedom. The average length of time in service for African Americans during the Revolution was four and a half years— eight times longer than the average period for white soldiers.

Individual service records verify this length of service by Black Americans, as does the only surviving personnel document of the war that specifically accounts for the number of African Americans in the Continental army. In the George Washington papers in the U.S. Library of Congress, there is only one known report of the number of Black men assigned on a specific date to the major portion of the rebel army.

It is titled "Return of Negroes in the Army, 24th Regt. 1778" and signed by Adj. Gen. Alexander Scammell. The document, only one page, reveals that 755 Black men were serving in the various brigades of the Continental army.[1] During this period the Continental army contained its lowest number of total troops, with only 7,600 in the ranks. Thus; during one of the most desperate periods of the rebellion, nearly 10 percent of the rebel soldiers fighting for American liberty were Black.

Figures on the number of Black rebel sailors are even more obscure

---

[1]The document includes those brigades under command of Washington that had fought in the Battle of Monmouth the previous June. The Rhode Island Regiment, with its large number of Black soldiers, and the various militia units on duty in their home states are not included.

than those who were soldiers. The U.S. Department of the Navy estimates that about 1,500 African Americans served during the Revolution aboard Continental or state vessels or privateers—about 10 percent of the total number of rebel participants in the war.

The Second Continental Congress, operating from its first meeting in 1775 for six years with no actual congressional authority, drafted articles in 1777 that formed a loose confederation in which each state had one vote and committees could formulate and execute laws. These Articles of Confederation left most powers to the states, including authority over commerce, taxes, and courts. The thirteen states did not ratify them until four years later, in 1781, shortly before the Battle of Yorktown.

After Yorktown, Congress, acting under the ratified Articles of Confederation, focused on the military and actually began reductions even before the British exited New York. Because the rebel military required the greatest outlay of funds, Congress looked to lower costs by reducing the number of men in the army, navy, and Marine Corps as quickly as possible.

Within weeks after Yorktown, the United States began to decommission its ships and withdraw privateer letters of marque. By December 31, 1781, the Continental navy was down to two vessels, the frigates *Alliance* and *Deane*. The following March 17, Congress ordered all naval vessels and privateers to return to their home ports. On June 3, 1785, Congress authorized the sale of the last remaining U.S. Navy ship, the *Alliance*.

During this same period, Continental marines were discharged as they completed their enlistments. The last marine left active duty in September 1783.

State militias mostly returned to an inactive status back in their home districts shortly after the surrender of Cornwallis. The Continental army maintained a force of only a few thousand to continue the siege of the remaining British at the ports of Savannah, Charleston, and New York. The more British troops sailed away, the smaller Washington's army became.

Congress and Americans in general opposed a large standing Regular Army because of its expense and the belief that power, political and military, should remain a function of the states rather than the federal government. On September 24, 1783, three weeks after the signing of the Treaty of Paris, Congress directed General Washington to discharge "such parts of the Federal Army now in service as he shall deem proper and expedient."

Washington immediately dismissed all Continental forces not directly involved in maintaining the siege of New York. When the last British troops departed two months later, Washington discharged the remainder of his army except for one infantry regiment and a battalion of artillery, a total of 600 men, to guard military supplies stored at West Point and at other forts.

On June 2 of the following year, Congress ordered Gen. Henry Knox, who had replaced Washington as commander of the army, to discharge the troops now in the service to the United States, except twenty-five privates to guard the stores at Fort Pitt and fifty-five to guard the stores at West Point and other magazines, with a proportionable number of officers, no officers to remain in service above the rank of captain.

As an explanation for reducing the U.S. Army to only eighty enlisted men, Congress declared: "Standing armies in time of peace are inconsistent with the principles of republican governments, dangerous to the liberties of a free people, and generally convert into destructive engines for establishing despotism."

Opportunities for slaves to earn their freedom through military service disappeared as soldiers of the Continental army rejoined civilian society. Despite loyal service in the Revolution, African Americans found that the postwar military held no rewards for them. The authorized number of fewer than 100 soldiers in the Regular Army was restricted to whites only. The states, which maintained most of their powers under the Articles of Confederation, enacted and enforced their own rules on Black service in their militias. These regulations varied from state to state in a manner similar to before and during the war.

In the North, where slavery was coming to an end, state legislatures still generally excluded Black Americans, free or slave, from military service. Connecticut rejected all Black men from militia service in 1784, and Massachusetts did the same the following year. Southern states barred all slaves from their militias but varied in their policies for freemen. On October 14, 1784, the Virginia legislature passed a bill requiring "all free persons between the ages of eighteen and fifty years" to be "enrolled or formed into companies."

The Articles of Confederation, barely adequate to hold the country together and govern its people during the Revolution, proved entirely too weak and unpopular once peace prevailed. On May 25, 1787, state delegates met in Philadelphia "for the sole and expressed purpose of revising" the Articles of Confederation.

Despite their stated objective of meeting only to establish a new Constitution, the representatives also had to deal with current issues. Controversy reigned over the status of the territory reaching from Ohio to Wisconsin ceded by the British to the Americans in the Treaty of Paris. Ultimately, Congress agreed upon the Northwest Ordinance on July 13, 1787, which defined the rights and liberties of residents in the new lands. The ordinance provided measures for the areas to be subordinate to the federal government until they could claim a population of 60,000. They would then be allowed into the Union as a state with all the privileges and responsibilities of the original thirteen members.

The most important portion of the Northwest Ordinance for African Americans was Article 6,[2] which stated, "There shall be neither slavery nor involuntary servitude in said territory." The prohibition of slavery in the new territories was a victory for Black Americans and abolitionists, and many believed that the end of slavery in the United States was near.

Except for time to discuss and vote on the Northwest Ordinance, the representatives spent seventeen long weeks debating the future of their country. Ultimately they agreed to a firm union of the states governed by executive, legislative, and judicial branches.

Much of the discussion and division of the delegates revolved around slavery issues. Southern representatives wanted to count their slaves in their population figures, which decided the number of each states' congressional representatives. Northerners resisted, saying that taxes would have to be administered using the same population numbers. Finally the two sides compromised and included in Article I, Section II, of the Constitution measures to include all free persons and indentured servants (most of whom were white) in the population figures but to exclude Native Americans altogether. "All others" (i.e., Black people),[3] were to be included as three-fifths of their total numbers.

In Section IX of Article I the Constitution provided its greatest concession to African Americans. Although most of the northern delegates lobbied to end the importation of slaves immediately, the southern representatives stood fast. Again, compromise prevailed to produce measures to end the importation of slaves, labeled "such persons" in the article, no later than "prior to the year 1808"—a distant twenty years in the future.

Representatives of the states with large slave populations also ensured that the Constitution include in Article IV, Section II, provisions that "no person held to service" who escaped to a free state would be free. Rather, escapees would be "delivered up on claim of the party to whom such service or labor may be due" and returned to their owners.

[2]Article 6 of the Northwest Ordinance is in Appendix O.
[3]In this section, as well as in the rest of the Constitution, the delegates managed not once to specifically mention slavery or Black people. Sections specifically relating to African Americans in the Constitution appear in Appendix P.

Under provisions of the Constitution, George Washington took the oath of office as the first president of the United States on April 30, 1789. Thomas Jefferson became the first secretary of state, Alexander Hamilton the secretary of treasury, and Henry Knox the secretary of war. Knox's army remained small, increasing to about 600 during his first year in office and to 1,200 the following year.

The United States remained politically opposed to a large standing army in peacetime and had few funds to maintain one if they had so desired. While money for an army was short, manpower for so few units was not. With ample white volunteers, the U.S. Army had no need for African Americans. On May 8, 1792, Congress made the exclusion of Black men from the army official by resolving that military service was restricted to "free able-bodied white male citizens."

The resulting militia laws of each state generally reflected the congressional resolution and barred Black men from enlistment. Paradoxically, only in the South, where small white and large Black populations still produced a military manpower need, did states ignore the "whites only" restriction. In Georgia and South Carolina freemen continued to enlist as laborers, pioneers, and musicians, and some slaves served in militia units when their owners "hired out" their slaves for military support duties. In North Carolina free Black men could enlist in the militia and serve in a variety of positions until 1812, when restrictions limited them to duty only as musicians.

On July 11, 1798, Congress authorized the reestablishment of the Marine Corps but excluded "negroes, mulattoes, or Indians" from enlisting. The marines, able to meet their recruitment objectives with whites, did not allow Black men to enlist for the next century and a half, until the manpower requirements and political changes of World War II forced them to open their ranks to African Americans.

Shortly after the establishment of the U.S. Department of the Navy, Secretary Benjamin Stoddert echoed the marine order of no "negroes, mulattoes, or Indians" when he took office in August 1798. However, the new navy faced difficulties the other services did not. The army was a land force that required few soldiers, and there was little competition for their services. The navy, though, had to compete with the emerging American merchant and fishing fleets for experienced sailors who could cope with the hardships and dangers of life at sea.

As a result, African Americans steadily found opportunities available in the post-Revolution navy. There is no evidence that Stoddert's order received much attention, and if a ban against recruitment of Black sailors ever did exist, it was of short duration. In fact, during the time of the order and for several years afterward, names of Black seamen appeared on nearly every U.S. Navy ship's crew list, including that of its primary warships, the *Constitution* and the *Constellation*.

The Revolutionary War produced huge contrasting results for white and Black Americans. The war yielded land, resources, and most important, independence for white Americans to establish personal fortunes and to enrich and empower their nation. Within a century, the United States would become a world power; shortly after the centennial celebration of its independence, Americans became the world's most dominant economic and military power.

Rewards for African Americans were not as significant. Although Black Americans had played a part in achieving victory, they did not share equally in the benefits of independence. During the war itself, Black people enjoyed a degree of acceptance and opportunity previously unknown in America. The need for their services in the military and behind the lines by both the Americans and the British provided new chances for employment, advancement, and freedom.

As a reward for military service and as a result of abolition in the northern states, the number of free Black Americans in the United States increased from only a few thousand in 1776 to 60,000 in 1790 and to 180,000 in 1810. That is not to say that the enslaved population decreased. Actually, due to legal and illegal importation of additional slaves and natural procreation, the slave population of the United States steadily increased until it reached over 3.5 million—more than seven times the number during the Revolution—just prior to the beginning of the Civil War in 1861.

Once the Revolution was over, however, many Americans saw Black people not as partners in winning their country's independence but as investment property to increase the wealth of their owners. The northern states, influenced by abolitionists but acting primarily because slavery had not proved economically feasible, generally outlawed the practice during or shortly after the Revolution and began measures to gradually free those currently held in bondage.

The southern states rewarded slaves with freedom for their military service during the Revolution but remained reluctant to free the majority of what was to many their most valuable property. Slaves labored throughout the war to produce food and other supplies needed by the rebel army and navy. When hostilities ceased, they continued their work to rebuild and to advance their owners' fortunes.

In the decade immediately following the war, southerners found slavery only marginally profitable because of the lack of markets either in the United States or overseas for their raw agricultural products. This economic downturn, combined with the moral stance of abolitionists and the recognition by some that Black Americans had contributed to the war, might have led to an end to the practice of slavery if not for still another revolution—this one characterized by inventions and industrial technology rather than bullets and bayonets.

As early as 1750, British inventors had perfected machines for the mass production of textiles and techniques of harnessing steam power to run their factory systems. This technology gradually spread, but during and immediately after the Revolutionary War, the United States remained an agricultural nation with little industry. This changed with the arrival of Samuel Slater in Rhode Island in 1791. Supported by Quaker capitalist Moses Brown, Slater assembled the first machinery in America that would spin thread from cotton.

All Slater and Brown needed to make their fortune was an ample supply of raw materials. The soil of the southern states readily grew cotton, but separating the seed from the short fibers was a slow, labor-intensive process. In 1793, Yale-educated Eli Whitney journeyed to Georgia from his Massachusetts home to serve as a tutor. Within ten days after his arrival, he recognized the limitations of cotton production and invented an engine, or "gin," to separate seed from fiber that was fifty times more efficient than the hand process.

Whitney profited little from his cotton gin because the process was so simple that others soon copied his design. When southerners began shipping ginned product to mills in the North, cotton became king, planters and mill owners became wealthy, and Black people found themselves more burdened with increased demands even as owners bought additional slaves to work the plantations.

More slaves increased the wealth of owners but also added to their fears of a Black rebellion. Southerners enacted more elaborate and restrictive slave codes to control *every* aspect of African American life and defended slavery as the source of their individual and state affluence. Slavery became a cornerstone of their political stance and agenda.

Although African Americans had made some advances as a result of the Revolution, specifically the abolition of slavery in the northern states and the Northwest Territory, as a whole their status as a race decreased during the decades following the war. Slaves still labored from dawn to dusk and faced the constant threat of severe punishment for minor infractions. Slave families existed at the pleasure of owners and always faced the possibility that owners would sell one or more members. Freemen could not vote, had limited rights to own property, and at times found themselves re-enslaved at the will of their neighbors.

The simple fact was, if born a slave in the North during the Revolution, an African American would have to reach adulthood before receiving his or her freedom. If born a slave in the South during America's war for independence, a Black child would almost surely die in bondage. The practice of slavery in the United States would not come to an end until the Thirteenth Amendment to the Constitution took effect at the end of the Civil War in 1865—ninety years after the first African American died in the fight for liberty in the American Revolution. It would take another hundred years and the Civil Rights Movement of the 1960s for the clause that "all men are created equal" to fully apply to African Americans.

The Revolutionary War demonstrated that Black Americans could and would contribute to the military on land and at sea and that whites would choose to ignore them until necessity forced open the ranks. This pattern of willingness and discrimination would prevail for about two centuries. Only in times of war did whites allow Black Americans into uniform despite the fact that African Americans made significant contributions to victory in the Civil War, the Indian Wars, the Spanish American War, World War I, and World War II as they served in segregated units with white officers.

On July 6, 1948, Pres. Harry Truman issued Executive Order 9981. It declared that "there shall be equality of treatment and opportunity for all persons in the armed services without regard to race, color, religion, or national origin." Integration of the armed forces continued through the Korean War of the early 1950s. During the Vietnam War of the 1960s, Black Americans served in every capacity and with every rank. When the United States took action against Iraq in Operation Desert Storm in 1990–1991, Gen. Colin Powell, the first Black chairman of the Joint Chiefs of Staff, was the senior U.S. officer in uniform.

Despite these advances by African Americans in the U.S. Armed Forces, the original sacrifice of Black people and their contributions toward winning America's independence from Great Britain remain unrecognized. In 1986, Congress formally authorized the Black Revolutionary War Patriots Foundation to solicit money from nongovernment sources to build a memorial on the Mall in Washington, D.C. On March 1, 1998, the U.S. Mint offered a commemorative coin featuring Crispus Attucks on one side and a "Black Colonial family" on the other. Part of the proceeds was to go to the monument construction fund. As of the end of 1998, a groundbreaking ceremony for the monument was finally scheduled for 1999. It took another fifteen years, however, before the National Liberty Memorial was fully approved by Congress. It has yet to be built.

Appendix A

Important Dates in African American Participation in the Revolutionary War

1619
August English colonists purchase first slaves in North America at Jamestown.

1638
December 12 Ship *Desire* delivers first slaves to New England in Boston.

1639
January 16 Virginia General Assembly bars arming of slaves.

1640
July 9 Virginia colonial court rules on differences between white and Black indentured servants.

1688
February 18 Society of Friends in Pennsylvania publish the "Germantown Protest."

1712
April 7 Slave revolt in New York City

1739
September 9 Slave revolt in South Carolina

1741
February 28 Slave revolt in New York City

1770
March 5 Boston Massacre
June 28 Quaker Anthony Benezet opens first nonsegregated school in Philadelphia.

1772

June 22   Mansfield Decision abolishes slavery in England.

1773

December 16   Boston Tea Party

1774

September 5   First Continental Congress convenes in Philadelphia.

October 2   Continental Congress votes to discontinue slave trade after December 1.

November 2   Slave revolt in St. Andrew's Parish, Georgia.

1775

March 8   Thomas Paine publishes *African Slavery in America.*

April 14   First American Abolition Society elects officers.

April 18   Paul Revere and William Dawes set off on their midnight ride.

April 19   Battles of Lexington and Concord.

May 1   Americans capture Fort Ticonderoga.

May 10   Second Continental Congress convenes in Philadelphia.

June 15   Second Continental Congress appoints George Washington commander in chief of the army.

June 17   Battle of Bunker Hill.

July 3   Prince Hall establishes the first Black Mason Lodge in Boston.

July 9   Continental army orders recruiters not to enlist any "stroller negro, or vagabond."

October 13   Congress authorizes the formation of the Continental navy.

November 7   The earl of Dunmore issues proclamation offering freedom to slaves who desert their rebel owners to join the British.

November 10   Continental Marines founded. South Carolina legislature authorizes the hiring of slaves to build fortifications, with wages going to their owners.

December 9   Battle of Great Bridge, Virginia.

December 14   Congress forms Marine Committee to govern the navy.

December 30   General Washington reverses the Continental army policy barring enlistment of free Black men.

1776

March 17   British evacuate Boston and sail to Nova Scotia.

July 4   Declaration of Independence.

August 6   Lord Dunmore ends his efforts to retake Virginia for the Crown and sails to England.

August 27	Battle of Long Island, New York.
September 5	Continental Congress adopts first uniforms for the navy and marines.
September 12	Americans evacuate New York City.
September 16	Battle of Harlem Heights, New York.
October 28	Battle of White Plains, New York.
December 25–26	Washington crosses Delaware River and surprises Hessians at Trenton.

1777

January 2	Battle of Princeton, New Jersey.
February 6	Treaties of commerce and alliance signed between the United States and France.
June 14	Congress adopts U. S. flag.
July 2	Vermont, a part of New York, abolishes slavery within its borders.
August 16	Battle of Bennington, Vermont.
September 11	Battle of Brandywine Creek, Pennsylvania.
October 4	British occupy Philadelphia.
October 17	Battle of Saratoga, New York.
November 15	Continental Congress adopts the Articles of Confedera-tion.

1778

February 14	Rhode Island passes a slave-enlistment act.
June 17	France officially enters the war against Great Britain.
June 18	British evacuate Philadelphia.
June 28	Battle of Monmouth, New Jersey.
July 29	French fleet joins rebels off Newport, Rhode Island.
August 11	Battle of Rhode Island.
August 24	Adjutant general report shows 755 Black men in Continental army.
December 29	British capture Savannah, Georgia.

1779

January 29	British occupy Augusta, Georgia.
February 16	Battle of Kettle Creek, Georgia.
March 14	Alexander Hamilton urges Congress to allow slaves to enlist.
March 16	Henry Laurens writes Washington supporting slave enlistments.
March 29	Congress encourages South Carolina and Georgia to enlist slaves.

May26   South Carolina rejects congressional recommendation to enlist Black men.

June 21   Spain declares war against Great Britain.

June 30   British general Henry Clinton proclaims freedom for slaves belonging to rebels who escape to his lines.

July 15–16   Battle of Stony Point, New York

September 23   John Paul Jones and his *Bon Homme Richard* defeat the British *Serapis.*

October 9   American-French force unsuccessfully attacks Savannah.

1780

May 12   British capture Charleston, South Carolina.

August 16   Battle of Camden, South Carolina.

October 7   Battle of King's Mountain, South Carolina.

1781

January 17   Battle of Cowpens, South Carolina.

March 15   Battle of Guilford Courthouse, North Carolina.

May 4   Black Rhode Island Regiment suffers heavy casualties at Point Bridge, New York.

October 6   American-French force begins siege of Yorktown, Virginia.

October 19   British surrender at Yorktown, Virginia.

1782

July 21   British evacuate Savannah, Georgia.

November 30   Rebel Americans and British sign Provisional Peace Agreement.

December 14   British evacuate Charleston, South Carolina.

1783

June 13   Black Rhode Island Regiment disbands.

May 6   Orangetown Conference.

September 3   War officially ends with Treaty of Paris.

November 25   British complete evacuation of New York City.

Appendix B

Slave Codes

"An Act for the Better Ordering and Governing of Negroes and Slaves"

The South Carolina colonial legislature passed this act in 1712. This appendix contains the introduction and twelve of the thirty-five sections. Other colonies, especially in the South, passed similar legislation.

Whereas, the plantations and estates of this Province cannot be well and sufficiently managed and brought into use, without the labor and service of negroes and other slaves; and forasmuch as the said negroes and other slaves brought unto the people of this Province for that purpose, are of barbarous, wild, savage natures, and such as renders them wholly unqualified to be governed by the laws, customs, and practices of the Province, but that it is absolutely necessary, that such other constitutions, laws and orders, should in this Province be made and enacted, for the good regulating and ordering of them, as may restrain the disorders, rapines and inhumanity to which they are naturally prone and inclined, and may also tend to the safety and security of the people of this Province and their estates; to which purpose;

I. Be it therefore enacted, by his Excellency, William, Lord Craven, Palatine, and the rest of the true and absolute Lords and Proprietors of this Province, by and with the advice and consent of the rest of the members of the General Assembly, now met at Charleston, for the Southwest part of this Province, and by the authority of the same, That all negroes, mulattoes, mestizoes or Indians, which at any time heretofore shall be brought [sic] and sold for slaves; and they, and their children, are hereby made and declared slaves, to all intents and purposes; excepting all such negroes, mulattoes, mestizoes or Indians, which heretofore have been, or hereafter shall be, for some particular merit, made and declared free, either by the Governor and council of this Province, pursuant to any Act or law of this Province, or by their respective owners or masters; and also, excepting all such negroes, mulattoes, mestizoes or Indians, as can prove they ought not to be sold for slaves. And in case any negro, mulatto, mestizo or Indian, doth lay claim to his or her freedom, upon all or any of the said accounts, the same shall be finally heard and determined by the Governor and council of this Province.

II. And for the better ordering and governing of negroes and all other slaves in this Province, be it enacted by the authority aforesaid, that no master, mistress, overseer, or other person whatsoever, that hath the care and charge of any negro or slave, shall give their negroes and other slaves leave, on Sundays, holidays, or any other time, to go out of their plantations, except such negro or other slave as usually wait upon them at home or abroad, or wearing a livery; and every other negro or slave that shall be taken hereafter out of his master's plantation, without a ticket, or leave in writing, from his master or mistress, or some other person by his or her appointment, or some white person in the company of such slave, to gain an account of his business, shall be whipped; and every person who shall not (when in his power), apprehend every negro or other slave which he shall see out of his master's plantation, without leave as aforesaid, and after apprehended, shall neglect to punish him by moderate whipping, shall forfeit twenty shillings, the one half to the poor, to be paid to the church wardens of the Parish where such forfeiture shall become due, and the other half to him that will inform for the same, within one week after such neglect; and that no slave may make further or other use of any one ticket than was intended by him that granted the same, every ticket shall particularly mention the name of every slave employed in the particular business, and to what place they are sent, and what time they return; and if any person shall presume to give any negro or slave a ticket in the name of his master or mistress, without his or her consent, such person so doing shall forfeit the sum of twenty shillings; one half to the poor, to be disposed of as aforesaid, the other half to the person injured, that will complain against the person offending, within one week after the offense committed. And for the better security of all such persons that shall endeavor to take any runaway, or shall examine any slave for his ticket, passing to and from his master's plantation, it is hereby declared lawful for any white person to beat, maim, or assault, and if such negro or slave cannot otherwise be taken, to kill him, who shall refuse to show his ticket, or, by running away or resistance, shall endeavor to avoid being apprehended or taken.

III. And be it further enacted by the authority aforesaid, that every master, mistress, or overseer of a family in this Province, shall cause all his negro houses to be searched diligently and effectually once every fourteen days, for fugitive and runaway slaves, guns, swords, clubs, and any other mischievous weapons, and finding any, to take them away, and cause them to be secured, as also for clothes, goods, and any other things and commodities that are not given them by their master, mistress, commander, or overseer, and honestly come by; and in whose custody they find any thing of that kind, and suspect or know to be stolen goods, the same they shall seize and take into their custody, and a full and ample description of the particulars thereof, in writing, within ten days after the discovery thereof, either to the provost marshall, or to the clerk of the parish for the time being, who is hereby required to receive the same, and to enter upon it the day of its receipt, and the particulars to file and keep to himself; and the clerk shall set upon the posts of the church door, and the provost marshall upon the usual public places, or places of notice, a short brief, that such lost goods are found; whereby, any person that hath lost his goods may the better come to the knowledge where they are; and the owner going to the marshall or clerk, and proving by marks or otherwise, that the goods lost belong to him, and paying twelve pence for the entry and declaration of the same, if the marshall or clerk be convinced that any part of the goods certified by him to be found, appertains to the party inquiring, he is to direct the said party inquiring to the place and party where the goods be, who is hereby required to make restitution of what is in being to the true owner; and every master, mistress or overseer as also the provost marshall or clerk, neglecting his duty in any the particulars aforesaid, and every neglect shall forfeit twenty shillings.

IV. And for the more effectual detecting and punishing such persons that trade with any slave for stolen goods, be it further enacted by the authority aforesaid, that where any person shall be suspected to trade as aforesaid, any justice of the peace shall have power to take from him suspected, sufficient recognizance, not to trade with any slave contrary to the laws of this Province; and if it shall afterwards appear to any of the justices of the peace, that such person hath, or hath had, or shipped off, any goods, suspected to be unlawfully come by, it shall be lawful for such justice of the peace to oblige the person to appear at the next general sessions, who shall be there obliged to make reasonable proof, of whom he bought, or how he came by, the said goods, and unless he do it, his recognizance shall be forfeited.

V. And be it further enacted by the authority aforesaid, that no negro or slave shall carry out of the limits of his master's plantation any sort of gun or fire arms, without his master, or some other white person by his order, is present with him, or without a certificate from his master, mistress, or overseer, for the same; and if any negro or slave shall be so apprehended or taken, without the limits aforesaid, with any gun or fire arms as aforesaid, such arms shall be forfeited to him or them that shall apprehend or take the same; unless the person who is the owner of the arms so taken, shall in three months time redeem the arms so taken, by paying to the person that took the same, the sum of twenty shillings.

VI. And be it further enacted by the authority aforesaid, that every master or head of any family, shall keep all his guns and other arms, when out of use, in the most private and least frequented room in the house, upon the penalty of being convicted of neglect therein, to forfeit three pounds.

VII. And whereas, great numbers of slaves which do not dwell in Charleston, on Sundays and holidays, resort thither, to drink, quarrel, fight, curse and swear, and profane the Sabbath, and using and carrying of clubs and other mischievous weapons, resorting in great companies together, which may give them an opportunity of executing any wicked designs and purposes, to the damage and prejudice of the inhabitants of this Province; for the preservation whereof, be it enacted by the authority aforesaid, that all and every constable of Charleston, separately on every Sunday, and the holidays at Christmas, Easter, and Whitsonside, together with so many men as each constable shall think necessary to accompany him, which he is hereby empowered for that end to press, under the penalty of twenty shillings to the person that shall disobey him, shall, together with such persons, go through all or any of the streets, and also round about Charleston, and as much further on the neck as they shall be informed or have reason to suspect any meeting or concourse of any such negroes or slave to be at that time, and to enter into any house, at

Charleston, or elsewhere, to search for such slaves, and as many of them as they can apprehend, shall cause to be publicly whipped in Charleston, and then to be delivered to the marshall, who for every slave so whipped and delivered to him by the constable, shall pay the constable five shillings, which five shillings shall be repaid the said marshall by the owner or head of that family to which the said negro or slave doth belong, together with such other charges as shall become due to him for keeping runaway slaves; and the marshall shall in all respects keep and dispose of such slave as if the same was delivered to him as a runaway, under the same penalties and forfeiture as hereafter in that case is provided; and every constable of Charleston which shall neglect or refuse to make search as aforesaid, for every such neglect shall forfeit the sum of twenty shillings.

VIII. And be it further enacted by the authority aforesaid, that no owner or head of any family shall give a ticket to any slave to go to Charleston, or from plantation to plantation, on Sunday, excepting it be for and about such particular business as cannot reasonably be delayed to another time, under the forfeiture of ten shillings; and in every ticket in that case given, shall be mentioned the particular business that slave is sent about, or that slave shall be dealt with as if he had no ticket.

IX. And be it further enacted by the authority aforesaid, that upon complaint made to any justice of the peace, of any heinous or grievous crime, committed by any slave or slaves, as murder, burglary, robbery, burning of houses, or any lesser crime, as killing or stealing meat or other cattle, maiming one the other, stealing of fouls, provisions, or such like trespasses or injuries, the said justice shall issue out his warrant for apprehending the offender or offenders, and for all persons to come before him that can give evidence; and if upon examination, it probably appearth, that the apprehended person is guilty, he shall commit him or them to prison, or immediately proceed to trial of the said slave or slaves, according to the form hereafter specified, or take security for his or their forthcoming, as the case shall require, and also to certify to the justice next to him, the said cause, and to require him, by virtue of this act, to associate himself to him, which said justice is hereby required to do, and they so associated, are to issue their summons to three sufficient freeholders, acquainting them with the matter, and appointing them a day, hour, and place, when and where the same shall be heard and determined, at which day, hour, and place, the said justices and freeholders shall cause the offenders and evidences to come before them, and if they, on hearing the matter, the said freeholders being by the said justices first sworn to judge uprightly and according to evidence, and diligently weighing and examining all evidences, proofs, testimonies, (and in case of murder only, if on violent presumption and circumstances) they shall find such negro or other slave or slaves guilty thereof, they shall give sentence of death, if the crime by law deserve the same, and forthwith by their warrant cause immediate execution to be done, by the common or any other executioner, in such manner as they shall think fit, the kind of death to be inflicted to be left to their judgement, and discretion; and if the crime committed shall not deserve death, they shall then condemn and adjudge the criminal or criminals to any other punishment, but not extending to limb or disabling him, without a particular law directing such punishment, and shall forthwith order execution to be done accordingly.

X. And in regard great mischiefs daily happen by petty larcenies committed by negroes and slaves of this Province, be it further enacted by the authority aforesaid, that if any negro or other slave shall hereafter steal or destroy any goods, chattels, or provisions whatsoever, of any other person than his master or mistress, being under the value of twelve pence, every negro or other slave so offending, and being brought before some justice of the peace of this Province, upon complaint of the party injured, and shall be adjudged guilty by confession, proof, or probable circumstances, such negro or slave so offending, excepting children, whose punishment is left wholly to the discretion of the said justice, shall be adjudged by such justice to be publicly and severely whipped, not exceeding forty lashes; and if such negro or other slave punished as aforesaid, be afterwards, by two justices of the peace, found guilty of the like crimes, he or they, for such his or their second offense, shall either have one of his ears cut off, or be branded in the forehead with a hot iron, that the mark thereof may remain; and if after such punishment, such negro or slave for his third offense, shall have his nose slit; and if such negro or other slave, after the third time as aforesaid, be accused of petty larceny, or of any of the offenses before mentioned, such negro or other slave shall be tried in such manner as those accused of murder, burglary, etc. are before by this act provided for to be tried, and in case they shall be found guilty a fourth time, of any the offenses before mentioned, then such negro or other slave shall be adjudged to suffer death, or other punishment, as the said justices shall think fitting; and any judgement given for the first offence, shall be a sufficient conviction for the first offence; and any after judgement after the first judgement, shall be a sufficient conviction to bring the offender within the penalty of the second offence, and so for inflicting the rest of the punishments; and in case the said justices and freeholders, and any or either of them, shall neglect or refuse to perform the duties by this act required of them, they shall severally, for such their defaults, forfeit the sum of twenty-five pounds.

XI. And be it further enacted by the authority aforesaid, that if any person shall send his negro out of this Province, that hath killed another negro or slave, such person shall pay unto the master or owner of such negro, the full value of such negro so killed as aforementioned; and in case any person shall send, or cause to be sent, his negro out of the Province, that hath killed any white person, knowing the negro to be guilty of such crime, he shall forfeit the sum of five hundred pounds, to the executors of the person killed; to be recovered by action of debt in the court of common pleas in this Province, the action to be brought at any time within one year after the fact committed.

XII. And it is further enacted by the authority aforesaid, that if any negroes or other slaves shall make mutiny or insurrection, or rise in rebellion against the authority and government of this Province, or shall make preparation of arms, powder, bullets or offensive weapons, in order to carry on such a mutiny or insurrection, or shall hold any counsel or conspiracy for raising such a mutiny, insurrection, or rebellion, the offenders shall be tried by two justices of the peace and three freeholders, associated together as before expressed in case of murder, burglary, etc., who are hereby empowered and required to try the said slaves so offending, and inflict death, or any other punishment, upon the offenders, and forthwith by their own warrant cause execution to be done, by the common or any other executioner, in such a manner as they shall think fitting; and if any person shall make away or conceal any negro or negroes, or any other slave or slaves, suspected to be guilty of the beforementioned crimes, and not upon demand bring forth the suspected offender or offenders, such person shall forfeit for every negro or negroes so concealed or made away, the sum of fifty pounds; provided nevertheless, that when and as often as any of the beforementioned crimes shall be committed by more than one negro, that shall deserve death, that then and in all such cases, if the Governor and council of this Province shall think fitting, and accordingly shall order, that only one or more of the said criminals should suffer death as exemplary, and the rest to be returned to the owners, that then, the owners of the negroes so offending, shall bear proportionably the loss of said negro or negroes so put to death, as shall be allotted to them by the said justices and freeholders; and if any person shall refuse his part so allotted him, that then, and in all such cases, the said justices and freeholders are hereby required to issue out their warrant of distress upon the goods and chattels of the person so refusing, and shall cause the same to be sold by public outcry, to satisfy the said money so allotted him to pay, and to return the overplus, if any be, to the owner; provided, nevertheless, that the part allotted for any person to pay for his part or proportion of the negro or negroes so put to death, shall not exceed one sixth part of his negro or negroes so excused and pardoned; and in case that shall not be sufficient to satisfy for the negro or negroes that shall be put to death, that the remaining sum shall be paid out of the public treasury of this Province.

Appendix C

Estimated American (White and Black) Population: 1760, 1770, 1780

Colony	1760	1770	1780
Maine	20,000	31,257	49,133
New Hampshire	39,093	62,396	87,802
Vermont	N.A.	10,000	47,620
Massachusetts	202,600	235,308	268,627
Rhode Island	45,471	58,196	52,946
Connecticut	142,470	183,881	206,701
New York	117,138	162,920	210,541
New Jersey	93,813	117,431	139,627
Pennsylvania	183,703	240,057	327,305
Delaware	33,250	35,496	45,385
Maryland	162,267	202,599	245,474
Virginia	339,726	447,016	538,004
North Carolina	110,442	197,200	270,133
South Carolina	94,074	124,244	180,000
Georgia	9,578	23,375	56,071
Kentucky	N.A.	15,700	45,000
Tennessee	N.A.	1,000	10,000
TOTAL	1,593,625	2,148,076	2,780,369

Appendix D

Estimated Black Population: 1760, 1770, 1780

(Percentage of state's total population in parenthesis.)

Colony	1760		1770		1780	
Maine	300	(1.5)	475	(1.5)	458	(1.0)
New Hampshire	600	(1.5)	654	(1.0)	541	(0.6)
Vermont			25	(0.2)	50	(0.1)
Massachusetts	4,566	(2.0)	4,754	(2.0)	4,822	(1.7)
Rhode Island	3,468	(7.0)	3,761	(6.4)	2,671	(5.0)
Connecticut	3,783	(2.6)	5,698	(3.0)	5,885	(2.0)
New York	16,340	(14.0)	19,112	(11.7)	21,054	(9.9)
New Jersey	6,567	(7.0)	8,220	(6.9)	10,460	(7.5)
Pennsylvania	4,409	(2.0)	5,761	(4.9)	7,855	(2.3)
Delaware	1,733	(5.0)	1,836	(5.1)	2,996	(6.6)
Maryland	49,004	(30.0)	63,818	(35.3)	80,515	(33.7)
Virginia	140,570	(41.0)	187,605	(41.9)	220,582	(41.0)
North Carolina	33,554	(30.0)	69,600	(35.3)	91,000	(33.7)
South Carolina	57,334	(60.9)	75,178	(60.5)	97,000	(53.9)
Georgia	3,578	(37.0)	10,625	(45.5)	20,831	(37.1)
Kentucky	N.A.		2,500	(15.0)	7,200	(16.0)
Tennessee	N.A.		200	(2.0)	1,500	(15.0)
TOTAL	325,806	(20.4)	359,822	(21.4)	575,420	(20.6)

Appendix E

The Deleted Clause of the Declaration of Independence

Thomas Jefferson included the following clause in his draft of the Declaration of Independence, submitted to the Continental Congress at Philadelphia. Representatives from South Carolina and Georgia so strenuously objected to it that Jefferson deleted it in order to preserve unity among the states.

He [King George III] has waged a cruel war against human nature itself, violating its most sacred rights of life and liberty in the persons of distant people who never offended him, captivating and carrying them into slavery in another hemisphere, or to incur miserable death in their transportation here. This piratical warfare, the opprobrium of Infidel powers, is the warfare of the Christian King of Great Britain. Determined to keep open a market where men should be bought and sold, he has prostituted his veto for suppressing every legislative attempt to prohibit or to restrain this execrable commerce. And that this assemblage of horrors might want no fact of distinguished caprice, he is now exciting those very people to rise in arms among us, and to purchase that liberty of which he has deprived them, thus paying off former crimes committed against the liberties of one people, with crimes which he urges them to commit against the lives of another.

Appendix F

Lord Dunmore's Proclamation

An original copy of the broadside (seventeen by eleven inches) is in the University of Virginia library. Other copies and facsimiles vary slightly in punctuation and capitalization.

By His Excellency the Right Honorable John, Earl of Dunmore, His Majesty's Lieutenant and Governor General of the Colony and Dominion of Virginia, and Vice Admiral of the same:

A Proclamation

As I have ever entertained hopes that an accommodation might have taken place between Great Britain and this Colony, without being compelled by my duty to this most disagreeable, but now absolutely necessary step, rendered so by a body of armed men, unlawfully assembled, firing on His Majesty's Tenders; and the formation of an army, and that army now on their march to attack His Majesty's troops, and destroy the well-disposed subjects of this Colony: To defeat such treasonable purposes, and that all such traitors and their abettors may be brought to justice, and that the peace and good order of this Colony may be again restored, which the ordinary course of the civil law is unable to effect, I have thought fit to issue this my Proclamation, hereby declaring, that until the aforesaid good purposes can be obtained, I do, in virtue of the power and authority to me given by His Majesty, determine to execute martial law, and cause the same to be executed throughout this Colony. And to the end that peace and good order may the sooner be restored, I do require every person capable of bearing arms to resort to His Majesty's standard, or be looked upon as traitors to His Majesty's Crown and Government, and thereby become liable to the penalty the law inflicts upon such offenses such as forfeiture of life, confiscations of lands, etc., etc., and I do hereby further declare all indentured servants, negroes, and others, (appertaining to Rebels) free, that are able and willing to bear arms, they joining His Majesty's troops, as soon as may be, for the more speedily reducing this Colony to a proper sense of their duty to His Majesty's Crown and dignity.

Given under my hand on board the ship *William,* off Norfolk, the 7th day of November, in the sixteenth year of His Majesty's reign [1775].

(Signed)

Dunmore

God save the King!

Appendix G

A Letter from Alexander Hamilton to John Jay Recommending Arming Slaves in South Carolina and Georgia

Middlebrook, New Jersey March 14, 1779

Dear Sir,

Col. Laurens, who will have the honor of delivering you this letter, is on his way to South Carolina, on a project, which I think, in the present situation of affairs there, is a very good one and deserves every kind of support and encouragement. This is to raise two, three, or four battalions of negroes; with the assistance of the government of that state, by contributions from the owners in proportion to the number they possess. If you should think proper to enter upon the subject with him, he will give you the details of his plan. He wishes to have it recommended by Congress to the state; and, as an inducement, that they would engage to take those battalions into Continental pay.

It appears to me, that an expedient of this kind, in the present state of Southern affairs, is the most rational, that can be adopted, and promises very important advantages. Indeed, I hardly can see how a sufficient force can be collected in that quarter without it; and the enemy's operations there are growing infinitely serious and formidable. I have not the least doubt, that the negroes will make very excellent soldiers, with proper management; and I will venture to pronounce, that they cannot be put in better hands that those of Mr. Laurens. He has all the zeal, intelligence, enterprise, and every other qualification requisite to succeed in such an undertaking. It is a maxim with some military judges, that with sensible officers soldiers can hardly be too stupid; and on this principle it is thought that the Russians would make the best troops in the world, if they were under other officers than their own. The King of Prussia is among the number who maintain this doctrine and has a *very* emphatical saying on the occasion, which I do not exactly recollect. I mention this, because I frequently hear it objected to the scheme of embodying negroes that they are too stupid to make soldiers. This is so far from appearing to me a valid objection that I think their want of cultivation (for their natural faculties are probably as good as ours) joined to that habit of subordination which they acquire from a life of servitude, will make them sooner to become soldiers than our white inhabitants. Let officers be men of sense and sentiment, and the nearer the soldiers approach to machines perhaps the better.

I foresee that this project will have to combat much opposition from prejudice and self-interest. The contempt we have been taught to entertain for the blacks, makes us fancy many things that are founded neither in reason nor experience; and an unwillingness to part with property of so valuable a kind will furnish a thousand arguments to show the impracticability or pernicious tendency of a scheme which requires such a sacrifice. But it should be considered that if we do not make use of them in this way, the enemy probably will; and that the best way to counteract the temptations they will hold out will be to offer them ourselves. An essential part of the plan is to give them their freedom with their muskets. This will secure their fidelity, animate their courage, and I believe will have a good influence upon those who remain, by opening a door to their emancipation.

This circumstance, I confess, has no small weight in inducing me to wish the success of the project; for the dictates of humanity and true policy equally interest me in favor of this unfortunate class of men.

While I am on the subject of Southern affairs, you will excuse the liberty I take in saying, that I do not think measures sufficiently vigorous are pursuing for our defense in that quarter. Except the few regular troops of South Carolina, we seem to be relying wholly on the militia of that and two neighboring states. These will soon grow impatient of service, and leave our affairs in miserable situation. No considerable force can be uniformly kept up by the militia, to say nothing of the many obvious and well-known inconveniences that attend this kind of troops. I would beg to suggest, sir, that no time ought to be lost in making a draught of militia to serve a twelve-month period, from the states of North and South Carolina and Virginia. But South Carolina, being *very* weak in her population of whites, may be excused from the draught, on the condition of furnishing the Black battalions. The two others may furnish about three thousand, five hundred men, and be exempted, on that account, from sending any succors to this army. The states to the northward of Virginia, will be fully able to give competent supplies to the army here; and it will require all the force and exertions of the three states I have mentioned, to withstand the storm which has arisen, and is increasing in the South.

The troops drafted, must be thrown into battalions, and officered in the best possible manner. The best supernumerary officers may be made use of as far as they will go. If arms are wanted for their troops, and no better way of supplying them is to be found, we should endeavor to levy a contribution of army upon the militia at large. Extraordinary exigencies demand extraordinary means. I fear this Southern business will become a very grave one.

With the truest respect and esteem,
I am, sir, your most obedient servant,

(Signed)
Alex. Hamilton

Appendix H

The Rhode Island Slave Enlistment Act
(February 14, 1778)

Whereas, for preservation of the rights and liberties of the United States, it is necessary that the whole powers of Government should be exerted in recruiting the Continental battalions; and whereas His Excellency General Washington hath enclosed to this State a proposal made to him by Brigadier General Varnum, to enlist into the two battalions, raising by this state, such slaves as should be willing to enter into the service; and whereas history affords us frequent precedents of the wisest, the freest, and bravest nations having liberated their slaves, and enlisting them as soldiers to fight in defense of their country; and also, whereas, the enemy, with a great force, have taken possession of the capital and of a great part of this State; and this State is obliged to raise a very considerable number of troops for its own immediate defense, whereby it is in a manner rendered impossible for this State to furnish recruits for the said two battalions without adopting the said measure so recommended:

It is voted and resolved, that every able-bodied negro, mulatto, or Indian man slave, in this State, may enlist into either of the said two battalions to serve during the continuance of the present war with Great Britain; that every slave so enlisting shall be entitled to and receive all bounties, wages, and encouragements allowed by the Continental Congress to any soldier enlisting into their service.

It is further voted and resolved, that every slave so enlisting shall, upon his passing muster before Colonel Christopher Greene, be immediately discharged from the service of his master or mistress, and be absolutely free, as though he had never been incumbered with any kind of servitude or slavery. And in such case such slave shall, by sickness or otherwise, be rendered unable to maintain himself, he shall not be chargeable to his master or mistress, but shall be supported at the expense of the State.

And whereas slaves have been by the laws deemed the property of their owners; and therefore compensation ought to be made to the owners for the loss of their service, it is further voted and resolved that there be allowed, and paid by this State to the owner, for every such slave so enlisting, a sum according to his worth; at a price not exceeding one hundred and twenty pounds for the most valuable slave, and in proportion for a slave of less value; provided the owner of said slave shall deliver up to the officer who shall enlist him the clothes of the said slave; or otherwise he shall not be entitled to said sum.

And for settling and ascertaining the value of such slaves, it is further voted and resolved, that a committee of five be appointed, to wit: one from each county; any three of whom to be a quorum, to examine the slaves who shall be so enlisted, after they shall have passed muster, and to set a price upon each slave according to his value, as aforesaid.

It is further voted and resolved, that upon any able-bodied negro, mulatto, or Indian slave, enlisting as aforesaid, the officer who shall so enlist him, after he has passed muster as aforesaid, shall deliver a certificate thereof to the master or mistress of said negro, mulatto, or Indian slave; which shall discharge him for the service of said master or mistress as aforesaid.

It is further voted and resolved, that the committee who shall estimate the value of any slave as aforesaid, shall give a certificate of the sum at which he may be valued, to the owner of said slave; and the General Treasurer of this State is hereby empowered and directed to give unto the owner of said slave his promissory note, as Treasurer, as aforesaid, for the sum of money at which he shall be valued as aforesaid, payable on demand, with interest, as the rate of six percent per annum; and that said notes which shall be so given, shall be paid with the money which is due this State, and is expected from Congress; the money which has been borrowed out of the General Treasury by this Assembly being first replaced.

Appendix I

The Rhode Island Assembly Protest Against Enlisting Slaves
(February 14, 1778)

We the subscribers, beg leave to dissent from the vote of the Lower House ordering a regiment of negroes to be raised for the Continental service, for the following reasons; viz.

1st, Because in our opinion, there is not sufficient number of negroes in the State who have an inclination to enlist, and would pass muster, to constitute a regiment; and raising several companies of blacks would not answer the purposes intended; and therefore the attempt to constitute said regiment would prove abortive, and be fruitless expense to the State.

2d, The raising such a regiment upon the footing proposed would suggest an idea, and produce an opinion in the world, that the State has purchased a band of slaves to be employed in the defense of the rights and liberties of our country; which is wholly inconsistent with those principles of liberty and constitutional government for which we are so ardently contending; and would be looked upon by the neighboring States in a contemptible point of view, and not equal to their troops; and they would, therefore, be unwilling that we should have credit for them as for an equal number of white troops; and would also give occasion to our enemies to suspect that we are not able to procure our own people to oppose them in the field, and to retort upon us the same kind of ridicule we so liberally bestowed upon them on account of Dunmore's regiment of blacks; or possibly might suggest to them the idea of employing black regiments against us.

3d, The expense of purchasing and enlisting said regiment, in the manner proposed, will vastly exceed the expenses of raising an equal number of white men; and, at the same time, will not have the like good effect.

4th, Great difficulties and uneasiness will arise in purchasing the negroes from the masters; and many of the masters will not be satisfied with any prices allowed.

Appendix J

General Henry Clinton's Proclamation

By His Excellency Sir Henry Clinton, General and Commander-in-Chief of all his Majesty's Forces, within the colony laying on the Atlantic Ocean, from Nova Scotia to West Florida, inclusive:

PROCLAMATION

Whereas, the enemy have adopted a practice of enrolling negroes among their troops, I do hereby give notice, that all negroes taken in arms, or upon any military duty, shall be purchased for a stated price; the money to be paid to the captors.

But I do most strictly forbid any person to sell or claim right over any negro, the property of a rebel, who may take refuge with any part of this army; and I do promise every negro who shall desert the rebel standard full security to follow within these lines any occupation which he shall think proper.

Given under my hand, at headquarters, Philipsburgh, the 30th day of June 1779.

H. Clinton
By His Excellency's Command
John Smith, Secretary

Appendix K

British Impressment of African Americans:
Letter from Sir James Wright to Lord George Germain
(His Majesty's Principal Secretary of State)

December 1, 1780
Savannah, Georgia

My Lord,

Inclosed Your Lordship has the triplicate of my letter No. 32 and in consequence of the power vested in me, by the Bill which I assented to on the 30th of October last, I ordered out upward of 400 negroes, who have been at work fortifying the town of Savannah ever since that day.

We are making five redoubts and batteries and there is to be a parapet made of fascines and earth from the river at each end and on the back of the town. This parapet is ten feet high and seven feet high with a ditch on the outside fifteen feet wide at the top, ten feet deep, and sloping to the bottom three feet. I think the redoubts will be finished and each parapet about half done, or say the whole four feet high by Christmas and I expect the works will be entirely finished in all by January. This my Lord is a most inconvenient thing and a heavy tax on the people, being one fourth part of all their male slaves for near or quite three months, and when the work is complete I shall send your Lordship a plan of the whole.

The present state of our strength will appear to your Lordship from my former letters and from the enclosed addresses of Members of His Majesty's Council.

The late law also enables me to call out and arm negroes in defense of the province and to exercise further power over the militia, but this only in time of alarms actually fired and there are several things provided for which we thought necessary in these yet very perilous times.

I have the honor to be with perfect esteem
My Lord, Your Lordships most obliged and obedient servant
James Wright

Appendix L

British Army Command Instructions for the Office Established to Receive the Pay of Negroes Employed in Different Departments

(South Carolina, 1781)

I. Returns to be given in to the pay-masters by the Heads of Departments, of the negroes employed in different Departments, by families, specifying the numbers, their owners' names, and if in arms against Government or if Loyalists.

II. Their wages as fixed by a former order: eight pence per day for common laborers, and eighteen pence per day for artificers; two women to be considered and paid equal to one laboring man; to be lodged in the hands of the pay-masters, quarterly, by the Heads of Departments, in order to pay Loyalists for the use of their slaves, to clothe them all and to establish a fund for future services.

III. The receipts of the Heads of Departments to be vouchers to the pay-masters for clothing supplied the negroes.

IV. All the negroes to have their clothing made up in uniform; and all negroes to be taken up who have not the proper tickets from the pay-masters.

V. A certain fixed allowance of money to be paid quarterly, upon a certificate of their deserving it being given by the foreman or overseer, under which they have worked, countersigned by the Head of the Department. To every common laborer and to every two women one dollar per month, to every artificer, two dollars per month; which allowance is to be ascertained by the tickets granted from the pay-office, specifying if an artificer or common laborer.

VI. The pay-masters to muster all the negroes, once a month, and when a negro absents himself from any Department the pay-masters are to be reported to in writing, by the Head of the Department, which report is to be produced to the Auditor of Accounts quarterly, and a copy of these accounts to be delivered to all the Heads of Departments, who are also to be supplied with new tickets, quarterly.

Appendix M

Lord Dunmore's Letter to
Sir Henry Clinton
(February 2, 1782)

Earl of Dunmore to Sir Henry Clinton
Charleston, South Carolina
February 2, 1782

Sir:

I was in hopes of having the pleasure of delivering the enclosed letter in person, but the fleet in which I came out is not proceeding to New York, being advised, and thinking it unsafe to hazard a further voyage northward, at this season of the year, with so large a fleet. . . .

I arrived here the 21st of December; having no employment, I made it my business to converse with every one that I thought capable of giving me any good information of the real situation of this country; and every one that I have conversed with think, and I must own, my own sentiments perfectly coincide with theirs, that the most efficacious, expeditious, cheapest, and certain means of reducing this country to a proper sense of their duty is in employing the blacks, who are, in my opinion, not only better fitted for service in this warm climate than white men, but they are also better guides, may be got on much easier terms, and are perfectly attached to our sovereign. And, by employing them, you cannot devise a means more effectual to distress your foes, not only by depriving them of their property, but by depriving them of their labor. You in reality deprive them of their existence; for, without their labor, they cannot subsist; and, from my own knowledge of them, I am sure they are as soon disciplined as any set of raw men that I know of.

What I would further propose is, that the officers of the Provincials, who are swarming in the streets here, perfectly idle, should be employed to command these men, with the rank they now have.

I would also propose, at first, to raise only ten thousand blacks, to give them white officers, but to fill up the vacancies of the non-commissioned officers now and then with Black people, as their services should entitle them to it.

In order to induce the negroes to enlist, I would propose to give each man one guinea and a crown, with a promise of freedom to all that should serve during the continuance of the war; and, that they may be fully satisfied that this promise will be held inviolate, it must be given by the officer appointed to command them, he being empowered to so, in the most ample manner, by your Excellency.

Appendix N

Official Notes on Conference Between General George Washington and Sir Guy Carleton
(Orangetown, New York, May 6, 1783)

Sir Guy Carleton observed . . . that in this embarkation a number of negroes were comprised. General Washington thereupon expressed his surprise that after what appeared to him an express stipulation to the contrary in the Treaty . . . to which Sir Guy Carleton replied. . . . He principally insisted that he conceived it could not have been the intention of the British Government by the Treaty of Peace to reduce themselves to the necessity of violating their faith to the negroes who came into the British lines under the proclamation of his predecessors in command, that he forbore to express his sentiments on the propriety of these proclamations but that delivering up the negroes to their former masters would be delivering them up some possibly to execution and others to severe punishment which in his opinion would be a dishonorable violation of the public faith pledged to the negroes in the proclamations that if the sending off the negroes should hereafter be declared an infraction of the treaty, compensation must be made by the Crown of Great Britain to the owners, that he had taken measures to provide for this by directing a register to be kept of all the negroes who were sent off specifying the name, age, and occupation of the slave and the name and place of residence of his former master.

General Washington again observed that he conceived this conduct on the part of Sir Guy Carleton a departure both from the letter and spirit of the articles of peace and particularly mentioned a difficulty that would arise in compensating the proprietors of negroes admitting this infraction of the treaty could be satisfied by such a compensation as Sir Guy Carleton had alluded to, as it was impossible to ascertain the value of the slaves from any fact or circumstance which may appear in the register, the value of a slave consisting chiefly in his industry and sobriety and General Washington further mentioned a difficulty which would attend identifying the slave supposing him to have changed his own name or to have given in a wrong name of his former master. In answer to which Sir Guy Carleton said that as the negro was free and secured against his master he could have no inducement to conceal either his own true name or that of his master. Sir Guy Carleton then observed that he was not by the treaty held to deliver up any property but was only restricted from carrying it away and therefore admitting the interpretation of the treaty as given by General Washington to be just, he was notwithstanding pursuing a measure which would operate most for the security of proprietors, for if the negroes were left to themselves without care or control from him numbers of them would very probably go off and not return to the parts of the country they came from, or clandestinely get on board the transports in manner which it would not be in his power to prevent; in either of which cases an inevitable loss would ensue to the proprietors but as the business was now conducted they had at least a chance for compensation; and concluded the conversation on this subject by saying that he imagined that the mode of compensating as well as the accounts and other points with respect to which there was no express provision made by the treaty must be adjudged by commissioners to be hereafter appointed by the two nations.

Appendix O

The Northwest Ordinance
(July 13, 1787)

ARTICLE 6

There shall be neither slavery nor involuntary servitude in the said territory, otherwise than in punishment of crimes whereof the party shall have been duly convicted: Provided always, that any person escaping into the same, from whom labor or service is lawfully claimed in any one of the original States, such fugitive may be lawfully reclaimed and conveyed to the person claiming his or her labor or service as aforesaid.

Appendix P

The U.S. Constitution and African Americans
(1787)

ARTICLE I, SECTION II, PARAGRAPH 3

Representatives and direct taxes shall be apportioned among the several states which may be included in this Union, according to their respective numbers, which shall be determined by adding to the whole number of free persons, including those bound to service for a term of years [apprentices and indentured servants], and excluding Indians not taxed, three-fifths of all other persons [slaves].

ARTICLE I, SECTION IX, PARAGRAPH 1

The migration or importation of such persons as any of the states now existing shall think proper to admit, shall not be prohibited by the Congress prior to the year 1808; but a tax or duty may be imposed on such importation, not exceeding ten dollars for each person.

ARTICLE IV, SECTION II, PARAGRAPH 3

No person held to service or labor in one state, under the laws thereof, escaping into another, shall, in consequence of any law or regulation therein, be discharged from such service or labor, but shall be delivered up on claim of the party to whom such service or labor may be due.

Sources

The following bibliography includes those sources that are available in most university and major metropolitan libraries. Other related information is accessible in the National Archives and in the records centers for the states that participated in the Revolution.

BOOKS

Acomb, Evelyn M., (trans. and ed.). *The Revolutionary Journal of Baron Ludwig Von Clasen 1780–1783*. Chapel Hill, N.C.: University of North Carolina Press, 1958.

Adams, Russell. *Great Negroes, Past and Present*. Chicago: Afro-Am Publishing, 1969.

Aptheker, Herbert. *The American Revolution*. New York: International Publishers, 1960.

———. *Early Years of the Republic*. New York: International Publishers. 1976.

———. *The Negro in the American Revolution*. New York: International Publishers, 1940.

———. *Negro Slave Revolts in the United States: 1526–1860*. New York: International Publishers, 1939.

———. *To Be Free: Studies in American Negro History*. New York: International Publishers, 1948.

Bartlett, Josiah. *Letters of Josiah Bartlett, William Whipple, and Others*. Philadelphia: Adams Co., 1889.

Baurmeister, Carl L. *Revolution in America: Confidential Letters and Journals: 1776–1784*. New Brunswick, N.J.: Rutgers University Press, 1957.

Berg, Fred A. *Encyclopedia of Continental Army Units, Battalions, Regiments, and Independent Corps*. Harrisburg, Pa.: Stackpole Books, 1972.

Berlin, Ira. *Many Thousands Gone: The First Two Centuries of Slavery in North America*. Cambridge, Mass.: Belknap Press, 1998.

Boatner, Mark M. III. *Encyclopedia of the American Revolution*. New York: David McKay, 1966.

Bolster, W. Jeffery. *Black Jacks: African American Seamen in the Age of Sail*. Cambridge, Mass.: Harvard University Press, 1997.

Bolton, Charles K. *The Private Soldier Under Washington.* New York: Charles Scribner's Sons, 1902. Reprint, Williamstown, Mass.: Corner House Publishers, 1976.

Brawley, Benjamin. *A Social History of the Negro.* New York: Collier, 1970.

Buchanan, John. *The Road to Guilford Courthouse: The American Revolution in the Carolinas.* New York: John Wiley, 1997.

Buckley, Robert N. *Slaves in Red Coats: The British West India Regiments, 1775–1815.* New Haven, Conn.: Yale University Press, 1979.

Bullock, James. *Black Patriots of the American Revolution.* Princeton, N.J.: Carolingian Press, 1969.

Chastellux, Marquis de. *Travels in North America in the Years 1780, 1781, and 1782.* Chapel Hill, N.C.: University of North Carolina Press, 1963.

Claghorn, Charles E. *Women Patriots of the American Revolution: A Biographical Dictionary.* Metuchen, N.J.: Scarecrow Press, 1991.

Clark, William B. et al., eds. *Naval Documents of the American Revolution.* 10 vols. Washington, D.C.: Naval Historical Center, 1966–1996.

Coggins, Jack. *Ships and Seamen of the American Revolution.* Harrisburg, Pa.: Stackpole Books, 1969.

Conniff, Michael L., and Thomas J. Davis. *Africans in the Americas.* New York: St. Martin's Press, 1994.

Cooley, Timothy M. *Sketches of the Life and Character of the Rev. Lemuel Haynes, A. M., for Many Years Pastor of a Church in Rutland, Vt., and Late in Granville, New York.* New York: J. S. Taylor, 1839.

Crow, Jeffery J. *The Black Experience in Revolutionary North Carolina.* Raleigh, N.C.: Department of Cultural Resources, 1977.

David, Jay, and Elaine Crane, eds. *The Black Soldier: From the American Revolution to Vietnam.* New York: William Morrow, 1971.

Davis, Burke. *Black Heroes of the American Revolution.* San Diego, Calif.: Harcourt Brace Jovanovich, 1991.

Davis, Lenwood G., and George Hill, eds. *Blacks in the American Armed Forces, 1776–1983: A Bibliography.* Westport, Conn.: Greenwood Press, 1985.

Day, William Howard. *The Loyalty and Devotion of Colored Americans in the Revolution and the War of 1812.* Boston: R. F. Wallcut, 1861.

Douglass, Frederick. *Oration, Delivered in Corinthian Hall, Rochester.* Rochester, N.Y.: Lee, Mann, 1852.

Draper, Lyman C. *King's Mountain and Its Heroes: History of the Battle of King's Mountain, October 7th, 1780.* Cincinnati: Peter G. Thomson, 1881.

Drimmer, Melvin, ed. *Black History: A Reappraisal.* Garden City, N.Y.: Doubleday, 1968.

———. *Issues in Black History.* Dubuque, Iowa: Kendall Hunt, 1987.

Drotning, Phillip T. *Black Heroes in Our Nation's History.* New York: Cowles Book Co., 1969.

Dupuy, Trevor N., and Gay M. Hammerman, eds. *People and Events of the American Revolution.* New York: Bowker, 1974.

Eckenrode, Hamilton J., ed. *List of Revolutionary Soldiers in Virginia*. Richmond, Va.: Davis Bottom, 1912.

Elting, John. *American Army Life*. New York: Charles Scribner's Sons, 1982.

Emanuel, Myron. *Faces of Freedom: Crispus Attucks, Benjamin Banneker; Gabriel Prosser; James Forten*. New York: Firebird Books, 1971.

Farr, James Barker. *Black Odyssey: The Seafaring Traditions of Afro-Americans*. New York: Peter Lang, 1989.

Fishel, Leslie H. Jr., and Benjamin Quarles. *The Negro American: A Documentary History*. New York: William Morrow, 1967.

Fleming, Thomas. *Give Me Liberty: Black Valor in the Revolutionary War*. New York: Scholastic Book Services, 1971.

Foner, Philip S. *History of Black Americans: From Africa to the Emergence of the Cotton Kingdom*. Westport, Conn.: Greenwood Press, 1975.

———. *Blacks in the American Revolution*. Westport, Conn.: Greenwood Press, 1976.

Fortescue, John W. *A History of the British Army*. 13 vols. London: Macmillan, 1899–1930.

Fowler, William M. Jr. *Rebels Under Sail: The American Navy During the Revolution*. New York: Charles Scribner's Sons, 1976.

Franklin, John H. *From Slavery to Freedom*. New York: Knopf, 1967.

Frey, Sylvia. *Water From the Rock: Black Resistance in the Revolutionary Period*. Princeton, N.J.: Princeton University Press, 1991.

Garrison, William L. *The Loyalty and Devotion of Colored Americans in the Revolution and the War of 1812*. Boston: R. F. Wallcut, 1861.

Gelb, Norman. *Less Than Glory*. New York: G. P. Putnam's Sons, 1984.

Gephart, Ronald M. *Periodical Literature on the American Revolution*. Washington, D.C.: Library of Congress, 1971.

Gilmer, George R. *Sketches of Some of the First Settlers of Upper Georgia*. Baltimore: Baltimore Genealogical Publishing, 1965.

Greene, Robert E. *Black Courage, 1775–1783: Documentation of Black Participation in the American Revolution*. Washington, D.C.: National Society of the Daughters of the American Revolution, 1984.

———. *Black Defenders of America: 1775–1973*. Chicago: Johnson Publishing Co., 1974.

Guthrie, James M. *Camp-Fires of the Afro-Americans*. Philadelphia: AfroAmerican Press, 1899.

Gwathmey, John H., ed. *Historical Register of Virginians in the Revolution*. Richmond, Va.: Dietz Press, 1938.

Hammond, Isaac W., ed. *The State of New Hampshire Rolls of Soldiers in the Revolutionary War*. 4 vols. Concord, N.H.: State Printers, 1885–1889.

Heitman, Francis B. *Historical Register of Officers of the Continental Army During the War of the Revolution, April, 1775 to December; 1783*. Washington, D.C.: W. H. Lowdermilk, 1893.

Hornsby, Alton Jr. *Chronology of African-American History: Significant Events and People from 1619 to the Present*. Detroit: Gale Research Inc., 1991.

Horton, James O., and Lois E. Horton. *In Hope of Liberty: Culture, Community, and Protest Among Northern Free Blacks, 1700–1860.* New York: Oxford University Press, 1997.

Hurd, John C. *The Law of Freedom and Bondage in the United States.* 2 vols. Boston: Little, Brown, 1858.

Jackson, Luther P. *Virginia Negro Soldiers and Seamen in the Revolutionary War.* Norfolk, Va.: Guide Quality Press, 1944.

Johnson, Jesse J. *Black Armed Forces Officers: 1736–1971.* Hampton, Va.: Hampton Institute, 1970.

———. *The Black Soldier Documented: 1619–1815.* Hampton, Va.: Hampton Institute, 1970.

———. *A Pictorial History of Black Servicemen: Missing Pages in United States History.* Hampton, Va.: Hampton Institute, 1970.

Jordan, Winthrop. *White Over Black: American Attitudes Toward the Negro, 1550–1812.* Chapel Hill, N.C.: University of North Carolina Press, 1968.

Kaminkow, Marion and Jack. *Mariners of the American Revolution.* Baltimore: Magna Carta Book Co., 1967.

Kaplan, Sidney, and Emma N. Kaplan. *The Black Presence in the Era of the American Revolution.* Rev. ed. Amherst, Mass.: University of Massachusetts Press, 1989.

Katz, William L., ed. *The Negro Soldier: Missing Pages in Our History.* Boston: R. F. Wallcut, 1861.

Kidder, Frederic. *History of the Boston Massacre, March 5, 1770.* Albany, N.Y.: J. Munsell, 1870.

Lanning, Michael L. *The African American Soldier: From Crispus Attucks to Colin Powell.* Secaucus, N.J.: Birch Lane Press, 1997.

Lerner, Gerda, ed. *Black Women in White America.* New York: Random House, 1972.

Lesser, Charles H., ed. *The Sinews of Independence: Monthly Strength Reports of the Continental Army.* Chicago: University of Chicago Press, 1976.

Livermore, George. *An Historical Research Respecting the Opinions of the Founders of the Republic on Negroes as Slaves, as Citizens, and as Soldiers.* Boston: J. Wilson and Son, 1862. Reprint, New York: Amo Press, 1969.

Locke, Mary S. *Anti-Slavery in America from the Introduction of the African Slaves to the Prohibition of the Slave Trade, 1619–1808.* Boston: Ginn and Co., 1901.

Lowell, Edward J. *The Hessians.* Williamstown, Mass.: Corner House, 1970.

MacDonald, William. *Select Charters and Other Documents Illustrative of American History, 1606–1775.* Littleton, Colo.: Fred B. Rothman, 1993.

MacGregor, Morris J., and Bernard C. Nalty. *Blacks in the United States Armed Forces: Basic Documents.* 13 vols. Wilmington, Del.: Scholarly Resources, 1977.

Marrant, John. *A Narrative of the Lord's Wonderful Dealings with John Marrant.* London: Gilbert and Plummer, 1785.

Matloff, Maurice, ed. *American Military History.* Washington, D.C.: U. S. Army, 1969.

McAllister, J. T. *Virginia Militia in the Revolutionary War.* Hot Springs, Va.: McAllister Publishing Co., 1913.

McManus, Edgar J. *A History of Negro Slavery in New York.* Syracuse, N.Y.: Syracuse University Press, 1966.

Miller, Nathan. *Sea of Glory: A Naval History of the American Revolution.* Annapolis, Md.: Naval Institute Press, 1992.

Moebs, Thomas T. *Black Soldiers—Black Sailors—Black Ink: Research Guide on African Americans in U.S. Military History.* Chesapeake Bay, Md.: Moebs Publishing Co., 1994.

Montross, Lynn. *Rag, Tag and Bobtail: The Story of the Continental Army 1775–1783.* New York: Harper & Brothers, 1952.

Moore, Frank. *Diary of the American Revolution.* 2 vols. New York: New York Times, 1969.

Moore, George H. *Historical Notes on the Employment of Negroes in the American Army of the Revolution.* New York: Charles T. Evans, 1862.

Moore, Wilbert E. *American Negro Slavery and Abolition: A Sociological Study.* New York: Third Press, 1971.

Mullen, Robert W. *Blacks in America's Wars.* New York: Pathfinder, 1973.

Murray, Lindley. *Narratives of Colored Americans.* New York: William Wood and Co., 1877.

Mzack, Walter H. *George Washington and the Negro.* Washington, D.C.: Associated Publishers, 1932.

Nalty, Bernard C. *Strength for the Fight: A History of Black Americans in the Military.* New York: Free Press, 1986.

Nash, Gary B. *Forging Freedom: The Foundation of Philadelphia's Black Community, 1720–1840.* Cambridge, Mass.: Harvard University Press, 1988.

———. *Race and Revolution.* Madison, Wisc.: Madison House, 1990.

———. *Red, White, and Black: The Peoples of Early America.* Englewood Cliffs, N.J.: Prentice-Hall, 1974.

Neimeyer, Charles P. *America Goes to War: A Social History of the Continental Army.* New York: New York University Press, 1996.

Nell, William Cooper. *The Colored Patriots of the American Revolution, With Sketches of Several Distinguished Colored Persons: To Which Is Added a Brief Survey of the Conditions and Prospects of Colored Americans.* Boston: R. F. Wallcut, 1855.

———. *Property Qualifications or No Property Qualifications: A Few Facts From the Record of Patriotic Services of the Colored Men of New York, During the Wars of 1776 and 1812, With a Compendium of Their Present Business, and Property Statistics.* New York: Hamilton and Leonard, 1860.

———. *Services of Colored Americans in the Wars of 1776 and 1812.* Boston: Prentiss and Sawyer, 1851.

Nelson, Dennis D. *The Integration of the Negro in the U.S. Navy.* New York: Farrar, Straus, 1951.

Newman, Richard, ed. *Black Preacher to White America: The Collected Writings of Lemuel Haynes, 1774–1833.* Brooklyn, N.Y.: Carlson Publishing, 1990.

———. *Lemuel Haynes: A Bio-Bibliography.* New York: Lambeth Press, 1984.

Peckham, Alford S. *Lexington: Gateway to Freedom.* Lexington, Mass.: Lexington Chamber of Commerce, 1966.

Peterson, Clarence S. *Known Military Dead During the American Revolutionary War, 1775–1783.* Baltimore: Genealogical Publishing Co., 1967.

Peterson, Harold L. *The Book of the Continental Soldier.* Harrisburg, Penn.: Promontory Press, 1968.

Phillips, Ulrich B. *American Negro Slavery.* Gloucester, Mass.: Peter Smith, 1959.

Powell, William S. *Dictionary of North Carolina Biography.* 4 vols. Chapel Hill, N.C.: University of North Carolina Press, 1979–1991.

Quarles, Benjamin. *The Negro in the American Revolution.* Chapel Hill, N.C.: University of North Carolina Press, 1961.

Raymond, Marcus D. *Colonel Christopher Greene: A Paper Read Before the Sons of the Revolution of New York.* Tarrytown, N.Y.: Argus Print, 1902.

Rider, Sidney S. *An Historical inquiry Concerning the Attempt to Raise a Regiment of Slaves by Rhode Island During the War of the Revolution.* Providence, R.I.: S. S. Rider, 1880.

Royster, Charles. *A Revolutionary People at War: The Continental Anny and American Character, 1775–1783.* Chapel Hill, N.C.: University of North Carolina Press, 1979.

Schoenfeld, Seymour J. *The Negro in the Armed Forces.* Washington D.C.: Associated Publishers, 1945.

Selby, John. *The Road to Yorktown.* New York: St. Martin's Press, 1976.

Shaw, George C. *John Chavis: 1763–1838.* Binghamton, N.Y.: Vail-Ballou Press, 1931.

Shaw, Henry I., and Ralph W. Donnelly. *Blacks in the Marine Corps.* Washington, D.C.: U.S. Marine Corps, 1988.

Slonaker, John. *The U. S. Anny and the Negro: A Military History Research Collection Bibliography.* Carlisle Barracks, Pa.: U. S. Army Military History Institute, 1971.

Smith, Myron J. *Navies in the American Revolution: A Bibliography.* Metuchen, N.J.: Scarecrow Press, 1873.

Southern, Eileen. *The Music of Black Americans.* New York: W.W. Norton, 1971.

Steiner, Bernard C. *History of Slavery in Connecticut.* Baltimore: Johns Hopkins Press, 1893.

Stewart, Robert A. *The History of Virginia's Navy of the Revolution.* Richmond, Va.: Mitchell and Hotchkiss, 1934.

Sweetman, Jack. *American Naval History.* Annapolis, Md.: Naval Institute Press, 1984.

Thompson, Buchanan P. *Spain: Forgotten Ally of the American Revolution.* North Quincy, Mass.: Christopher Publishing House, 1976.

Walker, James W. *The Black Loyalists: The Search for a Promised Land in Nova Scotia and Sierra Leone, 1783–1870.* New York: Africana Publishing Co., 1976.

Wesley, Charles H. *Richard Allen: Apostle of Freedom.* Washington, D.C.: Associated Publishers, 1969.

White, David O. *Connecticut's Black Soldiers: 1755–1783.* Chester, Conn.: Pequot Press, 1973.

Wilkes, Laura E. *Missing Pages in American History, Revealing the Services of Negroes in the Early Wars of the United States of America, 1641–1815.* Washington, D.C.: R. L. Pendleton Press, 1919. Reprint, New York: AMS Press, 1973.

Williams, George W. *History of the Negro Race in America from 1619–1880.* 2 vols. New York: Putnam's, 1883.

Wilson, Ellen G. *The Loyal Blacks.* New York: G. P. Putnam's Sons, 1976.

Wilson, Joseph T. *The Black Phalanx; A History of the Negro Soldiers in the Wars of 1775–1812, 1861–65.* Hartford, Conn.: American Publishing Company, 1890. Reprint, New York: Amo Press, 1968.

Winks, Robin W. *The Blacks in Canada.* New Haven, Conn.: Yale University Press, 1971.

Winslow, Eugene. *Afro-Americans '76: Black Americans in the Founding of Our Nation.* Chicago: Afro-Am Publishing, 1975.

Woodson, Carter G. *The Negro in Our History.* Washington, D.C.: Associated Publishers, 1922.

Young, Peter. *George Washington's Army.* Reading, Eng.: 1972.

Zobel, Hiller B. *The Boston Massacre.* New York: W.W. Norton, 1970.

PERIODICALS

Alexander, Arthur J. "How Maryland Tried to Raise Her Continental Quotas," *Maryland Historical Magazine* (September 1947): 184–196.

Andrews, Charles M. "Slavery in Connecticut," *Magazine of American History* (May 1889): 422–423.

Aptheker, Herbert. "Edward Griffin, Revolutionary Soldier," *Negro History Bulletin* (November 1949): 38, 45.

———. "Eighteenth Century Petitions of South Carolina Negroes," *Journal of Negro History* 31 (1946): 98–99.

———. "Negroes Who Served in Our First Navy," *Opportunity* (April 1940): 117.

Barnett, Paul. "The Black Continental," *Negro History Bulletin* (January 1970): 6–10.

Belton, Bill. "Prince Whipple: Soldier of the American Revolution," *Negro History Bulletin* (October 1973): 126–127.

Bettle, Edward. "Negro Slavery as Connected with Pennsylvania," *Historical Society of Pennsylvania* 1 (1826): 367–416.

Billington, Ray A. "James Forten: Forgotten Abolitionist," *Negro History Bulletin* (November 1949): 31–36.

Blakeley, Phyllis R. "Boston King: A Negro Loyalist Who Sought Refuge in Nova Scotia," *Dalhousie Review* (Autumn 1968): 347–356.

Boatner, Mark M. III. "The Negro in the American Revolution," *American History Illustrated* (August 1969): 36–44.

Bogin, Ruth. "The Battle of Lexington: A Patriotic Ballad by Lemuel Haynes," *William and Mary Quarterly* (October 1985): 499–504.

———. "Liberty Further Extended: A 1776 Antislavery Manuscript by Lemuel Haynes," *William and Mary Quarterly* (January 1983): 85–105.

Brill, Debra. "The Hessians," *American History* (November–December 1995): 20–24.

Brown, Wallace. "Negroes and the American Revolution," *History Today* (August 1964): 556–563.

Bull, Lisa A. "The Negro," *Historical journal of Western Massachusetts Supplement* (1976): 67–74.

Cantor, Milton. "The Image of the Negro in Colonial Literature," *New England Quarterly* (December 1963): 452–503.

Coleman, Charles W. "The Southern Campaign," *Magazine of American History 1* (1881): 201–216.

Collier, Thomas S. "The Revolutionary Privateers of Connecticut," *New London Historical Society, Records and Papers* 1 (1892): 3–45.

Colon, Noel P. "Rhode Island Negroes in the Revolution," *Rhode Island History* (Winter and Spring 1970): 52–53.

Cresto, Kathleen M. "The Negro: Symbol and Participant of the American Revolution," *Negro History Bulletin* (November–December 1976): 628–631.

Diman, J. Lewis. "The Capture of Prescott," *Rhode Island Historical Tracts* 1 (1877): 11–44.

Dole, Samuel T. "Windham's Colored Patriot," *Maine Historical Society Collections and Proceedings* 1 (1904): 316–321.

Eno, R. D. "The Strange Fate of the Black Loyalist," *American Heritage* 4 (1983): 102-109.

Fisher, J. B. "Who Was Crispus Attucks?," *American Historical Record* 1 (1872): 531–533.

Fisher, Ruth A. "Manuscript Materials Bearing on the Negro in the British Museum," *Journal of Negro History* 27 (1942): 83–93.

Fiske, John. "Crispus Attucks," *Negro History Bulletin* (March 1970), 58–68.

Fogg, John S. H. "Inquest on Michael Johnson Alias Crispus Attucks," *New England Historical and Genealogical Register* 44 (1890): 382–383.

Frey, Sylvia R. "The British and the Black: A New Perspective," *Historian* (February 1976), 225–238.

Fyfe, Christopher. "Thomas Peters: History and Legend," *Sierra Leone Studies* (December 1953): 4–13.

Gasperetti, Elio. "An Italo-American Newspaper's Obituary of a Negro Revolutionary War Veteran," *Negro History Bulletin* (December 1954): 58.

Gibbs, C. R. "The First Black Army Officer," *Armed Forces Journal International* (June 1975): 24.

Gobbel, Luther L. "The Militia in North Carolina in Colonial and Revolutionary Times," *Trinity College Historical Society, Historical Papers* 13 (1919): 35–61.

Gough, Robert J. "Black Men and the Early New Jersey Militia," *New Jersey History* (Winter 1970): 227–238.

Green, Samuel A. "Slavery at Groton in Provincial Times," *Massachusetts Historical Society Proceedings* 42 (1909): 196–202.

Greene, Lorenzo J. "The Negro in the Armed Forces of the United States," *Negro History Bulletin* (March 1951): 123–128.

———. "Some Observations on the Black Regiment of Rhode Island in the American Revolution," *Journal of Negro History* (April 1952): 142–172.

Haarmann, Albert W. "American Provincial Corps Authorized by Lord Dunmore, 1775," *Journal of the Society for Army Historical Research* (Winter 1974): 254–255.

———. "The Siege of Pensacola: An Order of Battle," *Florida Historical Quarterly* (January 1966): 193–199.

Hadaway, William S. "Negroes in the Revolutionary War," *Westchester County Historical Society Quarterly Bulletin* (January 1930): 8–12.

Harrington, Henry F. "Anecdotes of Washington," *Godey's Magazine & Ladies Book* (June 1849): 427–428.

Harris, Janette H. "Crispus Attucks," *Negro History Bulletin* (March 1970): 69.

Hartgrove, W. B. "The Negro Soldier in the American Revolution," *Journal of Negro History* (April 1916): 110–131.

Hoffman, Elliott W. "Black Hessians: American Blacks as German Soldiers," *Negro History Bulletin* 44 (1981): 81–82, 91.

Holbrook, Stewart H. "The First American WAC: Deborah Sampson Gannet," *Negro Digest* (November 1944): 36–43.

Hudson, Cassie H. "John Chavis 1763–1838: A Social Psychological Study," *Journal of Negro History* (Spring 1979): 142–156.

Jackson, Luther P. "Virginia Negro Soldiers and Seamen in the American Revolution," *Journal of Negro History* (July 1942): 247–287.

Jasper, John. "Biggest Hoax in the Revolutionary War," *Afro-American* (October 21, 1965): 1.

Johnson, Cecil. "Expansion in West Florida, 1770–1779," *Mississippi Valley Historical Review* (March 1934): 481–496.

Jones, George F. "The Black Hessians: Negroes Recruited by the Hessians in South Carolina and Other Colonies," *South Carolina Historical Magazine* (October 1982): 287–302.

Kaplan, Sidney. "A Negro Veteran in Shay's Rebellion," *Journal of Negro History* (April 1948): 123–29.

King, Boston. "Memoirs of the Life of Boston King, A Black Preacher," *Arminian Magazine* 21 (1798): 107, 110.

Knight, Edgar W. "Notes on John Chavis," *North Carolina Historical Review* 7 (1930): 326–345.

Langley, Harold D. "The Negro in the Navy and Merchant Service: 1789–1860," *Journal of Negro History* (October 1967): 273–279.

Linebaugh, Peter, and Marcus Rediker. "The Many-Headed Hydra: Sailors, Slaves, and the Atlantic Working Class in the Eighteenth Century," *Journal of Historical Sociology* (September 1990): 225–253.

Lull, Francisco F., and J. Hefter. "The Spanish Louisiana Regiment in the Floridas, 1779–1781," *Military Collector and Historian* (Fall 1964): 79–80.

Mann, JoAnn. "Black Americans in the War for Independence," *Soldiers* (January 1975): 30–35.

Maslowski, Pete. "National Policy Toward the Use of Black Troops in the Revolution," *South Carolina Historical Magazine* (January 1972): 1–17.

Miller, William. "Effects of the American Revolution on Indentured Servitude," *Pennsylvania History* (July 1940): 131–141.

Moore, C. H. "Crispus Attucks," *New England Historical and Genealogical Register* 13 (1859): 300.

Morse, W. H. "Lemuel Haynes," *Journal of Negro History* (January 1919): 22–32.

Moss, Simon F. "The Persistence of Slavery and Involuntary Servitude in a Free State," *Journal of Negro History* (July 1950): 289–314.

Norton, Mary B. "The Fate of Some Black Loyalists of the American Revolution, *Journal of Negro History* (October 1973): 402–426.

O'Brien, William. "Did the Jennison Case Outlaw Slavery in Massachusetts?" *William and Mary Quarterly* (April 1960): 219–41.

Payne, A. H. "The Negro in New York Prior to 1860," *Howard Review* I (1923): 23-35.

Pennington, Edgar L. "East Florida in the American Revolution, 1775–1778," *Florida Historical Quarterly* (July 1930): 24–46.

Phillips, David E. "Negroes in the American Revolution," *Journal of American History* 5 (1911): 143–146.

Porter, Dorothy B. "The Black During the Era of the Revolution," *Smithsonian* (August 1973): 52–57.

Pugh, Robert C. "The Revolutionary Militia in the Southern Campaign," *William and Mary Quarterly* (April 1957): 154–175.

Quarles, Benjamin. "The Colonial Militia and Negro Manpower," *Mississippi Valley Historical Review* (March 1959): 743–752.

———. "A Group Portrait: Black America at the Time of the American War," *Ebony* (August 1975): 44–50.

————. "Lord Dunmore as Liberator," *William and Mary Quarterly* (October 1958): 494–507.

————. "The Significance of the Revolutionary War for Black Americans," *Black Heritage* (November–December 1981): 25–35.

Rantoul, Robert S. "Negro Slavery in Massachusetts," *Historical Collections* 14 (1887): 81–100.

Reddick, Lawrence A. "The Negro Policy of the United States Army, 1775–1945," *Journal of Negro History* (January 1949): 9–29.

Reid, Maryann. "Is This Mission Impossible?" *Black Enterprise* (August 1996): 16.

Rider, Sidney S. "The Rhode Island Black Regiment of 1778," *Rhode Island Historical Tracts* 10 (1880): 1–86.

Roberts, Wesley A. "The Black Experience and the American Revolution," *Fides et Historia* 8 (1976): 50–62.

Savage, W. Sherman. "The Influence of John Chavis and Lunsford Lane on the History of North Carolina," *Journal of Negro History* (January 1940): 14–24.

Shaffer, E. T. "The Rejected Laurens: A Carolina Tragedy," *South Carolina Historical Association* 1 (1934): 12–24.

Smith, Jonathan. "How Massachusetts Raised Her Troops in the Revolution," *Massachusetts Historical Society Proceedings* 55 (1923): 345–370.

Smith, M. H. "Connecticut Slaves In Revolutionary Times," *Connecticut Magazine* (January 1905): 145–153.

Spector, Robert M. "The Quack Walker Cases: Slavery, Its Abolition, and Negro Citizenship in Early Massachusetts," *Journal of Negro History* (January 1968): 12–32.

Stickley, Julia W. "The Records of Deborah Sampson Gannet, Woman Soldier of the Revolution," *Prologue* (Winter 1972): 233–241.

Thum, Marcella. "Invisible Soldier in the Revolutionary War," *Black Collegian* (November–December 1975): 16–18.

Tyson, George F. Jr. "The Carolina Black Corps: Legacy of the Revolution, 1783–1798," *Review Interamericana* 4 (1975): 648–664.

Walker, James W. "Blacks as American Loyalists: The Slaves' War for Independence," *Historical Reflections* 2 (1975): 51–67.

Wax, Darold D. "Black Heroes of the American Revolution," *Crisis* (August–September 1976): 257–258.

————. "Black Heroes of the American Revolution," *Crisis* (December 1976): 360–362.

Weeks, Stephen B. "John Chavis: Ante-Bellum Negro Preacher and Teacher," *Southern Workman* (February 1914): 101–106.

Index

Connect with

Visit us online at
KensingtonBooks.com
to read more from your favorite authors, see books
by series, view reading group guides, and more.

for sneak peeks, chances to win books and prize packs,
and to share your thoughts with other readers.

facebook.com/kensingtonpublishing
twitter.com/kensingtonbooks

Tell us what you think!

To share your thoughts, submit a review,
or sign up for our eNewsletters, please visit:
KensingtonBooks.com/TellUs.